TOP
IN DER SCHULE

TESTBLOCK

5./6. Klasse

ENGLISCH

Grammatik

ullmann medien

Text und Satz: Susanne Lück, lückenlos, Köln
Projektleitung: Judith Krötz
Umschlaggestaltung: Stefanie Brüssel, Potsdam

Gesamtherstellung: Ullmann Medien GmbH, Potsdam
ISBN-13: 978-3-7415-0132-6

1* Vorwort mit Tipps zum richtigen Lernen

Liebe Schülerin, lieber Schüler,

in diesem Testblock findest du mit 166 Tests jede Menge Übungsmaterial für eine optimale Vorbereitung auf die nächste Klassenarbeit oder Vergleichsarbeit. Die klar strukturierte Form der Tests gibt dir die Möglichkeit, gezielt viele Übungen zu genau den Themen zu lösen, in denen du noch Schwierigkeiten hast und mehr Sicherheit erlangen willst. Die kurze Form eignet sich für kleine Übungseinheiten zwischendurch.

Es kommt aber nicht allein darauf an, wie viel du lernst, sondern auch wie du lernst und übst.

Hier findest du nun einige Tipps, die dich beim Lernen unterstützen sollen:

Der richtige Ort ...
Richte dir nach Möglichkeit einen dauerhaften Arbeitsplatz ein. Der Tisch sollte ausreichend groß und gut beleuchtet sein. Die benötigten Lernmaterialien solltest du stets in greifbarer Nähe haben. Zum Arbeiten sollte es möglichst ruhig sein. Achte auch auf eine gewisse Ordnung an deinem Arbeitsplatz. Räume also alles weg, was dich ablenkt! Für die Konzentration ist auch ein „freier Kopf" von Vorteil. Ein Spaziergang an der frischen Luft hilft oft, um im Anschluss wieder konzentriert arbeiten zu können.

... und Ruhe zum Lernen
Mal dir doch ein Stopp-Schild, das du zu deinen Lernzeiten an die Tür hängst, dann weiß deine Familie, dass du jetzt gerade nicht gestört werden möchtest, weil du für die Schule arbeitest.

Die richtige Einteilung von Lernzeit ...
Wenn du merkst, dass du oft keine Zeit für deine Hausaufgaben hast und diese nur schnell mal am Abend oder am Morgen erledigst, erstell dir eine Liste, in der du einträgst, wie viel Zeit du mit den einzelnen Beschäftigungen verbringst, z. B. Sport, Freunde, Fernsehen, Computer ... Dahinter kannst du eintragen, ob das so in Ordnung ist oder ob es auch kürzer hätte sein können. Das kann dir helfen zu entscheiden, wo du in Zukunft Zeit einsparen kannst.

... und Pausenzeit
Forscher haben herausgefunden, dass die Konzentration schnell abnimmt. Bereits nach einer halben Stunde bist du nur noch halb so leistungsfähig wie zu Beginn. Wenn du merkst, dass du müde wirst und dich nicht mehr richtig konzentrieren kannst, dann mach eine kurze Pause.

Täglich kleine Lernportionen statt Stress vor der Klassenarbeit
Es ist besser, den Stoff in kleinen Portionen zu lernen. So behältst du besser, was du gelernt hast und fühlst dich in der Klassenarbeit sicherer. Du merkst auf diese

Weise auch schneller, welche Themen noch nicht so gut sitzen und kannst rechtzeitig genau diese Themen wiederholen. Nimm dir also nicht zu viel auf einmal vor, denn dann ist die Gefahr groß, dass du dich überforderst und den Spaß am Lernen verlierst. Setze dir ein Ziel und teile dir dein Pensum in kleine, regelmäßig zu lernende Portionen ein, die dich schrittweise zum Ziel führen.

Nachhaltiges Lernen

Nachhaltiges Lernen ist gehirngerechtes Lernen. Die Lerninhalte sollen ins Langzeitgedächtnis gelangen. Nur kurz vor den Klassenarbeiten gepauktes Wissen gelangt meist nur ins Kurzzeitgedächtnis. Wenn du etwas wissen oder können möchtest, dann musst du es dir durch Üben und Wiederholen erarbeiten. Nur so gelangen Lerninhalte in dein Langzeitgedächtnis. Wenn du kontinuierlich Hausaufgaben machst und übst, hast du mehr davon und auch weniger Stress vor Klassenarbeiten. Es hilft auch, wenn du den im Unterricht behandelten Stoff direkt zu Hause nochmals durcharbeitest, dann festigt sich das neu Gelernte besser.

Aktives Lernen erleichtert das Behalten

Am besten lernst du, wenn du über mehrere Kanäle die Lerninhalte aufnimmst, also mehrere Eingänge zum Gehirn benutzt, zum Beispiel Lesen und Schreiben. Manche Schüler lernen auch besonders gut, wenn sie etwas hören. Dann könnte es hilfreich sein, z. B. komplizierte Formeln oder Regeln aufzunehmen und immer wieder zu hören. Auch ein Lernposter bringt die wichtigsten Inhalte immer wieder vor Augen und hilft, die Inhalte zu behalten. Am meisten kannst du behalten, wenn du selbst etwas machst, also zum Beispiel Tests bearbeitest oder ein Lernposter erstellst ... Auch mündliche Mitarbeit in der Schule ist gut geeignet, das Gelernte besser zu behalten.

Steuerung des eigenen Lernens ...

Nimm dir zu Beginn einer Woche Zeit, dir einen Plan zu überlegen, was du heute und in dieser Woche üben willst. In einen solchen Wochenplan sollten alle festen Termine wie Essenszeiten, sportliche Aktivitäten, sonstige Freizeitaktivitäten und ebenfalls feste Übzeiten eingetragen werden. Jetzt wird deutlich, dass feste Üb- oder auch Wiederholungszeiten eben vergleichbar mit anderen Terminen sind. Und bei dieser Planung einer neuen Woche kannst du rückblickend feststellen, inwieweit du deine Vorsätze umsetzen konntest und wo es dir nicht gelungen ist. Da solltest du kritisch nach den Gründen suchen.

Erstelle dir einen Lernkalender zur Planung vor Klassenarbeiten. Trage dort die Themen mit Datum ein, die du vor der Klassenarbeit wiederholen möchtest, dann kommt kurz vor der Klassenarbeit kein Stress auf. Wenn du bei einzelnen Themen noch Probleme hattest, notier dir auch das, dann kannst du später genau dieses Thema noch einmal wiederholen.

... für mehr Lernerfolg
Beginne mit etwas, was du gut kannst. Für Aufgaben, für die du viele Wiederholungen brauchst, plane mehrfach kurze Zeit ein. Wechsle mündliche und schriftliche Aufgaben ab. Wenn das, was du dir für heute vorgenommen hast, zu viel ist, verschiebe einen Teil auf den nächsten Tag. Lege dir z. B. nach Klassenarbeiten eine Liste an, wo du notierst, welche Fehler sich bei dir häufen und mit welchen Aufgabentypen oder Regeln du am meisten Probleme hast. Bearbeite und wiederhole diese Liste regelmäßig – du wirst sehen, dass du auf diese Weise bald Fortschritte erzielst.

Viel Erfolg beim Bearbeiten der 166 Tests wünscht dir

Prof. Dr. Ludwig Haag
Lehrstuhl für Schulpädagogik
Kulturwissenschaftliche Fakultät der Universität Bayreuth
Mitglied des Pädagogischen Beirats der Schülerhilfe Deutschland

Kurztipps für Eltern: Wie kann ich mein Schulkind beim Lernen unterstützen?

Erhalten Sie die Freude am Lernen: Geben Sie Ihrem Kind eine Rückmeldung, was es schon alles gelernt hat und loben Sie es für gute Leistungen.

Erziehen Sie zum selbstständigen Lernen: Je nach den individuellen Fähigkeiten Ihres Kindes sollten Sie ihm Autonomie und Entscheidungsfreiheit bei der Erledigung der eigenen Aufgaben zugestehen, z. B. wenn es um die Reihenfolge der zu erledigenden Hausaufgaben geht. Lassen Sie Ihr Kind selbst entscheiden, wann es Hilfe bei den Aufgaben benötigt.

Unterstützen Sie die Lernorganisation Ihres Kindes: Vereinbaren Sie Zeiten, zu denen regelmäßig die Hausaufgaben erledigt werden. Sorgen Sie für eine überschaubare Ordnung am Arbeitsplatz.

Erziehen Sie durch Lob: Positive Reaktionen fördern die Motivation und den Spaß am Erfolg. Loben Sie bei Erfolgen und üben Sie motivierende Kritik.

Ermöglichen Sie Lernerfolge: Regen Sie durch Fragen an, neue Entdeckungen zu machen. Strukturieren Sie die Lernerfahrungen und lenken Sie die Aufmerksamkeit Ihres Kindes. Wählen Sie die Aufgaben und das Lernpensum so aus, dass Ihr Kind Erfolgserlebnisse hat und dabei nicht überfordert ist.

Anleitung

Mit den Tests in diesem Block kannst du den in zwei Schuljahren behandelten Lernstoff üben und dich so ohne fremde Hilfe **auf Klassenarbeiten vorbereiten**. Vergleiche einfach deine Endergebnisse mit den **Lösungen** hinten im Lösungsteil. Dort findest du – rot unterlegt – auch die entsprechenden **Regeln**. Wenn du also einmal gar nicht weißt, wie du eine Aufgabe lösen sollst, schlag zuletzt dort nach. Schau aber vorher immer noch einmal in die Regelabschnitte in deinem eigenen Schulbuch oder Workbook!

Im Übrigen kannst du die Tests in diesem Block anstatt allein natürlich auch mit deinen Eltern, Geschwistern oder deiner Nachhilfelehrerin zusammen bearbeiten – gemeinsam lernt es sich ja bekanntlich viel schöner!

Dieser Block bietet einen **Querschnitt** durch den gesamten Unterrichtsstoff zweier Schuljahre. Nicht alle Schulen behandeln diesen Stoff aber in der gleichen Reihenfolge oder gleich schnell – orientiere dich also am **Inhaltsverzeichnis** auf den folgenden zwei Seiten und finde dort heraus, wo deine Klasse gerade steht und bei welchen Themen du noch unsicher bist.

Wie schnell du mit dem Block vorankommst, bestimmst ansonsten du allein. Als grobe Richtlinie kann gelten, dass du **pro Lerntag ein Blatt** bearbeiten kannst – das muss aber auch nicht sein. Jeder hat ein eigenes, individuelles Lerntempo, mit dem er oder sie sich wohl fühlt und nicht überfordert ist!

Das **Punktesystem**, mit dem hier alle Tests versehen sind, soll dir helfen, eigenständig zu arbeiten. Für richtige Lösungen erhältst du eine bestimmte Anzahl von Punkten, die du jeweils im Lösungsteil einsehen kannst. Trage nach jedem Test deine tatsächlich erreichte Punktzahl ein. Das soll dir bei der Entscheidung helfen, ob du **zum nächsten Thema vorrücken** kannst oder das gerade Bearbeitete **besser noch einmal** vertiefst. Hast du einen Test besonders gut gelöst, dessen Thema im nächsten noch einmal aufgegriffen wird, dann darfst du manchmal die direkt folgende Seite überspringen. Hast du nur wenig Punkte erreicht (eine Mindestpunktzahl wird dir jeweils unten auf der Seite angegeben), dann wiederholst du am besten den gerade gelösten Test. Ziel sollte es immer bleiben, dass du jeden einzelnen Test spätestens dann, wenn du ihn zweimal bearbeitet hast, so gut wie fehlerfrei lösen kannst.

Je nach **Schwierigkeitsgrad** werden die Tests der **Stufe 1, 2 oder 3** zugeordnet, was du an der Anzahl grau eingefärbter Kreise oben auf der Seite erkennen kannst. Fang immer mit dem einfachsten Schwierigkeitsgrad an.

Stufe 1

Stufe 2

Stufe 3

In den **Abschlusstests** hinten im Buch hast du die Möglichkeit, noch einmal die wichtigsten Anforderungen der gesamten zwei Unterrichtsjahre an einem Stück zu wiederholen. Diese löst du daher sinnvollerweise erst, nachdem du den Testblock ganz durchgearbeitet hast.

Ein Hinweis noch: Die Arbeit mit dem Textblock erspart es dir natürlich nicht, zusätzlich auch für Vokabeltests zu lernen! Achte also gut darauf, dass du die neuen englischen Wörter für jeden Test zu schreiben und auszusprechen lernst!

Test 1 Singular und Plural

Schwierigkeitsgrad: ● ○ ○

1. Setze diese Substantive in den Plural.

tree 's Baum

question 's Frage

nose 's Nase

pen 's stift

banana 's

glass es

house 's

window 's Fenster

bush es

fox 'es Fuchs

2. Setze diese Substantive in den Singular.

ladies ______

bees Bienen

halves halb

toys Spielzeug

diaries y Tagebuch

days ______

hobbies ______

dresses ______

lives Life

countries Land country

3. Setze diese Wortgruppen in den Plural.

a bus and a car The busses and the cars

a pear and a plum The pears and the plums

a plane and a bike The planes and the bikes

a girl and a baby The girls and the babies

a box and a pan The boxes and the pans

a minute and a second The minutes and the seconds

bearbeitet am: ______ erreichte Punktzahl: ______

Ab 21 erreichten Punkten kannst du mit Test 2 fortfahren, ab 25 mit Test 3.

Test 2 Singular und Plural

Schwierigkeitsgrad: ● ● ○

1. Setze diese Substantive in den Plural.

wife	wives	sandwich	sandwiches
shelf	shelves	house	houses
daisy	daisies	window	windows
party	parties	fly	flies
witch	witches	church	churches
star	stars	orange	oranges
hand	hands	brush	brushes

2. Trage die fehlenden Pluralwörter in die Lücken ein.

In my room, my b_______________ are on the sh_______________ on the wall.

My mother and my father are my p_______________ .

I don't have any br_______________ , but two s_______________ .

On a farm, there are lots of a_______________ beginning with "c": ch_______________

and co_________ and often ca_________ .

3. Welche dieser Pluralendungen werden wie [iz] ausgesprochen? Unterstreiche sie.

flakes	faces	apples	brakes	tomatoes
noses	pages	candles	toes	bridges
hedges	shoes	mazes	cases	tables
ropes	centres	clothes	braces	spices

bearbeitet am: __________ erreichte Punktzahl: __________

Ab 26 erreichten Punkten kannst du mit Test 3 fortfahren.

Test 3 Singular und Plural

Schwierigkeitsgrad: ● ● ○

1. Setze diese Substantive in den Plural.

woman ____________________ foot ____________________

mouse ____________________ man ____________________

tooth ____________________ child ____________________

2. Setze diese Substantive in den Singular.

sheep ____________________ geese ____________________

3. Setze diese Wortgruppen in den Plural.

one woman and one child — two w________ and four c____________________

one man's foot — two m________ 's f______________

one bad tooth — two ____________ ________________

one cat and one mouse — two c________ and eight m________________

one glass of water — three g__________ _____ ____________

one country and one man — many ______________ and many ________

4. Trage die fehlenden Wortteile in die Lücken ein.

Lad____________ and gentlem____________ , your dinner is ready.

Water, wine and other d____________ are served at the bar.

I have one nose, one mouth, two e____________ , two e____________

and 32 t____________ .

bearbeitet am: ____________ erreichte Punktzahl: ______

Ab 14 erreichten Punkten kannst du mit Test 4 fortfahren.

Test 4 Zählbare und nicht zählbare Substantive

Schwierigkeitsgrad: ● ○ ○

1. Welche dieser Substantive kann man als Paarwörter nur im Plural gebrauchen? Kreuze neben den reinen Pluralwörtern Wörtern das „P" an und notiere die Paarwörter noch einmal hintereinander auf den Linien.

shoes [P]	trousers [P]	glasses [P]	gloves [P]
tongs [P]	hands [P]	scissors [P]	shorts [P]
jeans [P]	socks [P]	lungs [P]	fingers [P]

____

____

2. Welche der folgenden Substantive lassen sich zählen und welche nicht? Trage sie in die richtige Spalte der Tabelle ein.

water glass tea news cup sugar peach

zählbar (*countable*)	nicht zählbar (*uncountable*)

3. Welche Wörter fehlen hier? Ergänze die englischen Pluralformen der Wörter in Klammern.

I cannot read well, I have lost my ____________________. (Brille)

I like to go to sleep dressed in my red ____________________. (Schlafanzug)

We should drink eight ____________________ of ____________________ every day. (Glas/Wasser)

Your clothes are torn. You need a new pair of ____________________. (Hose)

bearbeitet am: __________ erreichte Punktzahl: ______

Ab 15 erreichten Punkten kannst du mit Test 5 fortfahren, ab 18 mit Test 6.

Test 5 Zählbare und nicht zählbare Substantive

Schwierigkeitsgrad: ● ● ○

1. **Ein Blick in Sarahs Kleiderschrank: Ganz rechts siehst du, wie viele Stücke oder Paare von jedem Kleidungsstücke sie besitzt. Schreibe in vollständigen Sätzen auf, was sie alles hat, und setze ... *pairs of* davor, wo es passt.**

Sarah has got ______________________________ . /dresses (4)

She has got ______________________________ . /shoes (5)

She has got ______________________________ . /pyjamas (3)

She has got ______________________________ . /jeans (4)

She has got ______________________________ . /sunglasses (2)

She has got ______________________________ . /T-shirts (8)

2. **Übersetze die Sätze ins Englische.**

Wo ist die Schere? ______________________________ .

Sie mag meine neue Brille. ______________________________ .

Ich suche meine Hose. Ist sie hier?

____ .

3. **Bilde aus den Bestandteilen in den Kästen vier vollständige sinnvolle Sätze.**

The milk / My jeans / The scissors / The music	are / is	new / cold / loud / sharp

____ .

____ .

____ .

____ .

bearbeitet am: ________ erreichte Punktzahl: ____

Ab 11 erreichten Punkten kannst du mit Test 6 fortfahren.

Test 6 *s*-Genitiv

Schwierigkeitsgrad: ● ○ ○

1. **Verwende bei den folgenden Substantiven den *s*-Genitiv.**

Jerry / sister ______________________

your mother / car ______________________

Mr Frazer / dogs ______________________

the horse / colour ______________________

the dentist / chair ______________________

our teacher / glasses ______________________

Anne / book ______________________

our neighbour / newspaper ______________________

my grandmother / TV set ______________________

aunt Susie / friend ______________________

2. **Beantworte die Fragen in ganzen Sätzen mit dem *s*-Genitiv der Wörter in Klammern.**

Whose pen is this? It's ______________________ (Alice)

Is this your house? No, it's ______________________ (Muriel)

Is this your cap? ______________________ (Timmy)

Is this your brother's car? ______________________ (my mother)

Whose birthday is it? ______________________ (Fran)

Are these Ms Jenson's CDs? ______________________ (Mr Clay)

Are those your trainers? ______________________ (Philip)

Is this my drink? ______________________ (Jennifer)

bearbeitet am: __________ erreichte Punktzahl: __________

Ab 15 erreichten Punkten kannst du mit Test 7 fortfahren.

Test 7 *s*-Genitiv

Schwierigkeitsgrad: ● ● ○

1. **Verwende bei den folgenden Plural-Substantiven den *s*-Genitiv.**

the pupils / classroom ______________________

the policemen / motorbikes ______________________

the houses / roofs ______________________

her colleagues / haircuts ______________________

your doctors / orders ______________________

2. **Bilde erst den Plural der unterstrichenen Substantive und verwende dann den *s*-Genitiv.**

<u>my sister</u> / shoes ______________________

<u>my aunt</u> / presents ______________________

<u>her cat</u> / food ______________________

<u>the child</u> / toys ______________________

3. **Stelle die korrekten Fragen mit *whose*.**

______________________ ? It's my party.

______________________ ? It's my father's computer.

______________________ ? It's Maxwell's hammer.

______________________ ? These are Candy's stickers.

______________________ ? It's my friend's game.

______________________ ? That's your business.

______________________ ? Those are his chips.

bearbeitet am: ______ erreichte Punktzahl: ______

Ab 13 erreichten Punkten kannst du mit Test 8 fortfahren.

Test 8 *of*-Genitiv

Schwierigkeitsgrad: ● ○ ○

1. Verwende bei den folgenden Substantiven den *of*-Genitiv.

the house / the roof ______________________________

the door / the handle ______________________________

the garden / the size ______________________________

the mountain / the top ______________________________

the wine / the taste ______________________________

the word / the spelling ______________________________

our lesson / the beginning ______________________________

your photos / the quality ______________________________

their chair / the legs ______________________________

his plane model / the colour ______________________________

2. Verwende den *of*-Genitiv oder den *s*-Genitiv im Plural. Ergänze den Artikel vor dem Substantiv, wenn nötig.

the boys / toys ______________________________

the families / dogs ______________________________

the room / walls ______________________________

the closets / doors ______________________________

his teeth / colour ______________________________

their parents / houses ______________________________

the women / skirts ______________________________

bearbeitet am: __________ erreichte Punktzahl: ______

Ab 14 erreichten Punkten kannst du mit Test 9 fortfahren.

Test 9 *s*-Genitiv und *of*-Genitiv

Schwierigkeitsgrad: ● ●

1. **Finde heraus, zu wem oder zu was die Dinge rechts gehören, und verbinde sie. Schreibe dann jeweils den gesamten Genitivausdruck auf die Linien und entscheide, ob du *s*-Genitiv oder *of*-Genitiv verwenden musst. Ergänze den Artikel vor den Substantiven.**

computer	pages
the girls	bicycle
candle	haircuts
book	light
Billy	screen

The ______________________ of the ______________________

The ______________________ ______________________

____

____

____

2. **Übersetze die Sätze.**

Die Lehrerin der Schüler kommt aus London.

____.

Was ist am Ende des Monats?

____.

Die Farbe seiner Augen ist grün.

____.

bearbeitet am: ____________ erreichte Punktzahl: ______

Ab 6 erreichten Punkten kannst du mit Test 10 fortfahren.

Test 10 Unbestimmter und bestimmter Artikel

Schwierigkeitsgrad: ● ○ ○

1. Kreuze an, bei welchen Ausdrücken der bestimmte Artikel *the* wie [ði] ausgesprochen wird.

☐ the fish ☐ the alligator
☐ the apple ☐ the strawberry
☐ the exercise ☐ the book
☐ the nose ☐ the ears
☐ the trousers ☐ the boots
☐ the middle ☐ the end

2. *A* oder *an*? Setze den richtigen unbestimmten Artikel vor den Substantiven ein.

__________ aunt __________ mother
__________ question __________ answer
__________ father __________ uncle
__________ eternity __________ year

3. Setze den richtigen unbestimmten Artikel ein und trage ein, ob es sich beim folgenden Wort um eines mit Konsonant oder Vokal handelt.

	Denn das folgende Wort beginnt mit einem ...
__________ camel	____________________
__________ elephant	____________________
__________ monkey	____________________
__________ beautiful girl	____________________
__________ ugly doll	____________________

bearbeitet am: __________ erreichte Punktzahl: _____

Ab 24 erreichten Punkten kannst du mit Test 11 fortfahren, ab 29 mit Test 12.

Test 11 Unbestimmter und bestimmter Artikel

Schwierigkeitsgrad: ● ● ○

1. *A* oder *an*? Setze den richtigen unbestimmten Artikel vor den Gegensatzpaaren mit Adjektiv ein.

______________ young kitten	______________ old horse
______________ happy pupil	______________ unhappy teacher
______________ easy test	______________ difficult exercise
______________ cheap earring	______________ expensive scarf
______________ stupid mistake	______________ intelligent answer
______________ interesting story	______________ boring book
______________ hard start	______________ soft landing
______________ happy pupil	______________ unhappy teacher

2. **Fülle die Lücken mit dem richtigen bestimmten oder unbestimmten Artikel aus.**

– I have ______________ sore throat today, and ______________ fever, and ______________ headache, too. I think I caught ______________ cold.

Can you bring me ______________ large orange and ______________ ripe banana?

– Yes, but I'm in ______________ hurry. I must leave ______________ house in ______________ minute.

– Just bring me ______________ orange then. I will eat ______________ apple later, I know we have some left in ______________ kitchen.

– I'm afraid you can't go to ______________ theatre tomorrow night.

– You're right, that's ______________ pity.

bearbeitet am: ______________ erreichte Punktzahl: ______

Ab 24 erreichten Punkten kannst du mit Test 12 fortfahren.

Test 12 Unbestimmter und bestimmter Artikel

Schwierigkeitsgrad: ● ○ ○

1. **Bilde aus den Namens- und Instrumentenpaaren vollständige Sätze mit Artikeln.**

Jackie	guitar
Vanessa	violin
Her brother	trumpet

Jackie plays ____ .

____ .

____ .

2. **Bilde aus den Namens- und Berufspaaren vollständige Sätze mit Artikeln.**

My mother	baker
Your father	hairdresser
Dr Johnson	doctor

My mother is ____ .

____ .

____ .

3. **Übersetze die Sätze und achte auf die richtige Verwendung der Artikel.**

Timmy kann Klavierspielen.

____ .

Mr Black ist Landwirt.

____ .

Ich spiele oft Gitarre.

____ .

bearbeitet am: __________ erreichte Punktzahl: ______

Ab 7 erreichten Punkten kannst du mit Test 13 fortfahren.

Test 13 Unbestimmter und bestimmter Artikel

Schwierigkeitsgrad: ● ● ○

1. **Dennis and Kevin vergleichen ihre Geburtstagsgeschenke. Setze den *unbestimmten* Artikel in der richtigen Form in die Lücken ein. Achtung: Manche Lücken müssen leer bleiben.**

– I got ______________ remote-controlled helicopter and ______________ airplane for my birthday. They go very fast, and you must have ______________ lot of practice to fly them.

– Well, I got ______________ interesting new computer games and ______________ expensive new mp3 player for my birthday. My old one was broken, but ______________ mp3 players are not cheap, so I was really surprised I got ______________ new one.

– Yes, I'd love to have ______________ player, too! Did you have ______________ enormous party?

– Of course! It wouldn't be ______________ birthday without ______________ party!

2. **Urlaubspost von Lynn! Setze den *bestimmten oder* den *unbestimmten* Artikel in der richtigen Form in die Lücken ein. Achtung: Manche Lücken bleiben wieder leer.**

Dear Vicky, how are you? Here in Spain everything is fine, ______________ weather is great, and ______________ sun is shining a lot. Before ______________ breakfast I go for ______________ swim in ______________ hotel pool, and after ______________ lunch at ______________ beach I go swimming in ______________ sea. ______________ shops down there sell ______________ best ice cream ever. After ______________ supper in ______________ evening, we play ______________ card games, or sometimes I play ______________ guitar. My mother says she never wants to get back to ______________ work, but I will like to be back in ______________ school soon. I miss you and ______________ others from our class. Love, Lynn

bearbeitet am: ______________ erreichte Punktzahl: ______________

Ab 23 erreichten Punkten kannst du mit Test 14 fortfahren.

Test 14 Das Adjektiv

Schwierigkeitsgrad: ● ○ ○

1. **Unterstreiche alle Adjektive.**

on	window	tomato	red	run
new	car	take	eggs	rich
like	donkey	after	reason	table
milk	above	now	interesting	fine
hide	throw	hat	dark	off

2. **Suche zu jedem Substantiv das passende Adjektiv und verbinde die beiden. Schreibe die Begriffe dann mit dem unbestimmten Artikel (wenn nötig) noch einmal auf die Linien.**

high	hair
fast	story
short	tower
blond	trousers
funny	train
exciting	football game

a ______________________ ______________________

________ ______________________ ______________________

________ ______________________ ______________________

________ ______________________ ______________________

________ ______________________ ______________________

________ ______________________ ______________________

bearbeitet am: __________ erreichte Punktzahl: ______

Ab 25 erreichten Punkten kannst du mit Test 15 fortfahren, ab 30 mit Test 16.

Test 15 Das Adjektiv

Schwierigkeitsgrad: ● ○ ○

1. Suche aus den Adjektiven oben diejenigen heraus, die die aufgeführten Gegenstände unten beschreiben, und notiere dann Substantiv und passendes Adjektiv zusammen mit dem unbestimmten Artikel.

red	dark	cold	orange
hot	easy	little	soft

summer	fire engine	baby	lesson
carrot	pillow	winter	night

______________________ ______________________

______________________ ______________________

______________________ ______________________

______________________ ______________________

2. Bilde aus den Wörtern jeder Reihe jeweils einen vollständigen Satz und schreibe die Sätze auf. Wo stecken die Adjektive? Unterstreiche sie.

colourful – summer clothes – are wearing – the children

are – nice – my friend's parents

a – a– small cat – after – white dog – is running

your – look - new – glasses – good

____ .

____ .

____ .

____ .

bearbeitet am: __________ erreichte Punktzahl: ______

Ab 10 erreichten Punkten kannst du mit Test 16 fortfahren.

Test 16 Das Adjektiv

Schwierigkeitsgrad: ● ● ○

1. **Bilde jeweils das gegenteilige Adjektiv und schreibe es mit dem unbestimmten Artikel auf.**

a cheap jacket ______________________

a clever boy ______________________

a full cup ______________________

a rich woman ______________________

a hot day ______________________

an interesting movie ______________________

2. **Notiere je zwei Adjektive, die deiner Meinung nach zu diesen Substantiven passen.**

cars ______________________

school ______________________

comic books ______________________

fresh fruit ______________________

3. **Lies dir diese Behauptungen gut durch und kreuze „richtig" oder „falsch" an.**

	richtig	falsch
Adjektive stehen immer vor ihrem Bezugswort.	☐	☐
Adjektive geben stets Eigenschaften wieder.	☐	☐
Adjektive stehen nur mit Substantiven.	☐	☐
Adjektive beziehen sich auch auf Pronomen.	☐	☐
Adjektive verändern im Englischen ihre Form je nach Bezugswort.	☐	☐

bearbeitet am: ______ erreichte Punktzahl: ______

Ab 16 erreichten Punkten kannst du mit Test 17 fortfahren.

Test 17 Das Adjektiv

Schwierigkeitsgrad: ● ● ●

1. **In welchen Sätzen finden sich attributiv gebrauchte Adjektive, in welchen prädikativ gebrauchte? Trage die Buchstaben der Sätze in die richtige Tabellenspalte ein.**

A. The white rabbit is eating a carrot.

B. Nice work, Josh!

C. You look fantastic!

D. Andy is a good cook.

E. Her perfume smells wonderful.

F. Can I have two green apples, please?

G. Your chair is big.

H. 7 is my lucky number!

attributiv	prädikativ

2. **Übersetze die Sätze ins Englische und trage in die Kästchen „A" für attributiven, „P" für prädikativen Gebrauch des Adjektivs ein.**

Beverly hat ein Paar grüne Socken.

______________________________. ☐

Das Mittagessen schmeckt gut.

______________________________. ☐

Anne fühlt sich schlecht.

______________________________. ☐

bearbeitet am: ______ erreichte Punktzahl: ______

Ab 12 erreichten Punkten kannst du mit Test 18 fortfahren.

Test 18 Steigerung von Adjektiven

Schwierigkeitsgrad: ● ○ ○

1. **Bilde die regelmäßigen Komparative und Superlative.**

	Komparativ	Superlativ
small	______	______
warm	______	______
great	______	______
large	______	______
fine	______	______
fat	______	______
lucky	______	______
busy	______	______
pretty	______	______
tired	______	______
interesting	______	______

2. **Übersetze die Sätze ins Englische.**

Benny ist vorsichtiger.

______________________________.

Dein Auto ist das schnellste.

______________________________.

Heute ist das Wetter heißer.

______________________________.

bearbeitet am: ______ erreichte Punktzahl: ______

Ab 20 erreichten Punkten kannst du mit Test 19 fortfahren.

Test 19 Steigerung von Adjektiven

Schwierigkeitsgrad: ● ● ○

1. **Bilde die unregelmäßigen Komparative und Superlative.**

	Komparativ	Superlativ
far	______________	______________
bad	______________	______________
good	______________	______________
quiet	______________	______________

2. **Bilde einfache Vergleichssätze mit der richtigen Steigerungsform der Adjektive.**

	→	
Superman	strong	Spiderman
Snow White's hair	dark	Cinderella's hair
Tower Bridge	famous	London Eye
Sherlock Holmes	tall	Miss Marple
Marge Simpson	thin	Homer Simpson
Avatar	successful	*Titanic*

Superman is ______________________ than Spiderman.

____ .

____ .

____ .

____ .

____ .

bearbeitet am: ______ erreichte Punktzahl: ______

Ab 11 erreichten Punkten kannst du mit Test 20 fortfahren, ab 13 mit Test 21.

Test 20 Steigerung von Adjektiven

Schwierigkeitsgrad: ● ● ○

1. **Trage die fehlenden Formen in die Lücken aus.**

Grundform	Komparativ	Superlativ
lazy	______	______
______	harder	______
boring	______	______
______	______	busiest
great	______	______
______	worse	______
______	happier	______
______	______	best
funny	______	______
terrible	______	______

2. **Kimmy ist Siegerin bei allem! Steigere die Adjektive und fülle die Lücken aus.**

I am tall. Lena is ______________________ . Kimmy is

______________________ .

My hair is long. Selina's hair is ______________________ . Kimmy's hair is

______________________ .

My shoes are expensive. Janine's shoes are ______________________ .

Kimmy's shoes are ______________________ .

bearbeitet am: ______ erreichte Punktzahl: ______

Ab 21 erreichten Punkten kannst du mit Test 21 fortfahren.

Test 21 Steigerung von Adjektiven

Schwierigkeitsgrad: ● ● ●

1. Vergleiche die beiden genannten Substantive und bilde aus ihnen und dem Adjektiv jeweils zwei sinnvolle Vergleichssätze: Einen mit dem Komparativ und einen zweiten mit *not as ... as ...* Achtung: Vergiss die richtigen Artikel nicht!

tasty: chips / soup

Chips are ______________________________ than soup.

Soup is ____ chips.

high: Tower of London / Eiffel tower

____ .

____ .

elegant: French cafés / Irish pubs

____ .

____ .

hot: Sahara desert / North Sea

____ .

____ .

exact: stop watch / grandfather clock

____ .

____ .

good: movie / football

____

____ .

bearbeitet am: __________ erreichte Punktzahl: __________

Ab 10 erreichten Punkten kannst du mit Test 22 fortfahren.

Test 22 Das Adverb

Schwierigkeitsgrad: ● ○ ○

1. Bilde die korrekten Adverbien aus folgenden Adjektiven.

clear	______	gentle	______
funny	______	clever	______
horrible	______	hopeful	______
fantastic	______	secret	______
simple	______	exciting	______
sweet	______	basic	______
nice	______	heavy	______

2. Welches Adverb passt zu welchem Verb? Verbinde die zueinander passenden Paare und notiere die Wortpaarungen zusammen auf den Linien.

walk	well
shout	hungrily
smile	happily
play the piano	slowly
eat	angrily

______

______

______

______

______

bearbeitet am: ______ erreichte Punktzahl: ______

Ab 15 erreichten Punkten kannst du mit Test 23 fortfahren.

Test 23 Das Adverb

Schwierigkeitsgrad: ● ● ○

1. **Bilde die korrekten Adverbien zu den Gegensatzpaaren. Welches Wortpaar fehlt am Ende noch? Achtung: Es sind unregelmäßig gebildete Formen dabei.**

good	______	bad	______
warm	______	cold	______
hard	______	soft	______
late	______	early	______
slow	______	fast	______
loud	______	quiet	______
sad	______	______	______

2. **Adjektiv oder Adverb – erkennst du den Unterschied? Setze das fehlende Wort ein.**

quick	Adjektiv	She is ______ .
	Adverb	She comes ______ .
good	Adjektiv	This is a ______ joke.
	Adverb	You tell it ______ .
loud	Adjektiv	He is a ______ boy.
	Adverb	He often talks ______ .
slow	Adjektiv	He has a ______ car.
	Adverb	He drives it ______ .
careful	Adjektiv	She is a ______ mother.
	Adverb	She watches her children ______ .

bearbeitet am: ______ erreichte Punktzahl: ______

Ab 20 erreichten Punkten kannst du mit Test 24 fortfahren.

Test 24 Das Adverb

Schwierigkeitsgrad: ● ● ●

1. **Übersetze die Sätze.**

Jason ist ein guter Fußballspieler.

____ .

Er übt/trainiert hart.

____ .

Melissa schwimmmt sehr schnell.

____ .

Sie ist eine gute Schwimmerin.

____ .

Es ist schon spät. Fast Mitternacht!

____ .

2. **Adjektiv oder Adverb? Vervollständige den Lückentext.**

Hi Jenny, I am your ________________ (neu) pen-pal from Germany. First I want to tell you something about me, then I would like to learn some ________________ (interessant) things about you. My name is Lea. I can dance and sing ________________ (gut) and I like riding horses. I have a ________________ (groß) pony called Lisa. Lisa looks really ________________ (hübsch). She can run very ________________ (schnell) and jump very________________ (hoch). So tell me about you – are you a ______________ (gut) dancer or singer, too? Dou you like ______________ (lang) pony rides? Write back ______________ (schnell), please! Your friend, Lea

bearbeitet am: __________ erreichte Punktzahl: ______

Ab 12 erreichten Punkten kannst du mit Test 25 fortfahren.

Test 25 Steigerung von Adverbien

Schwierigkeitsgrad: ● ● ○

1. **Ergänze die fehlenden Formen der Adjektive oder Adverbien in der Steigerungstabelle. Achtung: Entscheide zuerst, ob es sich um Adjektiv oder Adverb handelt!**

Grundform	Komparativ	Superlativ
lazily	____________	____________
____________	harder	____________
boringly	____________	____________
____________	____________	most busily
____________	____________	greatest
badly	____________	____________
____________	more simply	____________
happy	____________	____________

2. **Fülle die Lücken aus. Benutze die passenden Grund- und Steigerungsformen von Adjektiv oder Adverb der Wörter in Klammern.**

Beverly feels ____________ (good) than last week.

My aunt Susan drives ____________ (fast) than my dad. Dad is a much ________________________ (careful) driver than his sister.

I think that was a ____________ (good) play. They all acted very ____________ (good).

When Philip came into the room, Joanna started to talk ____________ ____________ (nervous) than before.

Can you please be a little ____________ (quick)? We're all waiting here!

bearbeitet am: ____________ erreichte Punktzahl: ______

Ab 18 erreichten Punkten kannst du mit Test 26 fortfahren.

Test 26 Steigerung von Adverbien

Schwierigkeitsgrad: ● ● ●

1. **Übersetze die hier aufgeführten Formen von Adjektiven und Adverbien und setze sie in der richtigen Form in die passenden Lücken ein.**

schneller als	älter als	den schlimmsten	schrecklichen	gesünder als
neueste	schlimmer als	am kleinsten	am gesündesten	größer als
höher als	gesunde	der beste	leicht	

I had ______________________ day of the year.

I woke up with a ______________ headache, and then someone stole my ______________________ „Green Day" CD at school. That was even ______________________ the pain.

Tim's sister is ______________________ him, but nevertheless he is ______________________ her. Their little brother is ______________________ of the whole family. But he grows ______________________ any baby I know.

My dad eats ______________________ me and my brothers, but my mom eats ______________________ of us all. We children cannot stand all this ______________________ food.

Can Max not jump ______________________ Ben? He said he were ______________________ jumper of the class. And I believed him so ______________________!

bearbeitet am: __________ erreichte Punktzahl: ______

Ab 11 erreichten Punkten kannst du mit Test 27 fortfahren.

Test 27 Personalpronomen

Schwierigkeitsgrad: ● ○ ○

1. Unterstreiche in den Sätzen die Personalpronomen und übersetze diese.

She is coming home. ____________________

We are on our way to school. ____________________

It takes some time. ____________________

Must I go to school today? ____________________

He is on the phone. ____________________

You are late again, Stephen. ____________________

It's finished! ____________________

You, Viv and Anne, sit down! ____________________

I can call again later. ____________________

Now they are listening. ____________________

Do they know we live here? ____________________ / ____________________

2. Gillians Mutter macht Gillian schulfertig. Einige Sachen fehlen leider noch. Beantworte die Fragen für Gillian und ersetze dabei die Substantive durch Personalpronomen.

Where is your Jacket? ____________________ is on the chair.

Where is your exercise book? ____________________ is in my schoolbag.

Where are your glasses? ____________________ are on the table.

Where is your lunch money? ____________________ is in my pocket.

Where are your keys? ____________________ are in my jacket.

Where is the bus? ____________________ is outside at the bus stop.

bearbeitet am: ____________ erreichte Punktzahl: ______

Ab 23 erreichten Punkten kannst du mit Test 28 fortfahren.

Test 28 Personalpronomen

Schwierigkeitsgrad: ● ○ ○

1. ***She, he*** **oder** ***it*****? Kreuze das passende Personalpronomen zu den Subjekten an**

Personalpronomen	she	he	it
the carpet			
Ms O'Casey			
the cow			
Robert			
our cat Felix			
your sister			
my uncle			

2. Setze die passenden Pronomen in die Lücken ein.

"Hello Lucy. It's good to see ______________________ !"

"Good morning, Sandy. How are ______________________ ?"

"______________________'m fine, and ______________________ ?

How is Christopher, is ______________________ feeling better?"

"Yes, ______________________ is well again. How about little Ella,

is ______________________ okay?"

"Yes, ______________________ is fine, thank you. All three children are fine,

______________________ are taking piano lessons now."

"Good! Well, ______________________ have to hurry."

"Okay, see ______________________ !"

bearbeitet am: ____________ erreichte Punktzahl: ______

Ab 13 erreichten Punkten kannst du mit Test 29 fortfahren.

Test 29 Personalpronomen

Schwierigkeitsgrad: ● ● ○

1. Fülle die Lücken mit den entsprechenden Objekt- und Subjektformen der Personalpronomen aus.

I	→	____________	it	→	____________
you	→	____________	____________	→	us
she	→	____________	you	→	____________
____________	→	him	they	→	____________

2. Das Wörtchen *you* hat viele deutsche Bedeutungen. Was bedeutet es jeweils in diesen Sätzen? Such die korrekte Übersetzung aus den vorgegebenen Wörtern heraus und trage sie auf den Linien ein.

du | dir | dich | ihr | euch | Sie | Ihnen

You have two dogs, Emily, right? ____________

Do **you** want to go, dear? ____________

You must excuse me, Mr Lawson. ____________

See **you** later, boys! ____________

May I see **you** after class, Ms Mifflin? ____________

Can I help **you**, sir? ____________

I love **you**, darling! ____________

I give **you** the bags, Ethan! ____________

I trust **you**, Uncle Stephen. ____________

Where are **you** going on holiday, children? ____________

bearbeitet am: ____________ erreichte Punktzahl: ____________

Ab 15 erreichten Punkten kannst du mit Test 30 fortfahren.

Test 30 Personalpronomen

Schwierigkeitsgrad: ● ● ○

1. **Noah ist schusselig. Nichts kann er finden, und immer muss er andere fragen! Ergänze die fehlenden Objektpronomen.**

Where is my red model plane?	I can't find ____________.
Where are my Chucks?	I can't find ____________.
Where is mum?	I can't find ____________.
Where is my homework?	I can't find ____________.
Where are you, dad?	I can't find ____________.
Where is my friend Danny?	I can't find ____________.
Where are you going?	Wait for ____________!

2. **Fülle die Lücken mit den fehlenden Pronomen. Achtung: Hier werden Subjekte *und* Objekte ersetzt.**

What would ____________ like to do, girls? – Let ____________ play some volleyball!

Where is Alex? I can't see ____________ anywhere. Perhaps ____________ is in the garden.

Hey, dad, let ____________ play football! – Sorry, Jacob ____________ can't. I've hurt my foot. ____________ hurts terribly.

Mr and Ms Miller are at not home now. But ____________ will come back tonight.

Poor Mia! ____________ forgot to do some grocery shopping, and now ____________ freezer is completely empty. ____________ is a pity!

Come here, sweetheart, and give ____________ a kiss!

bearbeitet am: ____________ erreichte Punktzahl: ______

Ab 15 erreichten Punkten kannst du mit Test 31 fortfahren.

Test 31 Possessivpronomen

Schwierigkeitsgrad: ● ○ ○

1. **Ersetze die unterstrichenen Ausdrücke durch die passenden Possessivbegleiter.**

Bella's boyfriend	____________ boyfriend
Mr Good's shop	____________ shop
Aaron's and Ava's books	____________ books
the fireman's boots	____________ boots
my mother's toothbrush	____________ toothbrush
the monkey's tree	____________ tree

2. **Bilde Sätze, indem du die Wortpaare mit Possessivbegleiter verwendest.**

dad	→	car	Emma	→	cat
Ms Honeychurch	→	roses	grandpa	→	slippers
Michael and Andy	→	bikes	three girls	→	bags
some dogs	→	bones	two parents	→	baby

There is dad with his car.

There is ____________________ with ____________________ roses.

There are ____________________ with ____________________ .

____

____

____

____

____

bearbeitet am: __________ erreichte Punktzahl: ______

Ab 11 erreichten Punkten kannst du mit Test 32 fortfahren.

Test 32 Possessivpronomen

Schwierigkeitsgrad: ● ● ○

1. **Setze den richtigen Possessivbegleiter in die Lücken ein. Die Übersetzungen in Klammern helfen dir.**

Lily is looking for ________________ (ihre) glasses. ________________ (Ihre) sister is helping her. They are looking in the living room and in Lily's room and in ________________ (ihrem) closet, also in ________________ (ihrer) parents' bedroom – nothing! Lily calls up to ________________ (ihre) mother: "We can't find ________________ (meine) glasses, where are they?" ________________ (ihre) mother says: "Call ________________ (deinen) dad, he's at ________________ (seinem) office. Perhaps he knows, where you put ________________ (deine) glasses." Lily calls ________________ (ihren) father, but he doesn't know, where they are, either. Finally, ________________ (ihre) sister finds Lily's glasses on the garden table in ________________ (ihrem) garden.

2. **Fülle die Lücken mit den Possessivpronomen aus, die zu den jeweiligen Possessivbegleitern passen – oder umgekehrt.**

my → ________________ ________________ → ours

your → ________________ your → ________________

________________ → hers their → ________________

his → ________________

3. **Wie viele Möglichkeiten gibt es, im Englischen das Wörtchen „sie/Sie" auszudrücken?**
Wenn du alle Verwendungen auch noch aufzählen kannst, gibt's einen dicken Extrapunkt!

1 Möglichkeit ☐ 3 Möglichkeiten ☐ 5 Möglichkeiten ☐

bearbeitet am: ________ erreichte Punktzahl: ________

Ab 18 erreichten Punkten kannst du mit Test 33 fortfahren.

Test 33 Possessivpronomen

Schwierigkeitsgrad: ● ● ○

1. *Its* oder *it's*? *Your* oder *you're*? Kannst du den Stolperfallen entgehen? Trage die richtige Form ein.

This chair is useless. ________________ leg is broken. ________________ a pity!

Have you lost ________________ watch? ________________ late again!

I think ________________ very clever! ________________ plan sounds great.

________________ five o'clock already! The dog needs ________________ food.

This shirt is beautiful, ________________ true. ________________ colour looks good.

________________ feeling cold? No wonder, ________________ coat is much too thin!

________________ bus is leaving soon. Don't forget ________________ bag!

2. Setze die richtigen Possessivbegleiter und -pronomen in die Lücken ein.

I am looking for ________________ seat. I don't think this one is ________________ ,

because it isn't ________________ seat row number. Perhaps it is over there, next to

________________ seat, Alyssa! Is ________________ in row number 13?

Escuse me, madam, is this ________________ suitcase? I took it by mistake, because it

looks just like ________________ . I'm sorry, I will go find ________________ own

luggage right away.

Let me see ________________ passport, sir. And open ________________ bags

for us, please. What about that backpack over there? Is it ________________ , too?

I don't think he is sleeping enough. ________________ eyes look very tired.

bearbeitet am: ________________ erreichte Punktzahl: ________

Ab 21 erreichten Punkten kannst du mit Test 34 fortfahren.

Test 34 Demonstrativpronomen

Schwierigkeitsgrad: ● ○ ○

1. Fülle die Lücken mit den richtigen Demonstrativpronomen.

__________________ here is a mouse, and __________________ over there is a rat.

__________________ here are my cookies, and __________________ over there are yours.

__________________ potatoes here and __________________ green beans over there are too old, I won't buy them.

__________________ is my plate, and __________________ one at the other end of the table is your plate.

__________________ are my Magic cards, and __________________ on the table are yours.

__________________ was your idea last week, and __________________ is my idea today!

Is __________________ white dog yours? Mine is __________________ black one on the lawn.

__________________ girl on the chair in the back is my girlfriend.

2. Ergänze die passenden Demonstrativpronomen im Singular oder Plural.

this hat – __________________ hats

__________________ child – those children

that woman – __________________ women

this plane – __________________ planes

__________________ orange – these oranges

this lady – __________________

__________________ – those pages

that house – __________________

__________________ – these families

bearbeitet am: __________ erreichte Punktzahl: ______

Ab 19 erreichten Punkten kannst du mit Test 35 fortfahren.

Test 35 Demonstrativpronomen

Schwierigkeitsgrad: ● ● ○

1. **Jessica hat einen neuen Austauschschüler zu Besuch, und er stellt ihr viele Fragen zum Haus. Sieh dir ihre Antworten an und ergänze die fehlenden Demonstrativpronomen.**

Carlos: What do you call ________________ room here? Jessica: It's the bathroom.

Carlos: And what are ________________ things here called? Jessica: They're toothbrushes.

Carlos: What is ________________ thing on the hook? Jessica: It's a towel.

Carlos: What is ________________ room where you cook? Jessica: It's our kitchen.

Carlos: And what are ________________ things you eat with? Jessica: They're forks.

Carlos: Whose room is ________________ one over there? Jessica: It is my room.

Carlos: What's ________________ book on your bed? Jessica: It's a storybook.

2. ***This, these, that* oder *those*? Setze das richtige Demonstrativpronomen ein.**

– Look at ________________ shirt! I think it's nice. But ________________ shirt on the left looks nice, too. Do you like ________________ shirt better than ________________ one on the left?

– I'm not sure. But I really like ________________ trousers over there.

– Would you like to buy ________________ two cheap DVDs here, or ________________ one expensive DVD?

– I think I'll buy ________________ special offer DVD of *Avatar*. It' on sale in the back.

– Just look at ________________ mess here! Put ________________ dirty socks in the washing and ________________ jumper on the floor, too!

– Mum, ________________ is *my* room. I live here, and I can live with clothes on the floor.

– O stop it! Just put them on ________________ chair in the corner, and I will get them.

bearbeitet am: ________ erreichte Punktzahl: ________

Ab 16 erreichten Punkten kannst du mit Test 36 fortfahren.

Test 36 *one/ones*

Schwierigkeitsgrad: ● ○ ○

1. **Ersetze die unterstrichenen Begriffe durch *one* oder *ones* und notiere den letzten Satzteil noch einmal vollständig.**

Look at all those puppies! Which puppy would you like?

Which ________________ would you like?

I don't know, which DVD to borrow – this DVD or that DVD?

____

Which way to the station – this street to the left, or that street to the right?

____

What kind of crisps do you like better – paprika-flavoured crisps, or salted crisps?

____

I am looking for ripe strawberries – where can I find very ripe strawberries?

____

2. **Unterstreiche selbst die Begriffe, bei denen ein Ersatz durch *one* oder *ones* sinnvoll ist, und schreibe das richtige Ersatzwort, wenn es eines gibt, neben den Satz.**

– Can I try on that bikini?

– Which bikini?

– That yellow bikini in the window.

– It's a little too large, isn't it? Have you got a smaller yellow bikini?

– No, I don't think so. We have no other yellow bikinis.

– Can I try on the orange bikini on that rack there?

– Oh, this bikini fits perfectly. I will take it.

bearbeitet am: ____________ erreichte Punktzahl: ______

Ab 8 erreichten Punkten kannst du mit Test 37 fortfahren, ab 10 mit Test 38.

Test 37 *one/ones*

Schwierigkeitsgrad: ● ○ ○

1. Ergänze *one* oder *ones*.

Which dress should she wear? The green __________ or the black __________?

You don't need all your old toys! Let's keep only the __________ you really play with.

You can eat these carrots. The other __________ are bad.

He has got many T-shirts, but he wears only the black __________.

There are two crayons in her pencil case: a hard __________ and a soft __________.

Which movie should we watch? The __________ at the Rex, or the __________ at the Metropol?

Here's your Halloween candy: the sweets on the left are Tristan's and the __________ on the right are Leah's.

I know all the books on your shelf, but I don't know the __________ next to your bed.

No, the small car in front of the shop window isn't mine. It's the big black __________ next to it.

There are three rules: two old __________ and a new __________ .

I like going to the movies, but I don't like all films – there are some good __________ and there are some bad __________.

You don't like that kind of pie? Come on, try this __________!

Not all pupils wear glasses – only the __________ with weak eyes.

Can you give me one of your balloons? I'd like the green __________!

bearbeitet am: __________ erreichte Punktzahl: __________

Ab 15 erreichten Punkten kannst du mit Test 38 fortfahren.

Test 38 Regelmäßige Verben

Schwierigkeitsgrad: ● ○ ○

1. **Unterstreiche alle Verben im Text, auch die Hilfsverben.**

In Great Britain, people have Christmas on the 25th of December. Children find their presents in their socks – they call them "Christmas stockings". They can open their presents early in the morning, and in the evening, they eat their Christmas dinner, which is often turkey. For dessert they have "Christmas pudding", a very sweet fruit cake. Some children cannot sleep well the night before Christmas. They think they must wait a very long time, until Christmas morning arrives. If there is snow for Christmas, British children also like to build snowmen.

2. **Schreibe alle Verben aus dem Gespräch unten heraus auf die Linien. Denke auch an die Hilfsverben und mögliche abgekürzte Formen.**

– Can you tell me, where my exercise book is?
– No, sorry, do you need it now?
– Yes, there is a maths test tomorrow, and I must do the exercises.
– Why can't you do them later?
– I need to go to football practice later.
– Okay. I can help you look for it.
– Thank you, that's nice.

____

____

3. **Füge die passenden Verben aus der Liste in der richtigen Personalform in die Lücken ein.**

start like forget be give do give

Our English teacher ________________ a nice lady.

I never ________________ my homework for her.

My brother ________________ his maths teacher best.

She ________________ not ________________ them much homework.

School ________________ at nine.

bearbeitet am: ________ erreichte Punktzahl: ________

Ab 30 erreichten Punkten kannst du mit Test 39 fortfahren.

Test 39 Regelmäßige Verben

Schwierigkeitsgrad: ● ○ ○

1. Sortiere die Wörter je nach Wortart in die passenden Tabellenspalten ein.

swim	remember	totally	jam	leg	knee	run
quickly	well	purple	grey	quiet	strong	forget
feel	make	idea	bitter	mistake	dolphin	wildly

nouns	adjectives	adverbs	verbs

2. Ergänze die fehlenden Stammformen dieser regelmäßigen Verben.

infinitive	simple past	past participle
turn	__________	__________
__________	jumped	__________
play	__________	__________
paint	__________	__________
wave	__________	__________
__________	__________	enjoyed
__________	walked	__________
__________	__________	promised

bearbeitet am: erreichte Punktzahl:

Ab 30 erreichten Punkten kannst du mit Test 40 fortfahren.

Test 40 Unregelmäßige Verben

Schwierigkeitsgrad: ● ○ ○

1. Ergänze die fehlenden Stammformen dieser unregelmäßigen Verben.

infinitive	simple past	past participle
___	was, were	___
become	___	___
begin	___	___
___	bound	___
bite	___	___
___	___	blown
break	___	___
bring	___	___
___	built	___
burn	___	___
bought	___	___
___	___	caught
choose	___	___
come	___	___
___	cost	___
creep	___	___
___	___	cut
___	did	___

bearbeitet am: ________ erreichte Punktzahl: ____

Ab 32 erreichten Punkten kannst du mit Test 41 fortfahren.

Test 41 Unregelmäßige Verben

Schwierigkeitsgrad: ● ○ ○

1. Ergänze die fehlenden Stammformen dieser unregelmäßigen Verben.

infinitive	simple past	past participle
____________	drew	____________
____________	dreamt/dreamed	____________
____________	drank	____________
drive	____________	____________
eat	____________	____________
fall	____________	____________
____________	felt	____________
____________	____________	fought
find	____________	____________
fly	____________	____________
____________	____________	forbidden
forget	____________	____________
get	____________	____________
____________	gave	____________
go	____________	____________
grow	____________	____________
have	____________	____________
____________	heard	____________

bearbeitet am: ____________ erreichte Punktzahl: ______

Ab 32 erreichten Punkten kannst du mit Test 42 fortfahren.

Test 42 Unregelmäßige Verben

Schwierigkeitsgrad: ● ○ ○

1. Ergänze die fehlenden Stammformen dieser unregelmäßigen Verben.

infinitive	simple past	past participle
hold	______	______
______	______	hurt
______	______	kept
know	knew	known
learn	______	______
______	left	______
______	______	let
lose	______	______
make	______	______
______	met	______
pay	______	______
______	______	put
______	______	read [red]
ride	______	______
______	______	said
see	______	______
______	sent	______
show	______	______

bearbeitet am: ______ erreichte Punktzahl: ______

Ab 32 erreichten Punkten kannst du mit Test 43 fortfahren.

Test 43 Unregelmäßige Verben

Schwierigkeitsgrad: ● ● ○

1. Ergänze die fehlenden Stammformen dieser unregelmäßigen Verben.

infinitive	simple past	past participle
sing	______	______
sit	______	______
______	______	slept
______	spoke	______
______	______	spent
stand	______	______
steal	______	______
______	______	swum
take	______	______
______	______	taught
tell	______	______
think	______	______
throw	______	______
______	understood	______
wake	______	______
wear	______	______
______	won	______
write	______	______

bearbeitet am: ______ erreichte Punktzahl: ______

Ab 32 erreichten Punkten kannst du mit Test 44 fortfahren.

Test 44 *be* – Bejahung und Verneinung

Schwierigkeitsgrad: ● ○ ○

1. Fülle die freien Felder in der Tabelle mit den fehlenden Lang- und Kurzformen von *be* aus.

BEJAHUNG		VERNEINUNG	
lange Form	Kurzform	lange Form	Kurzform
I am	______	I am not	______
______	you're	______	you aren't
she is	______	she is not	______
he is	______	he is not	______
it is	______	it is not	______
______	we're	we are not	______
they are	______	______	they aren't

2. Julia stellt sich ihrer Brieffreundin vor. Ergänze die fehlenden Formen von *be*. Verwende für den Brief ausschießlich die Langform.

Dear Alina,

my name ______ Julia. I ______ in fifth grade and live in a town in the North of England called Newcastle. I ______ 11 years old and have two brothers. They ______ both older than me, and we ______ a nice family. But I ______ happy to have a girl as a a penfriend now. How old ______ you? What ______ your hobby? My hobbies ______ books and horses. I put in a photo of myself. It ______ a pity that I haven't got a picture of you yet. Please send me one!

Yours, Julia

bearbeitet am: ______ erreichte Punktzahl: ______

Ab 20 erreichten Punkten kannst du mit Test 45 fortfahren.

Test 45 *be* – Bejahung und Verneinung

Schwierigkeitsgrad: ● ● ○

1. **Verneine die Fragen und stelle die Aussagen richtig. Verwende für die Gesprächssätze die Kurzform, wo es geht.**

– Are you from Scotland?

– No, I ______________________ from Scotland, I ____________ from Wales.

– Is that boy over there your brother?

– No, he ______________________ my brother, he ____________ my cousin.

– Are your parents teachers?

– No, ______________________________, they ____________ sales people.

– Are you and your brothers in the tennis team?

– ______________________________, we ____________ in the chess club.

2. **Bilde aus den Vorgaben plus der passenden Form von *be* ganze Aussagesätze.**

Susan / my name / + ? *be*

____.

my sister / over there / that / + ? *be*

____.

she / alone / not / + ? *be*

____.

and / with / some friends, too / you / + ? *be*

____.

bearbeitet am: ____________ erreichte Punktzahl: ____

Ab 10 erreichten Punkten kannst du mit Test 46 fortfahren.

Test 46 *be* – Fragen

Schwierigkeitsgrad: ● ○ ○

1. **Beantworte die Fragen in der Kurzform, wo es geht, sonst in der Langform.**

Are you in fourth grade? No, ______________________.

Is your dad at home? No, ______________________.

Are you good at sports? Yes, ______________________.

Is your sister called Eileen? No, ______________________.

Is the football match on Sunday? Yes, ______________________.

Am I late? No, ______________________.

Are we in trouble? No, ______________________.

Are they a strong team? Yes, ______________________.

Is Natalie your friend? No, ______________________.

2. **Stelle jetzt die zu den Antworten passenden Fragen.**

Are you ______________________? No, I'm not at school now.

Is he ______________________? Yes, he's in the kitchen.

______________________? No, she is not in the hospital.

______________________? Yes, they're at the movies.

______________________? Yes, we are on holiday.

______________________? Yes, you are a good reader.

______________________? No, that is not your scarf.

______________________?

No, I'm not the worst singer of the class!

bearbeitet am: __________ erreichte Punktzahl: __________

Ab 14 erreichten Punkten kannst du mit Test 47 fortfahren.

Test 47 *be* – Fragen

Schwierigkeitsgrad: ● ● ○

1. **Forme die Aussagen zu Fragesätzen um und gib die vorgegebene bejahende oder verneinende Kurzantwort.**

   Gabriel and Dylan are late for school. (yes)

   Are Gabriel and Dylan ____________________ ? Yes, ____________________ .

   This test is difficult. (no)

   ____________________ ? ____________________ .

   You are a pop music fan. (yes)

   ____________________ ? ____________________ .

   Hannah is happy. (no)

   ____________________ ? ____________________ .

2. **Bilde aus den Vorgaben plus der passenden Form von *be* ganze Fragesätze.**

   Henry / your name / + ? *be*

   ____ ?

   at the same school / we / + ? *be*

   ____ ?

   the party / on Saturday / + ? *be*

   ____ ?

   a guest / at that party / you, too / + ? *be*

   ____

   ____ ?

bearbeitet am: __________ erreichte Punktzahl: _____

Ab 10 erreichten Punkten kannst du mit Test 48 fortfahren.

Test 48 *be – there is/there are*

Schwierigkeitsgrad: ● ○ ○

1. Was gibt es alles bei Cathy zu Hause? Fülle die Lücken mit *there is* oder *there are*.

At home, ______________________ carpets in all rooms.

At home, ______________________ a fireplace in the living room.

At home, ______________________ two bathrooms.

At home, ______________________ a swing set in the garden.

At home, ______________________ chairs around the tables.

At home, ______________________ a grandfather clock in the hall.

At home, ______________________ four bedrooms.

At home, ______________________ a carport in the front.

At home, ______________________ lots of books on the shelves.

2. Beantworte die Fragen wie vorgegeben bejahrend oder verneinend.

Is there sugar in the corn flakes? (yes)

Yes, there is ____.

Is there milk in the fridge? (no)

____.

Are there chocolate cookies in your bag? (yes)

____.

Is there an alarm system in his expensive new car? (yes)

____.

____.

bearbeitet am: __________ erreichte Punktzahl: ______

Ab 11 erreichten Punkten kannst du mit Test 49 fortfahren.

Test 49 *be – there is/there are*

Schwierigkeitsgrad: ● ● ○

1. **Welche Tiere gibt es im Zoo zu sehen? Stelle die zu den Antworten passenden Fragen.**

Are there monkeys ?	Yes, there are monkeys at the zoo.
______________________________ ?	Yes, there is a rhino at the zoo.
______________________________ ?	No, there aren't bunnies at the zoo.
______________________________ ?	Yes, there are snakes at the zoo.
______________________________ ?	Yes, there is a polar bear at the zoo.
______________________________ ?	No, there isn't a whale at the zoo.
______________________________ ?	Yes, there are penguins at the zoo.

2. **Was gibt es alles in Andys Klassenraum? Bilde aus den Gegenständen und ihren Mengenangaben vollständige Sätze.**

blackboard (1)	windows (6)	door (1)	chairs (many)
desks (a lot)	posters (3)	lamps (2)	sponge (1)

There is one blackboard in the classroom.

______________________________ in the classroom.

______________________________ in the classroom.

______________________________ in the classroom.

______________________________ in the classroom.

______________________________ in the classroom.

______________________________ in the classroom.

______________________________ in the classroom.

bearbeitet am: ____________ erreichte Punktzahl: ____

Ab 11 erreichten Punkten kannst du mit Test 50 fortfahren.

Test 50 *have got* – Bejahung und Verneinung

Schwierigkeitsgrad: ● ○ ○

1. **Lukes Familie hat viele Sachen. Zähle auf, wer was besitzt, und setze dabei in die Lücken *have got* und *has got* ein.**

Luke ______________________ a computer in his room.

Luke's sister Betsy ______________________ two hamsters.

Luke's mum and dad ______________________ 400 DVDs.

Luke and Betsy ______________________ a red and a green bicycle.

The family ______________________ a dog named Lassie.

The dog ______________________ a new leash.

2. **Hier geht es um Familienmitglieder. Wer hat welche Verwandten und wer nicht? Lies die Namen und Stichwörter und ergänze dann die Sätze. Verwende bei allen Verneinungen die Kurzform *hasn't got*.**

Josh: one brother, no sister, one father, one mother, two uncles, no aunts
Sam: no brother, no sister, no father, one mother, three uncles, two aunts
Nell: no brothers, one sister, two fathers, one mother, no uncles, one aunt

Josh ______________________ a brother but he ______________________

a sister. He ______________________ a father and a mother.

Sam ______________________ a father, but he ______________________
three uncles.

Nell ______________________ a brother but she ______________________

a sister. She ______________________ two fathers!

Josh ______________________ two uncles, but he ______________________
an aunt.

Sam ______________________ a sister, but he ______________________
two aunts.

bearbeitet am: __________ erreichte Punktzahl: __________

Ab 15 erreichten Punkten kannst du mit Test 51 fortfahren, ab 17 mit Test 52.

Test 51 *have got* – Bejahung und Verneinung

Schwierigkeitsgrad: ● ○ ○

1. Gib die passenden Antworten mit Formen von *be* und *have got* in der Kurzform.

Have you got many friends at school?	Yes, I have.
Have you got a favourite subject?	No, ______________________.
Are you in fifth grade?	Yes, ______________________.
Have you got good grades in English?	Yes, ______________________.
Is your class a big class?	Yes, ______________________.
Are you happy with all your teachers?	No, ______________________.
Have you got a new school bag?	Yes, ______________________.
Are you in the school band?	Yes, ______________________.
Have you got a guitar?	No, ______________________.
Have you got a computer?	Yes, ______________________.
Is your maths teacher okay?	No, ______________________.

2. Kreuze jeweils die richtige Antwort an.

Der englische Audruck *have got* sagt aus, dass jemand etwas hat im Sinn von ...

besitzen ☐ vorhaben ☐ behalten ☐

Bei Kurzanworten entfällt ...

das *have* ☐ das *got* ☐ das Apostroph ☐

Es gibt <u>keine</u> Kurzform des Ausdrucks bei ...

verneinenden Kurzantworten ☐ bejahenden Kurzantworten ☐ Fragen ☐

bearbeitet am: ____________ erreichte Punktzahl: ______

Ab 11 erreichten Punkten kannst du mit Test 52 fortfahren.

Test 52 *have got* – Bejahung und Verneinung

Schwierigkeitsgrad: ● ● ○

1. Bilde aus den Satzteilen in den Feldern vollständige, sinnvolle Sätze.

Ms Peters	have got	four big airports
Jonathan and Olivia	has got	a bone to chew
Cornwall		a lot of beaches
Mark's dog		new school bags
London		a good job
the new girl in class		a nice hair band

____.

____.

____.

____.

____.

____

____.

2. Übersetze die Sätze und verwende dabei die Kurzform.

Ich habe gute Noten in Englisch.

____.

Ihr habt einen größeren Garten.

____.

Er hat ein sehr kleines Auto.

____.

bearbeitet am: ______ erreichte Punktzahl: ______

Ab 7 erreichten Punkten kannst du mit Test 53 fortfahren.

Test 53 *have got* – Fragen

Schwierigkeitsgrad: ● ○ ○

1. **Schau dir Aufgabe 2 aus Test 50 noch einmal an und gib die richtigen Kurzantworten.**

Has Josh got a sister? ______________________________ .

Has Sam got three uncles? ______________________________ .

Has Nell got a mother? ______________________________ .

Has Nell got a brother? ______________________________ .

Has Josh got an aunt? ______________________________ .

Has Sam got a sister? ______________________________ .

Has Josh got a father? ______________________________ .

Has Nell got an aunt? ______________________________ .

2. **Stelle nun die zu den Antworten passenden Fragen.**

______________________________ ? Yes, Nell has got two fathers.

______________________________ ? No, Sam hasn't got a brother.

______________________________ ? Yes, Josh has got two uncles.

______________________________ ? No, Josh hasn't got an aunt.

______________________________ ? No, Nell hasn't got an uncle.

______________________________ ? Yes, Sam has got a mother.

______________________________ ? Yes, Nell has got a mother, too.

______________________________ ? No, Sam hasn't got a father.

______________________________ ? Yes, Nell has got an aunt.

______________________________ ? Yes, Josh has got a brother.

bearbeitet am: __________ erreichte Punktzahl: ______

Ab 15 erreichten Punkten kannst du mit Test 54 fortfahren.

Test 54 *have got* – Fragen

Schwierigkeitsgrad: ● ● ○

1. **Bilde aus den Aussagesätzen Fragesätze und gib eine Kurzantwort wie vorgegeben.**

Tony has got 100 CDs. (yes)

______________________________? ______________________________.

Zoey has got a twin sister. (no)

______________________________? ______________________________.

The brothers have got a TV set. (no)

______________________________? ______________________________.

We've got time. (yes)

______________________________? ______________________________.

You've got sunglasses. (yes)

______________________________? ______________________________.

2. **Jetzt geht es um dich! Was hast du? Beantworte die Fragen selbst mit Kurzantworten.**

Have you got a brother? ______________________________.

Have you got a lot of computer games? ______________________________.

Have you got a pet? ______________________________.

Have you got a blue pen? ______________________________.

Have you got a bicycle? ______________________________.

Have you got two sisters? ______________________________.

Have you got many T-shirts? ______________________________.

Have you got a good friend? ______________________________.

bearbeitet am: __________ erreichte Punktzahl: __________

Ab 15 erreichten Punkten kannst du mit Test 55 fortfahren.

Test 55 *have* im Satz

Schwierigkeitsgrad: ● ○ ○

1. **Verbinde die zueinander passenden Satzteile und notiere die entstandenen Sätze dann vollständig auf den Linien.**

Molly	have	a shower	Saturday night
Mr and Ms Kent	has	a dinner party	every morning
the class	has	a meeting	on Thursdays
the directors	have	two long breaks	on a schoolday

____

____

____

____

____

____

2. **Bilde aus den Aussagesätzen Fragesätze und umgekehrt.**

We have breakfast together.

____ ?

Do you have fun in front of your computer?

____ .

Nicholas has football practice every Wednesday.

____

____ ?

bearbeitet am: ____________ erreichte Punktzahl: ______

Ab 6 erreichten Punkten kannst du mit Test 56 fortfahren.

Test 56 *have* im Satz

Schwierigkeitsgrad: ● ● ○

1. **Matt schreibt seiner Freundin aus dem Ferienlager. Setze die fehlenden Formen von *have* oder *have got* in die Lücken seines Briefes ein.**

Dear Rachel,

I really ______________________ fun here at summer camp. My days are so busy that I ______________________ much time to write, sorry. Let me tell you about my day: We get up at seven o'clock and ______________________ breakfast. I usually ______________________ toast and a glass of orange juice. Then we go outside and ______________________ a little football match. I ______________________ my own football here with me, so we take Brandon's ball. Then we ______________________ lunch. In the afternoon, we play games or build things or ______________________ swimming lessons. I ______________________ quiet nights, because I ______________________ a bed for myself here. That's all for now. I hope you ______________________ a lot of fun, too! Yours, Matt

2. **Übersetze die Sätze. Achte auf den unterschiedlichen Gebrauch von *have* und *have got*.**

Ich habe heute Basketball-Training.

____ .

Nimmst du samstags ein Bad?

____ .

Meine Großeltern haben kein Auto.

____ .

bearbeitet am: ____________ **erreichte Punktzahl:** ______

Ab 11 erreichten Punkten kannst du mit Test 57 fortfahren.

Test 57 *do* – als Vollverb und Hilfsverb

Schwierigkeitsgrad: ● ○ ○

1. **Setze die richtige Form des Vollverbs *do* ein.**

My brothers ______________________ a lot of sports.

Linda ______________________ her shopping after lunch.

Lucas ______________________ his homework every day.

I ______________________ the washing, and you ______________________ the ironing.

2. **Verneine die Fragen in der Langform. Verwende bei deinen Antworten die Umschreibung mit *do* als Hilfsverb.**

Do you live in East Berlin?

No, I ____________________ ____________________ live in East Berlin.

Does he go to school on Saturdays?

____.

Do they like Italian food?

____.

3. **Verneine die Fragen in der Kurzform von *do* als Hilfsverb.**

Does Nina go swimming? ______________________________.

Do you like him? ______________________________.

Do your parents drive there often? ______________________________.

Does it hurt? ______________________________.

Do we know any Scottish towns? ______________________________.

bearbeitet am: __________ erreichte Punktzahl: __________

Ab 11 erreichten Punkten kannst du mit Test 58 fortfahren.

Test 58 *do* – als Vollverb und Hilfsverb

Schwierigkeitsgrad: ● ● ○

1. Übersetze die Sätze. Achte auf die richtige Umschreibung mit *do*.

Ich lebe nicht in Manchester.

____.

Meine Freunde mögen Fußball nicht.

____.

Er macht seine Hausaufgaben nicht.

____.

Unsere Katze isst keinen Fisch.

____.

2. Davids Eltern fahren übers Wochenende weg. Was verbieten sie ihm, währendessen zu tun? Forme aus den Verboten ganze Befehlssätze.

eat sweets
have a party
forget to water the flowers
leave the door open
watch TV late
drink Coke

____!

____!

____!

____!

____!

____!

bearbeitet am: ____________ erreichte Punktzahl: ______

Ab 8 erreichten Punkten kannst du mit Test 59 fortfahren.

Test 59 *do* – Fragen

Schwierigkeitsgrad: ● ○ ○

1. Im Restaurant. Stelle die zu den Antworten passenden Fragen.

____ ?
Yes, I like cheese cake.

____ ?
No, she doesn't eat meat.

____ ?
No, they don't serve tea here.

____ ?
Yes, we have coffee.

____ ?
No, I don't want to pay.

____ ?
Yes, they take credit cards.

2. Wer tut was? Verbinde die zueinander passenden Satzteile und notiere die entstandenen (sinnvollen) Fragesätze dann vollständig auf den Linien.

Do	cows	write	a lake
Do	your friend	eat	jazz music
Does	Newcastle	have	grass
Does	pupils	listen to	with pencils

____ ?

____ ?

____ ?

____ ?

bearbeitet am: ____________ erreichte Punktzahl: ______

Ab 8 erreichten Punkten kannst du mit Test 60 fortfahren, ab 10 mit Test 61.

Test 60 *do* – Fragen

Schwierigkeitsgrad: ● ○ ○

1. Füge die Satzteile in der richtigen Reihenfolge zu vollständigen Fragesätzen zusammen. Ergänze sie jeweils um das Hilfsverb *do* in der richtigen Form. Vergiss das richtige Satzzeichen am Ende nicht.

he / before bedtime / watch television

____

____

she / going on holidy / like / in Italy

____

____

their homework / on time / they / do / always

____

____

I / speak / in class / too loudly

____

____

Jen and Nick / come home / early / on weekdays

____

____

like / swimming / in the lake / in the morning / you

____

____

bearbeitet am: __________ erreichte Punktzahl: _____

Ab 5 erreichten Punkten kannst du mit Test 61 fortfahren.

Test 61 „können"

Schwierigkeitsgrad: ● ○ ○

1. **Was kannst du und was nicht? Bilde aus den geeigneten Satzteilen ganze Sätzen mit *can* oder *cannot* bzw. *can't*.**

swim / in the sea / in the soup

____.

____.

repair / a space ship / a bike

____.

____.

visit / planet Mars / Great Britain

____.

____.

drink / lemon water / motor oil

____.

____.

2. **Beantworte die Fragen wie vorgegeben mit der richtigen Kurzform von *can*.**

Can you tell me the way to Bath? (no) Sorry, no ____________________.

Can your teacher play football? (yes) ____________________.

Can Annika sing well? (no) ____________________.

Can Paul and Louis speak Spanish? (no) ____________________.

Can I come in? (yes) ____________________.

bearbeitet am: ____________ erreichte Punktzahl: ______

Ab 11 erreichten Punkten kannst du mit Test 62 fortfahren.

Test 62 „können"

Schwierigkeitsgrad:

1. Wer kann was in der Schülerband? Stelle die zu den Antworten passenden Fragen.

____? Yes, I can play the piano.

____? No, Jim can't play the guitar.

____? Yes, Angie can sing well.

____? No, Chris can't play the drums.

____? Yes, Payton can play the bass.

____? Yes, we can rock.

____? Yes, you can join us.

2. Setze *can, can't, could* oder *couldn't* ein.

_____________________ you pass me the salt, please?

Your sisters _____________________ do a lot of magic tricks, that's great!

When I was a boy, I _____________________ stand on my hands.

You _____________________ use my old computer, but you

_____________________ have the new one, I need it myself!

Last summer, I _____________________ swim, but now I've been to swimming

class and now I _____________________ swim.

I _____________________ buy the red bathing suit, but I also _____________________

buy the blue one. I _____________________ buy both suits, because I don't have enough money.

bearbeitet am: __________ erreichte Punktzahl: __________

Ab 14 erreichten Punkten kannst du mit Test 63 fortfahren.

Test 63 „können"

Schwierigkeitsgrad: ● ● ●

1. **Dazugelernt – erst konnten sie es nicht, jetzt können sie es! Welche englischen Formen von „können" passen in die Aussagen über die Kinder? Nenne jeweils alle Lösungen.**

Last year Anna ______________________ go to Boston as an exchange student, because she was ill. But this year she ______________ go.

When he was one year old, Brian ______________________ speak clearly. But now he is three and ______________ speak very well.

Jenny ______________________ run 800 m before. But she practiced and this time she ______________ run 800 m really fast.

Right now Charles ______________________ play the piano very well yet. But he has a new teacher and ______________ play much better than he ______________ last year.

2. **Übersetze die Sätze. Teils gibt es mehrere Möglichkeiten. Vergiss die Satzzeichen nicht.**

Das Baby kann noch nicht laufen.

____

Sophia könnte kein Fleisch essen.

____

Können Sie mein Auto reparieren?

____

Kannst du mir helfen?

____

bearbeitet am: __________ erreichte Punktzahl: __________

Ab 11 erreichten Punkten kannst du mit Test 64 fortfahren.

Test 64 „dürfen"

Schwierigkeitsgrad: ● ● ○

1. *Can* oder *may*? Setze die richtigen Formen beider Hilfsverben ein. Teils passen zwei Formen.

A. ______________________ I come in, please?

B. Yes, you ______________________ use our toilet.

C. After hospital Ms Sweetly ______________________ walk again now.

D. No, you ______________________ play in the street, Sammy and Ellis!

2. Ordne den Sätzen aus Aufgabe 1 aus den möglichen eine passende Bedeutung zu und schreibe sie auf die Linien.

Erlaubnis	Verbot	Fähigkeit	Bitte

A. ______________________

B. ______________________

C. ______________________

D. ______________________

3. Verbote, Verbote! Verneine die Anfragen der Schüler an den Schulleiter.

May we use our mobile phones in school? No, you ______________________!

May we leave the grounds during lunch break? ______________________!

May we be late to class in the morning? ______________________!

4. Stelle nun die passenden Fragen zum Verbot.

______________________ No, you mustn't smoke in school!

______________________ No, he mustn't talk in class!

______________________ No, they mustn't fight in the halls!

bearbeitet am: ________ erreichte Punktzahl: ________

Ab 11 erreichten Punkten kannst du mit Test 65 fortfahren.

Test 65 „dürfen"

Schwierigkeitsgrad: ● ● ●

1. **Entscheide, wann *can/can't* oder *may/mustn't* passt und wann die Umschreibung mit *be allowed to* gewählt werden muss. Manchmal passen mehrere Formen.**

Now that he is twelve, my brother ______________________________ go to school on his bike.

When I was smaller, I ______________________________ go out to play, because it was too dangerous.

Don't go, Sid! You know, we ______________________________ leave the house, when mum is gone!

Not too long ago, French children ______________________________ to drink wine with their meals.

2. **Früher durften sie nicht, jetzt haben sie die Erlaubnis! Welche englischen Formen von „dürfen" passen in diese Aussagen? Nenne jeweils alle Lösungen.**

When I was nine, I ______________________________ to

stay up after nine o'clock. Now I ______________________________ to stay up until eleven.

Alice ______________________________ to go out after school last

year. Now she ______________________________ stay out until five o'clock, if there is no homework.

3. **Übersetze die Sätze. Es gibt dafür mehrere Möglichkeiten. Vergiss die Satzzeichen nicht.**

Kinder dürfen auf dem Rasen spielen.

____

Hunde durften nicht an den Strand gehen.

____

bearbeitet am: ____________ erreichte Punktzahl: ______

Ab 9 erreichten Punkten kannst du mit Test 66 fortfahren.

Test 66 „müssen"

Schwierigkeitsgrad: ● ● ○

1. **Die Mutter ermahnt ihre Kinder, was sie am Tag alles erledigen müssen. Setze die richtige Form von *must* mit dem passenden Verb aus der Reihe oben in die Lücken ein.**

be – wash – buy – show – drink

Eric, you ______________________________ your hands.

Oliver ______________________________ at home by four.

Kat, you ______________________________ your tea.

Eric ______________________________ some catfood.

You all ______________________________ me your homework.

2. **Maya ist krank. Was muss sie nun tun bzw. braucht sie nicht zu tun? Und was darf sie auf keinen Fall tun? Setze die richtigen Hilfsverben ein, wo möglich in der Kurzform.**

Maya ____________________ take her medicine.

She ____________________ stay in bed.

She ____________________ go to school or do her homework.

She ____________________ let a doctor examine her.

She ____________________ play outside.

She ____________________ do any housework.

3. **Kreuze die korrekte Kurzform der *Verneinung* dieses Satzes an.**

I must get up early for school.

Verneinung:

I mustn't get up early for school. ☐
I can't get up early for school. ☐
I needn't get up early for school. ☐

bearbeitet am: ________ erreichte Punktzahl: ________

Ab 10 erreichten Punkten kannst du mit Test 67 fortfahren.

Test 67 „müssen"

Schwierigkeitsgrad: ● ● ●

1. Forme die Aussagen zu Fragesätzen um und umgekehrt.

They had to help me.

____ ?

He needn't listen to her.

____ ?

Must I wait here?

____ .

2. Welche englischen Formen von „müssen" oder „brauchen nicht" bzw. „dürfen nicht" passen in die Lücken des Gesprächs? Nenne jeweils alle Lösungen, die möglich sind.

"I ____________________ go to bed early yesterday, I felt so tired."

"Then you ____________________ hear what happened later."

"Oh no! You ____________________ tell me that, I ____________________

know all that right now. Come on, we ____________________ hurry!"

"Okay, you're right. I ____________________ be late for school again,

I ____________________ get good grades this year!"

3. Übersetze die Sätze. Es gibt dafür teils mehrere Möglichkeiten. Denk an die Satzzeichen.

Musstet ihr lange warten?

____

Wir müssen im Bus sitzen.

____

bearbeitet am: __________ erreichte Punktzahl: __________

Ab 8 erreichten Punkten kannst du mit Test 68 fortfahren.

Test 68 *can, may, must*

Schwierigkeitsgrad: ● ● ○

1. Ordne den Beispielsätzen aus den möglichen Bedeutungen eine passende zu und trage die richtigen Kennbuchstaben in die Kästchen ein.

A. Aufforderung	B. Notwendigkeit	C. Erlaubnis	D. Verbot	E. Fähigkeit	F. Bitte

Ned had to walk the dog. ☐

May I have the sugar, please? ☐

You must be there on time! ☐

You can watch TV tonight. ☐

Visitors mustn't touch the paintings. ☐

After a year of piano lessons Anna could play Beethoven. ☐

2. Ordne die Hilfsverben zu Gegensatzpaaren und trage sie vor und hinter den Pfeilen ein.

can – needn't – must – may – mustn't – can't

can ⟷ ____________________

____________________ ⟷ ____________________

____________________ ⟷ ____________________

3. Trage die richtigen Hilfsverben aus Aufgabe 2 in die Lücken ein und ordne ihnen dann den passenden Kennbuchstaben aus Aufgabe 1 zu.

Stop! You ____________________ feed the zoo animals, they could get sick. ☐

Adam is cool, he ____________________ hold his breath for two full minutes! ☐

Mr Jones is a baker, he ____________________ go to work at 4 a.m. every day. ☐

4. Notiere die korrekte Umschreibung (Grundform) für jedes Hilfsverb.

can ⟷ be ____________________ to.

may ⟷ ____________________

must ⟷ ____________________

bearbeitet am: ________ erreichte Punktzahl: ________

Ab 15 erreichten Punkten kannst du mit Test 69 fortfahren.

Test 69 Zeitangaben

Schwierigkeitsgrad: ● ● ●

1. **Setze die richtige Präposition für diese Zeitangaben ein.**

______ February	______ lunch
______ August, 10th	______ summer
______ Christmas	______ your birthday
______ the morning	______ two o'clock
______ the afternoon	______ midnight (nach)
______ the evening	______ next week (vor)
______ night	______ next week (bis)
______ 2011	______ day (bei)

2. **So sieht Sandys Tag aus. Setze die richtigen Präpositionen in die Lücken ein.**

Sandy wakes up ______ seven o'clock ______ the morning.

She has breakfast ______ eight and then leaves the house ______ breakfast.

School ends ______ four o'clock ______ the afternoon.

Sandy doesn't come home from school ______ five o'clock (vor).

______ dinner she tells her family about her day.

______ the evening she reads a little or watches TV.

______ weekends her days are different, of course.

______ Sundays she can sleep ______ ten o'clock (bis) or even ______ ten (nach), if she wants to.

bearbeitet am: ______ erreichte Punktzahl: ______

Ab 23 erreichten Punkten kannst du mit Test 70 fortfahren, ab 28 mit Test 71.

Test 70 Zeitangaben

Schwierigkeitsgrad: ● ● ○

1. **Welche Präposition ist mit welcher Zeiteinheit vereinbar? Ziehe Pfeile von den Präpositionen zu ihren möglichen Zeitangaben. Achtung: Oft passen mehrere!**

	nine o' clock
in	Saturdays
on	winter
at	dinner
after	Easter
	May, 22nd
	the morning

2. **Setze die richtigen Präpositionen ein.**

Jonas was born ____________________ 2004.

His birthday is ____________________ April, 1st.

His grandma's birthday is ____________________ the same month.

What's the weather like ____________________ April?

____________________ spring there is a lot of wind, but mostly ____________________ night.

It helps to start the party early, ____________________ two o'clock.

The children can eat birthday cake and play ____________________ (bis) five

____________________ the afternoon.

Then everyone goes home and must be in bed ____________________ (vor) ten, so they

will not be tired ____________________ the morning.

bearbeitet am: ______ erreichte Punktzahl: ______

Ab 20 erreichten Punkten kannst du mit Test 71 fortfahren.

Test 71 Ortsangaben

Schwierigkeitsgrad: ● ● ●

1. Setze die richtige Präposition für diese Ortsangaben ein.

________ the left

________ the room

________ front of the mirror

________ the TV set (neben)

________ the roof (unter)

________ the table (über)

________ the sofa (hinter)

________ the passage (durch)

2. Trage immer das Gegenteil der angegebenen Ortsangaben ein.

above the clouds ⟷ ________ the clouds

on the right ⟷ ________

behind the house ⟷ ________

into the garden ⟷ ________

up the street ⟷ ________

3. So sieht Carolines Zimmer aus. Setze die richtigen Präpositionen in die Lücken ein.

________ the right there is Caroline's desk with a chair ________ it. ________ the left there is her bed with a little lamp ________ it. There are two windows ________ her room, one ________ the left-hand wall, and one ________ the right-hand wall. Posters are hanging ________ all the walls. Caroline likes her room tidy. She puts her shoes neatly ________ her bed and has no clothes lying around ________ the floor. Her bed is made, and the covers are ________ it.

bearbeitet am: ________ erreichte Punktzahl: ________

Ab 20 erreichten Punkten kannst du mit Test 72 fortfahren, ab 23 mit Test 73.

Test 72 Ortsangaben

Schwierigkeitsgrad: ● ● ○

1. Setze die richtigen Präpositionen ein.

I can't find my keys. They are not __________ my bedroom and not __________ the kitchen. They're not __________ the shelves or __________ the fridge, either.

Did you look __________ (unter) your bed or __________ the TV set?

And what about __________ (unter) the magazines __________ the living room table?

Where is your brother? Is he not __________ home? He's not __________ his room or __________ the garden.

Did you look __________ the living room __________ the TV?

Gina wants to leave for school, but all her things are still __________ her room.

Her pencil case is __________ her desk, and her books are __________ (auf) her bed. Some pens are still lying __________ (vor) her computer.

2. Beantworte die Fragen mit den richtigen Präpositionen des Ortes.

Was ist das Gegenteil von *out of*? __________

Was zeigt an, dass jemand oder etwas in einem Raum ist? __________

Was bedeutet, dass etwas vor etwas anderem steht? __________

Was zeigt an, dass jemand oder etwas neben etwas anderem ist? __________

Was ist das Gegenteil von *under*? __________

bearbeitet am: __________ erreichte Punktzahl: __________

Ab 18 erreichten Punkten kannst du mit Test 73 fortfahren.

Test 73 Bildung und Gebrauch des *simple present*

Schwierigkeitsgrad: ● ● ●

1. **Setze die Verben ins *simple present.***

Sue (try) ____________ people (write) ____________

we (dance) ____________ the girl (watch) ____________

Tim (walk) ____________ Jane (buy) ____________

I (sleep) ____________ he (learn) ____________

the car (stop) ____________ she (know) ____________

2. **Setze jedes Verb aus der Reihe oben an die richtige Stelle im Text und bringe es ins *simple present.* Achtung: Achte auf Verneinungen und Fragen.**

play – like – sleep – live – not hear – go – think – not lie – have got – watch – fight

At night most people ____________.

I´ve got a dog. He ____________ to run and play.

(you) ____________ television often?

When she´s at school, she ____________ in her bed.

I ____________ three brothers. We ____________

in a small house, so we ____________ a lot.

My teacher ____________ I´m lazy.

You ____________ soccer very well.

____________ she ____________ to school in the afternoon?

My parents ____________ anything if I walk down the stairs carefully.

bearbeitet am: ____________ erreichte Punktzahl: ____________

Ab 18 erreichten Punkten kannst du mit Test 74 fortfahren.

Test 74 Bildung und Gebrauch des *simple present*

Schwierigkeitsgrad:

1. **Unterstreiche die Schlüsselwörter, die auf den Gebrauch des *simple present* hinweisen.**

yesterday	today	always	every weekend	usually	tomorrow	often
a month ago	seldom	last year	sometimes	next month	every August	never

2. **Übersetze die Sätze ins Deutsche.**

Every Monday I play soccer.

____ .

They seldom go to the movies.

____ .

Do you sleep at night?

____ .

My mother never watches TV.

____ .

I always eat rice with ketchup.

____ .

Sometimes I hate my sister.

____ .

You are often bored.

____ .

I usually drink tea in the morning.

____ .

bearbeitet am: erreichte Punktzahl:

Ab 13 erreichten Punkten kannst du mit Test 75 fortfahren.

Test 75 Bildung und Gebrauch des *simple present*

Schwierigkeitsgrad: ● ● ●

1. **Schreibe zu jeder Antwort die passende Frage auf.**

_______________ Yes, Mia likes her sister.

_______________ No, I don't eat meat.

_______________ Yes, your eyes are brown.

_______________ No, they don't watch TV on Sundays.

_______________ Yes, she plays table tennis.

_______________ No, we haven't got two cars.

2. **Verneine die folgenden Sätze.**

Snails go faster than horses. ⃠ _______________.

Kids drive their own cars. ⃠ _______________.

Trucks ar smaller than bikes. ⃠ _______________.

Animals talk to people. ⃠ _______________.

The sun shines at night. ⃠ _______________.

Donald Duck loves his uncle. ⃠ _______________.

Most old people love computers.

⃠ _______________.

The police rob a bank when they need money.

⃠ _______________.

Babies walk and talk right after birth.

⃠ _______________.

bearbeitet am: ______ erreichte Punktzahl: ______

Ab 12 erreichten Punkten kannst du mit Test 76 fortfahren.

Test 76 Bildung und Gebrauch des *simple present*

Schwierigkeitsgrad: ● ● ○

1. **Ergänze zu jedem Satz die passende der aufgeführten Zeitangaben.**

never – every year – at night – in the morning – on Sundays – in the afternoon

Sue has Sandwiches for breakfast ______________________ .

______________________ the moon shines into her bedroom.

She sometimes goes swimming with her sister ______________________ .

______________________ she goes on holiday with her grandparents.

She sleeps late ______________________ .

She ______________________ goes out without her purse.

2. **Bringe die Wörter in die richtige Reihenfolge und bilde ganze Sätze.**

never / you / late / are

____ .

always / forget / I / my homework

____ .

never / a book / read / you

____ .

usually / play / they / together

____ .

our bikes / sometimes / ride / we

____ .

bearbeitet am: ____________ erreichte Punktzahl: ______

Ab 9 erreichten Punkten kannst du mit Test 77 fortfahren.

Test 77 Bildung und Gebrauch des *present progressive*

Schwierigkeitsgrad: ● ○ ○

1. Setze die Verben im *present progressive* ein. Verwende die Langform.

We ______________________________ (have) a party.

The music ______________________________ (play).

My cat ______________________________ (purr).

My friends ______________________________ (eat) crisps.

Tina ______________________________ (have) some cake.

We ______________________________ (make) fun of her.

But she ______________________________ (laugh), too.

Now we ______________________________ (dance).

Everyone ______________________________ (join) in!

We ______________________________ (do) a funny dance.

The dancers ______________________________ (put) their hands up in the air!

All my friends ______________________________ (have) fun!

2. Bilde die Formen des *present progressive* für die folgenden Verben.

write	______________	meet	______________
lie	______________	let	______________
put	______________	see	______________
swim	______________	run	______________
wake	______________	carry	______________
hit	______________	come	______________

bearbeitet am: ______________ erreichte Punktzahl: ______

Ab 20 erreichten Punkten kannst du mit Test 78 fortfahren.

Test 78 Bildung und Gebrauch des *present progressive*

Schwierigkeitsgrad: ● ● ○

1. **Bilde aus den Satzteilen eine Frage im *present progressive*.**

you / work ____________________________________ ?

she / go / home ____________________________________ ?

we / meet / at school ____________________________________ ?

he / ask / for help ____________________________________ ?

they / play / games ____________________________________ ?

You / look / at me ____________________________________ ?

she / do / this / on purpose

____ ?

2. **Debbie hat Tanztraining und wird von einem Schulreporter interviewt. Trage die Antworten wie in dem Beispiel in ihrer langen Form ein.**

Is your dancing improving? Yes, it is improving.

Are you planning a dancing career?

Yes, ____ .

Are you stretching your muscles?

Yes, ____ .

Is your lesson starting now?

Yes, ____ .

Am I getting on your nerves?

Well, no, ______________________________________ .

bearbeitet am: __________ erreichte Punktzahl: ______

Ab 9 erreichten Punkten kannst du mit Test 79 fortfahren.

Test 79 Bildung und Gebrauch des *present progressive*

Schwierigkeitsgrad: ● ● ○

1. **In jedem Satz ist ein Wort zu viel. Streiche es.**

I'm coming go home now.

He is running on the lawn later.

They can are riding their bikes.

The teacher is listening to you tomorrow.

We always are eating Pizza right now.

I'm doing my homework usually now.

2. **So sieht Aidens Schulmorgen aus. Fülle die Lücken mit den Formen des *present progressive*.**

7 a.m.: I ______________________________ (get) up.

7.15: I ______________________________ (take) a shower and

______________________________ (brush) my teeth.

7.30: I ______________________________ (have) breakfast.

My mother ______________________________ (read) the newspaper.

7.45: I ______________________________ (walk) to the bus station.

7.55: I ______________________________ (sit) on the bus.

The bus ______________________________ (drive) me to school.

8.10: I ______________________________ (leave) the bus.

I ______________________________ (talk) to my friends.

8.15: We ______________________________ (enter) our classroom.

We ______________________________ (wait) for the teacher.

bearbeitet am: __________ erreichte Punktzahl: __________

Ab 15 erreichten Punkten kannst du mit Test 80 fortfahren.

Test 80 Bildung und Gebrauch des *present progressive*

Schwierigkeitsgrad: ● ● ○

1. Welche Schlüsselwörter findest du nicht im *present progressive*? Kreuze an.

- ☐ always
- ☐ a month ago
- ☐ now
- ☐ at this moment
- ☐ yesterday
- ☐ just

2. Sind die folgenden Sätze logisch? Geht das überhaupt? Übersetze und kreuze an.

The boy is running and sleeping. ☐ Das geht. ☐ Das geht nicht.

Übersetzung: ______________________________.

The dog is playing and barking. ☐ Das geht. ☐ Das geht nicht.

Übersetzung: ______________________________.

It is raining and the ground is dry. ☐ Das geht. ☐ Das geht nicht.

Übersetzung: ______________________________.

I'm reading and not listening to my mother. ☐ Das geht. ☐ Das geht nicht.

Übersetzung: ______________________________.

The man is driving his car and watching a film. ☐ Das geht. ☐ Das geht nicht.

Übersetzung: ______________________________.

She is playing the piano and the guitar. ☐ Das geht. ☐ Das geht nicht.

Übersetzung: ______________________________.

The cat is eating and purring. ☐ Das geht. ☐ Das geht nicht.

Übersetzung: ______________________________.

bearbeitet am: ________ erreichte Punktzahl: ________

Ab 14 erreichten Punkten kannst du mit Test 81 fortfahren.

Test 81 *simple present* versus *present progressive*

Schwierigkeitsgrad: ● ● ○

1. **Übersetze und mach dabei den Unterschied deutlich.**

I'm reading. ______________________________.

I read. ______________________________.

Kate is playing basketball. ______________________________.

Kate plays basketball. ______________________________.

He's eating fish. ______________________________.

He eats fish. ______________________________.

You are talking a lot. ______________________________.

You talk a lot. ______________________________.

2. **Benjamin spricht an seinem Handy. Setze das *simple present* oder *present progressive* ein.**

I ______________________ (like) to ride my bike every day. Do you want to know what I ______________________ (do) at this moment? I ______________________ (cycle) to the shop. I ______________________ (need) new brakes. I ______________________ (wait) now, because the mechanic ______________________ (talk) to another customer. The mechanic ______________________ (know) a lot about bikes. And he ______________________ (likes) me. Sometimes I ______________________ (get) smaller parts for free. Now the customer ______________________ (leave), but the mechanic ______________________ (talk) on the phone! ______________________ he (ignore) me? Ah no, he ______________________ (come) over. Okay, I have to go, bye!

bearbeitet am: __________ erreichte Punktzahl: __________

Ab 17 erreichten Punkten kannst du mit Test 82 fortfahren.

Test 82 *simple present* versus *present progressive*

Schwierigkeitsgrad: ● ● ●

1. **Übersetze ins Englische. Achte dabei auf die Signalwörter für *simple* und *progressive*!**

Normalerweise mag ich Gemüse.

____ .

Ich schreibe gerade eine E-Mail.

____ .

Manchmal werde ich wütend auf meine Eltern.

____ .

Guck mal, der Hund schläft auf der Couch! Normalerweise schläft er auf dem Fußboden.

____ .

Jeden Sonntag besuche ich meine Oma.

____ .

2. ***Simple present* oder *present progressive*? Trage die richtige Verbform ein.**

Hi, Leo. – Hi!? ____________________ (you / talk) to me?

Yes, I am. We ____________________ (go) to the same dancing class.

Oh, I ____________________ (see)! What ____________________ (be) your name?

I'm Nina. ____________________ (you / have) a mobile phone?

Yes, I ____________________ (have). Why?

I ____________________ (want / call) my mother, I ________________ (be) late.

Look, my mother ____________________ (come)! We ________________ (can / take) you with us.

bearbeitet am: __________ erreichte Punktzahl: ______

Ab 12 erreichten Punkten kannst du mit Test 83 fortfahren, ab 14 mit Test 84.

Test 83 *simple present* versus *present progressive*

Schwierigkeitsgrad: ● ● ●

1. **Trage die richtigen Formen des simple present oder *present progressive* ein.**

Is Ron at home? No, I'm sorry. He ______________________ (play) soccer at school.

Look, ______________________________________ (Paul and Sue / wear)

the same cardigan? Yes, they are. I wonder if they ______________________ (know) each other.

Do cats ______________________ (eat) fruit? No, cats don't eat fruit. They

______________________ (prefer) meat.

Oh, you ______________________ (read) a book. Do you ______________________

(read) a lot? Yes, I ______________________

What ______________________________________ (you / do)?

I ______________________ (clean) my desk.

______________________ Sarah ______________________ (argue) with

her friend? Yes, she is. Unfortunately, they ______________________ (argue) a lot.

2. **Schreibe all die Verben, die <u>meistens</u> im *simple present* stehen, heraus.**

eat – write – want – run – learn – like – listen – need – love – sit – know – laugh

____

____

____

____

____

bearbeitet am: ____________ erreichte Punktzahl: ______

Ab 15 erreichten Punkten kannst du mit Test 84 fortfahren.

Test 84 Bildung und Gebrauch des *simple past*

Schwierigkeitsgrad: ● ○ ○

1. Trage das *simple past* für die Verben ein. Kreuze alle regelmäßigen Verben an.

☐ sleep	______________	☐ laugh	______________
☐ talk	______________	☐ send	______________
☐ walk	______________	☐ keep	______________
☐ drive	______________	☐ put	______________
☐ get	______________	☐ read	______________
☐ go	______________	☐ buy	______________
☐ see	______________	☐ play	______________
☐ look	______________	☐ feel	______________

2. Trage alle Verbformen des *simple present* in die linke Spalte, die dazu passende Form des *simple past* in die rechte Spalte ein.

told – stand – sang – tell – build – wrote – caught – stood – catch – built – write – sing

simple present	*simple past*

bearbeitet am: erreichte Punktzahl:

Ab 23 erreichten Punkten kannst du mit Test 85 fortfahren.

Test 85 Bildung und Gebrauch des *simple past*

Schwierigkeitsgrad: ● ● ○

1. **Setze die richtigen Formen von *be* im *simple past* ein.**

Grace ______________________ tired this morning.

We ______________________ very worried.

______________________ you at school yesterday?

My dog ______________________ in his bed.

Last year, I ______________________ much smaller.

My teachers ______________________ on holiday.

My brother ______________________ ill.

There ______________________ an accident on the road.

Many people ______________________ there to watch.

You ______________________ at the swimming pool.

1. **Trage die richtigen Formen der Verben in Klammern im *simple past* ein.**

Last year, Tobias ______________________ (visit) a British school. The other kids ______________________ (ask) him a lot of questions. ______________________ (be) the questions hard for Tobias? No, they ______________________ (not be). The teachers ______________________ (explain) everything to him. When Tobias ______________________ (answer) a question, he ______________________ (say) something wrong. But nobody ______________________ (laugh). A girl even ______________________ (smile) at him. Then the teacher ______________________ (finish) the lesson, and Tobias ______________________ (play) soccer with the others.

bearbeitet am: ____________ erreichte Punktzahl: ______

Ab 17 erreichten Punkten kannst du mit Test 86 fortfahren.

Test 86 Bildung und Gebrauch des *simple past*

Schwierigkeitsgrad: ● ● ○

1. **Ergänze eine bejahende oder verneinende Kurzantwort.**

Did they watch TV last night?	No, they ______________________ .
Did you feel good when you visited your friend?	Yes, I ______________________ .
Did the concert last until 10 p.m.?	No, it ______________________ .
Did your father buy this book for you?	Yes, ______________________ .
Was your brother or your sister at home?	Yes, they ______________________ both at home.
Did you go to the movies on Sunday?	Yes, ______________________ to the movies on Sunday.

2. **Und nun stelle die zu den Antworten passenden Fragen.**

____ ? Yes, I went on holiday with my parents.

____ ? No, we didn't drive. We took a plane.

____ ? No, I didn't spend all my pocket money.

____ ? Yes, I made some friends.

____ ? Yes, I ate special food.

____ ? No, didn't see any wild animals.

____ ? Yes, I liked it there.

bearbeitet am: ____________ erreichte Punktzahl: ______

Ab 11 erreichten Punkten kannst du mit Test 87 fortfahren.

Test 87 Bildung und Gebrauch des *simple past*

Schwierigkeitsgrad: ● ● ●

1. Setze die Fragen ins *simple past*.

When do you get up? ______________________________ ?

Why do you throw away my bag? ______________________________ ?

What do you have for lunch? ______________________________ ?

Why do you take my shirt? ______________________________ ?

Where is Mom? ______________________________ ?

2. Setze die Verben ins *simple present*.

felt ____________________	drew ____________________
kept ____________________	hit ____________________
got ____________________	left ____________________
broke ____________________	drank ____________________

3. **Setze jede Verbform in der richtigen Form an die richtige Stelle.**

arrive – go – like – stay – be (2 x) – come – get – see – think – leave

Yesterday I ____________________ to a concert. It ____________________ great. I ____________________ my favourite singer. He ____________________ much smaller than I ____________________. But I ____________________ him anyway. I ____________________ until he ____________________ the stage. After the concert my mom ____________________ to ____________________ me, so I ____________________ at home safely.

bearbeitet am: __________ erreichte Punktzahl: __________

Ab 19 erreichten Punkten kannst du mit Test 88 fortfahren.

Test 88 Bildung und Gebrauch des *simple past*

Schwierigkeitsgrad: ● ● ●

1. **Ein Begriff aus der Reihe kann nicht mit dem *simple past* stehen. Streiche ihn durch.**

always sometimes never next year often seldom usually

2. **Formuliere Fragen nach den unterstrichenen Satzteilen.**

Tim went <u>to Turkey</u> with his parents.

____?

The family arrived at the hotel <u>at six o'clock</u>.

____?

<u>Tim</u> slept in a single bed room.

____?

<u>The beach</u> wasn't far away from the hotel.

____?

Tim met <u>some nice girls and boys</u> there.

____?

A man tried to impress <u>his wife</u> with his diving.

____?

The kids laughed, <u>because the man looked stupid</u>.

____?

At the end of the day Tim felt <u>happy</u>.

____?

bearbeitet am: erreichte Punktzahl:

Ab 13 erreichten Punkten kannst du mit Test 89 fortfahren.

Test 89 Bildung und Gebrauch des *past progressive*

Schwierigkeitsgrad: ● ● ●

1. Bilde jeweils die Verlaufsform.

do	______________	ride	______________
carry	______________	have	______________
swim	______________	run	______________
wake	______________	drive	______________

2. Woraus setzt sich das *past progressive* zusammen? Kreuze an.

A. Aus der Vergangenheit von *do* und der Verlaufsform. ☐

B. Aus der Vergangenheit von *do* und dem Infinitiv. ☐

C. Aus der Vergangenheit von *be* und der Verlaufsform. ☐

3. Fülle die Lücken mit den Formen des *past progressive* der oben stehenden Verben aus.

sing – write – walk – watch – do – have – dance

I ______________________________ an e-mail to my friend Frida, when my sister called.

I ______________________________ dinner and

______________________________ TV, when the doorbell rang.

They ______________________________ and

______________________________ along to the music, when it stopped.

We ______________________________ along the beach, when the rain started.

She ______________________________ her homework, when she remembered her basketball lesson.

bearbeitet am: ______________ erreichte Punktzahl: ______

Ab 13 erreichten Punkten kannst du mit Test 90 fortfahren.

Test 90 Bildung und Gebrauch des *past progressive*

Schwierigkeitsgrad: ● ● ○

1. **Setze die Verben aus der Reihe oben jeweils im *past progressive* an die richtige Stelle.**

walk – have – do – play – read – talk – dance – write – chat – ride

I ______________________ my homework. I ______________________ on the internet. I ______________________ a book. I ______________________ an e-mail. I ______________________ dinner with my parents. I ______________________ with my friend. I ______________________ the dog. I ______________________ the piano. I ______________________ my bike. I was ______________________ to my friend on the phone.

2. **Was passierte gestern gerade, als Mia nach Hause kam? Bilde aus den Satzteilen korrekte Fragen im *past progressive*.**

the cat / lie / on the sofa

____?

her father / listen / to music

____?

flowers / bloom / in the garden

____?

her grandma / bake / a cake

____?

bees / hum / in the bushes

____?

bearbeitet am: ____________ erreichte Punktzahl: ______

Ab 12 erreichten Punkten kannst du mit Test 91 fortfahren.

Test 91 Bildung und Gebrauch des *past progressive*

Schwierigkeitsgrad: ● ● ○

1. Ganz schön schlecht, der Klassenausflug! Gib die passenden Antworten in Langform.

When you were on the class trip, ...

... was the train going fast? No, the train wasn't going fast.

... were you enjoying the trip? No, ______________________.

... were you eating right? No, ______________________.

... was Pauline talking to you? No, ______________________.

... were you arguing with her? Yes, ______________________.

... were you getting along well with the others?

No, ______________________.

... were the teachers paying attention?

No, ______________________.

2. Vervollständige die Fragen im *past progressive* und gib Kurzantworten.

__________ you sleeping at 10 o'clock? No, I __________.

__________ your dog lying in your bed? Yes, __________.

__________ I writing a test, when you knocked? Yes, __________.

__________ you and Eli listening to music? No, __________.

__________ the Hendersons playing table tennis yesterday?

No, __________.

__________ Samantha playing the guitar when her brother called?

Yes, __________.

bearbeitet am: __________ erreichte Punktzahl: __________

Ab 15 erreichten Punkten kannst du mit Test 92 fortfahren, ab 18 mit Test 93.

Test 92 Bildung und Gebrauch des *past progressive*

Schwierigkeitsgrad: ● ● ○

1. **Bilde aus den Satzbestandteilen vollständige Sätze im *past progressive.***

Ben / read

____ .

Sarah / talk to / her friend

____ .

birds / fly / in the sky

____ .

the woman / drive / to Brussels

____ .

Christmas / come

____ .

2. **Setze die richtigen Formen des *past progressive* ein.**

It ____________________ (rain), while Lisa ____________________ (run) through the fields.

She ____________________ (practise) for her first marathon run.

She ____________________ (dream) about her success, so she

____________________ (not watch) her steps.

Suddenly she tripped and fell. Oh! Her ankle ____________________ (ache)!

She ____________________ (hold) her leg, when she saw she didn't have her phone.

While she ____________________ (wait), she sudenly heard a noise.

Someone ____________________ (come)!

bearbeitet am: __________ erreichte Punktzahl: ______

Ab 12 erreichten Punkten kannst du mit Test 93 fortfahren.

Test 93 Bildung und Gebrauch des *past progressive*

Schwierigkeitsgrad: ● ● ●

1. **Achtung: Zwei dieser Sätze kannst du nicht ins *past progressive* setzen! Wähle für jede Lücke die richtige Zeitform.**

Last night, Sarah ______________________________ (hike) in the mountains.

Suddenly, she ______________________________(meet) a bear.

The bear ______________________________ (growl).

Sarah ______________________________(scream).

The bear ______________________________ (look) into her eyes.

It ______________________________(show) her its teeth.

Sarah ______________________________ (shiver).

Then Sarah ______________________________ (wake up)!

2. **Übersetze und achte dabei auf die Signalwörter fürs *past progressive*.**

Ich habe den ganzen Tag Klavier gespielt.

____ .

Ich habe gerade gegessen, als du angerufen hast.

____ .

Was hast du gestern Abend gemacht?

____ .

Während ich gelesen habe, bist du plötzlich hereingekommen.

____

____ .

bearbeitet am: __________ erreichte Punktzahl: ______

Ab 10 erreichten Punkten kannst du mit Test 94 fortfahren.

Test 94 *simple past* versus *past progressive*

Schwierigkeitsgrad: ● ○ ○

1. Bilde die Formen der Verben im *simple past* und im *past progressive*.

	simple past	past progressive
steal	________	________
move	________	________
climb	________	________
think	________	________
do	________	________
speak	________	________
lose	________	________
wear	________	________
choose	________	________
burn	________	________

2. Welche Aussagen sind wahr? Kreuze „richtig" oder „falsch" an.

	richtig	falsch
A. Wenn man eine Geschichte in der Vergangenheit erzählt, benutzt man immer das *past progressive*.	☐	☐
B. Das *past progressive* benutzt man, wenn man eine Handlung beschreiben will, die in der Vergangenheit abläuft, aber zu einem bestimmten Zeitpunkt noch nicht abgeschlossen ist.	☐	☐
C. Das *simple past* bildet man mit *be* und der Verlaufsform.	☐	☐
D. Das *simple past* umschreibt man bei Fragen mit *did/didn't*.	☐	☐
E. Das *simple past* beschreibt abgeschlossene Handlungen.	☐	☐

bearbeitet am: ________ erreichte Punktzahl: ________

Ab 23 erreichten Punkten kannst du mit Test 95 fortfahren.

Test 95 *simple past* versus *past progressive*

Schwierigkeitsgrad: ● ● ●

1. Fülle die Lücken mit *simple past* oder *past progressive* der Verben in Klammern.

Last week, me and my parents ______________________ (go) on holiday.

While we ______________________ (sit) in a restaurant, our car

______________________ (be stolen). We ______________________ (be)

very shocked! While one policeman ______________________ (take)

notes, another one ______________________ (try) to be nice. He

______________________ (offer) me tea. While I ______________________

(drink), another policeman ______________________ (come) in. The

policemen ______________________ (talk) for a while, and my mother

______________________ (get) nervous. But then they

______________________ (promise) to look for our car very soon.

2. Trage die richtigen Formen ein.

While I ______________________ (watch) my favourite programme, the

TV set ______________________ (explode).

When my mother ______________________ (come) back from work, I

______________________ (cook) dinner.

When the accident ______________________(happen), you

______________________ (sit) in a café.

We ______________________ (get) angry, because he

______________________ (make) fun of us all day.

bearbeitet am: __________ erreichte Punktzahl: __________

Ab 13 erreichten Punkten kannst du mit Test 96 fortfahren.

Test 96 *simple past* versus *past progressive*

Schwierigkeitsgrad: ● ● ●

1. **Stelle die entsprechenden Fragen zu den Antworten. Achtung: Lies dir die Antworten sehr sorgfältig durch und achte genau darauf, wonach gefragt werden muss.**

____? No, I wasn't waiting all day.

____? Yes, he went to the soccer game.

____? I went to sleep about 10 o'clock.

____? I was reading, when you came home.

____? Yes, the music was playing very loud

____? No, they weren't running to school.

2. **Übersetze ins Englische und achte auf die Signalwörter.**

Plötzlich klopfte jemand ans Fenster. Ich öffnete es.

____.

Mein Freund stand da. Er lachte die ganze Zeit.

____.

Ich fragte: „Warst du heute Nacht hier?"

____.

Er sagte: „Ja, während du geschlafen hast."

____.

bearbeitet am: ____________ erreichte Punktzahl: ______

Ab 8 erreichten Punkten kannst du mit Test 97 fortfahren.

Test 97 Bildung und Gebrauch des *present perfect*

Schwierigkeitsgrad: ● ○ ○

1. Welche Aussage ist wahr? Kreuze „richtig" oder „falsch" an.

	richtig	falsch
A. Das *present perfect* beschreibt Zustände oder Aktionen, die in der Vergangenheit begonnen haben und sich bis in die Gegenwart auswirken.	☐	☐
B. Das *present perfect* wird mit *do* und der Verlaufsform gebildet.	☐	☐
C. Das *present perfect* beschreibt abgeschlossene Handlungen.	☐	☐
D. Das *present perfect* wird mit *have/has* und dem *past participle* gebildet.	☐	☐

2. Bilde das *present perfect* aus den aufgelisteten Verben

spend	__________	draw	__________
buy	__________	tell	__________
look	__________	ring	__________
talk	__________	arrive	__________
watch	__________	run	__________
go	__________	hit	__________
say	__________	be	__________
ask	__________	ride	__________
laugh	__________	fly	__________
cry	__________	write	__________
meet	__________	do	__________
read	__________	have	__________

bearbeitet am: __________ erreichte Punktzahl: _____

Ab 23 erreichten Punkten kannst du mit Test 98 fortfahren.

Test 98 Bildung und Gebrauch des *present perfect*

Schwierigkeitsgrad: ● ● ○

1. **Bilde aus den Satzbestandteilen vollständige Sätze im *present perfect* (Langform).**

I / miss / her / ever since

______________________________.

we / be / on holiday / for three weeks

______________________________.

I / forget / to write him

______________________________.

you / just / eat / all my pancakes

______________________________.

they / already / paint / the house

______________________________.

Paul / never / sleep / late

______________________________.

2. **Übersetze ins Englische und verwende dafür das *present perfect* (Kurzform).**

Ich bin müde, weil ich zu lange aufgeblieben bin.

______________________________.

Du bist glücklich, weil du lange geschlafen hast.

______________________________.

Er ist krank, weil er zu viel gegessen hat.

______________________________.

bearbeitet am: ______ erreichte Punktzahl: ______

Ab 8 erreichten Punkten kannst du mit Test 99 fortfahren.

Test 99 Bildung und Gebrauch des *present perfect*

Schwierigkeitsgrad: ● ● ○

1. **Ergänze die richtigen Verbformen im *present perfect.* Verwende die Kurzform, wo möglich.**

Oops! Sorry, I ______________________ (not notice) you.

It's okay. ______________________ (you / be) to London before?

No, I ______________________ (not have). What about you?

I______________________ (be) here four times already.

Wow! ______________________ (you / see) all the sights yet?

No, not all of them yet. I______________________ (never / visit) the Tower.

2. **Übersetze ins Deutsche.**

I've seen the new computer, and now I'm thinking about buying it.

____.

I have done the dishes. They are clean now.

____.

I've been friends with Pam for three years.

____.

I've been ill all week.

____.

I have asked John to go to the pharmacy, but he hasn't gone yet.

____.

I've never asked you to help me.

____.

bearbeitet am: __________ erreichte Punktzahl: __________

Ab 10 erreichten Punkten kannst du mit Test 100 fortfahren.

Test 100 Bildung und Gebrauch des *present perfect*

Schwierigkeitsgrad: ● ● ○

1. Setze die Verben in der richtigen Form ein und verneine jeweils mit der Kurzform.

speak – fly – drink – pay – explode – hear – grow

Have you ever bought an elephant? No, I haven't.

Have you ever ______________ an Australian talk? No, ______________ .

Has this dog ever ______________ English? No, ______________ .

Have trees ever ______________ 100 m tall? No, ______________ .

Have you ever ______________ blood? No, ______________ .

Has anyone ever ______________ to the sun? No, no one ______________ .

Has the earth ever ______________ before? No, ______________ .

Has she ever ______________ with stones at the supermarket? No, ______________ .

2. Bilde aus den Satzbestandteilen vollständige Sätze im *present perfect* (Langform).

they / just / catch /a big fish

____ .

he / do / his homework / not yet

____ .

we / never / go / on holiday / without our dog

____ .

you / spend / all your pocket money / already?

____ ?

bearbeitet am: ______ erreichte Punktzahl: ______

Ab 15 erreichten Punkten kannst du mit Test 101 fortfahren.

Test 101 Bildung und Gebrauch des *present perfect*

Schwierigkeitsgrad: ● ● ●

1. **Übersetze die Fragen und Antworten ins Englische und verwende dabei das *present perfect*. Achte besonders auf die *present perfect*-Formen für „können" und „müssen".**

Bist du schon zu Hause gewesen? Nein, ich bin noch nicht dort gewesen.

____ ?

____ .

Hast du schon einmal nach Italien fahren können? Nein, ich habe noch nicht fahren können.

____ ?

____ .

Hast du auf mich warten müssen? Ja, ich habe warten müssen, aber jetzt bist du da.

____ ?

____ .

2. **Verbinde immer die zwei zueinander passenden Sätze miteinander und trage vorn die richtigen Verbformen ein.**

My little sister ______________ (be) tired.	She's full now.
Mum ______________ (tell) him to stay home.	Our grades are good.
They ______________ (leave) the house.	Now she's asleep.
She ______________ (eat) all her sandwiches.	They are standing outside now.
We ______________ (study) a lot for the exam.	Now you know that I like you.
You ______________ (see) my diary.	But he doesn't want to.
I ______________ (work) too hard.	Now I'm tired.

bearbeitet am: ______________ erreichte Punktzahl: ______

Ab 11 erreichten Punkten kannst du mit Test 102 fortfahren.

Test 102 Bildung und Gebrauch des *present perfect progressive*

Schwierigkeitsgrad: ● ○ ○

1. Welche Aussagen über das *present perfect progessive* sind wahr? Kreuze an.

	richtig	falsch
A. Das *present perfect progressive* wird mit einer Form von *do* gebildet.	☐	☐
B. Das *present perfect progressive* wird mit einer Form von *be* gebildet.	☐	☐
C. Man verwendet für das *present perfect progressive* die Verlaufsform.	☐	☐

2. Forme die folgenden Sätze zum *present perfect progessive* um.

I'm waiting. ____________________.

He's diving. ____________________.

She's running. ____________________.

You're reading. ____________________.

We're talking. ____________________.

Sam's smiling. ____________________.

She's watching. ____________________.

I'm drinking. ____________________.

It's raining. ____________________.

We're drawing. ____________________.

You're playing. ____________________.

They're whispering. ____________________.

Sandy's swimming. ____________________.

bearbeitet am: __________ erreichte Punktzahl: __________

Ab 13 erreichten Punkten kannst du mit Test 103 fortfahren.

Test 103 Bildung und Gebrauch des *present perfect progressive*

Schwierigkeitsgrad: ● ● ○

1. **Ergänze die fehlenden Formen.**

present perfect	*present perfect progressive*	*present perfect*	*present perfect progressive*
has done	______________	have chosen	______________
have written	______________	has gone	______________
has thought	______________	have had	______________
have given	______________	has said	______________
has ridden	______________	have lead	______________
have thought	______________	has left	______________
has enjoyed	______________	have sung	______________

2. ***present perfect*** **oder** ***present perfect progessive*****? Fülle die Lücken mit den Langformen.**

I ______________________________ (finish) my homework quickly.

We ______________________________ (shop) all day, and

I ______________________________ (spend) a lot of money.

My dad ______________________________ (watch) TV for three hours.

The cat ______________________________ (try) to catch a mouse all day.

The cake ______________________________ (cool down) for two hours, but it's still warm.

She ______________________________ (know) him for a long time, but she still can't stand him.

I ______________________________ (bring) you the newspaper, so now you can tell me the news.

bearbeitet am: __________ erreichte Punktzahl: __________

Ab 18 erreichten Punkten kannst du mit Test 104 fortfahren.

Test 104 Bildung und Gebrauch des *present perfect progressive*

Schwierigkeitsgrad: ● ● ○

1. Setze die richtige Verbform (Kurzform) sowie jeweils *since* oder *for* ein.

I ________________ (be) a member of the chess club ________ three years.

________ eight o'clock this morning, she ________________ (study) for the exam.

We ________________ (talk) ________ three hours now.

Hey, I ________________ (wait) for you ________ two o'clock!

She ________________ (lie) in bed ________ a few days.

They ________________ (drive), ________ they left London.

I ________________ (not be) able to talk to you ________ a while.

2. Übersetze ins Englische und verwende dafür das *present perfect progressive* (Kurzform).

Seit drei Stunden spielt sie Computerspiele.

____.

Er sitzt seit 10 Uhr an seinem Schreibtisch.

____.

Der Hund bellt schon eine halbe Stunde!

____.

Seit mehr als zwei Stunden liest du jetzt dein Buch.

____

____.

bearbeitet am: __________ erreichte Punktzahl: ______

Ab 15 erreichten Punkten kannst du mit Test 105 fortfahren.

Test 105 Bildung und Gebrauch des *present perfect progressive*

Schwierigkeitsgrad: ● ● ●

1. **Bilde vollständige Sätze und Fragen im *present perfect* oder *present perfect progressive.***

Anne / study / her books / all day

____.

Robbie / not eat /since 8 o'clock

____.

we / just / write / a letter / to grandma

____.

they / dance / all night

____?

you / look at me / for 5 minutes now / Please stop!

____.

she / walk / around the store / since 10 o'clock

____?

2. **Übersetze ins Englische.**

Ich habe dieses Tier noch nie gesehen.

____.

Warst du schon mal in Frankreich?

____.

Ich warte hier seit Stunden!

____.

bearbeitet am: ____________ erreichte Punktzahl: ______

Ab 7 erreichten Punkten kannst du mit Test 106 fortfahren.

Test 106 Bildung und Gebrauch des *will future*

Schwierigkeitsgrad: ● ○ ○

1. **Setze folgende kurze Sätze ins *will future*.**

Alexa goes to town. ______________________________.

Zach goes with her. ______________________________.

They have breakfast. ______________________________.

I make them a sandwich. ______________________________.

Mr Anderson works for a big phone company.

____.

Me and my family like our new summer cottage.

____.

2. **Fülle die Lücken mit den Verben im *will future*. Verwende die Langform.**

You ______________ (eat) your sandwiches.

You ______________ (not stay) hungry all morning.

I ______________ (take) care that you ______________ (have) regular meals.

They ______________ (know) that you all ______________ (be) okay.

3. **Fülle die Lücken mit den Verben im *will future*. Verwende die Kurzform, wo es geht.**

I'm sure I______________ (marry), when I'm older.

______________ (you / marry) one day?

No, I ______________ (not marry). I______________ (live)

on my own and I______________ (mind) my own business!

bearbeitet am: ______________ erreichte Punktzahl: ______

Ab 14 erreichten Punkten kannst du mit Test 107 fortfahren.

Test 107 Bildung und Gebrauch des *will future*

Schwierigkeitsgrad: ● ● ○

1. **Wettervorhersage: Setze die fehlenden Formen der Verben in Klammern ein (Langform).**

The weather ______________________ (get) worse tomorrow. There ______________________ (be) a lot of clouds, and there ______________________ (not be) any sunshine. At night, it ______________________ (rain) a lot. I don't think we ______________________ (have) it very warm.

2. **Fülle die Lücken (Kurzform) und trage in die Kästchen ein, um was für eine Art Satz (A, B oder C) es sich handelt.**

A. Hoffnung **B.** Vermutung/Voraussage **C.** schnelle Entscheidung

You're hungry? I______________________ (cook) some pancakes. ☐

I hope my friends ______________________ (not forget) me. ☐

He______________________ (love) his presents, I'm sure. ☐

Don't be afraid, I______________________ (help) you. ☐

3. **Übersetze ins Englische.**

Er glaubt, Ashley kommt nächste Woche.

____.

Am Samstag wirst du vielleicht meine Freundin treffen.

____

____.

Ich gehe später nicht auf die Party.

____.

bearbeitet am: ________ erreichte Punktzahl: ________

Ab 13 erreichten Punkten kannst du mit Test 108 fortfahren, ab 16 mit Test 109.

Test 108 Bildung und Gebrauch des *will future*

Schwierigkeitsgrad: ● ● ○

1. **Bilde aus den Satzbestandteilen vollständige Sätze und Fragen im *will future*.**

Ms Howe / have / a new job / next month

____ .

she / prepare / files / for a lawyer

____ .

he / ask / her / to answer / his phone calls

____ ?

she / get / better payment / later

____ ?

2. **Beantworte die Fragen mit Kurzantworten.**

Will the Mercers go to New Zealand next year?	Yes, they ______________ go.
Will they live in Auckland?	No, they ______________ live there.
Will they visit a sheepfarm?	Yes, they ______________ .
Will there be rain in summer?	No, ______________ be rain.

3. **Stelle die zu den Antworten passenden Fragen.**

______________________________________ ? Yes, I will go on holiday to Spain.

______________________________________ ? No, I won't enjoy the long journey.

______________________________________ ? Yes, I will love to be out in the sun all day.

bearbeitet am: ______ erreichte Punktzahl: ______

Ab 9 erreichten Punkten kannst du mit Test 109 fortfahren.

Test 109 Bildung und Gebrauch des *will future*

Schwierigkeitsgrad: ● ● ●

1. **Stelle die zu den Antworten passenden Fragen.**

____ ? Yes, I will be in seventh form next year.

____ ? No, I won't have to take more maths lessons.

____ ? Yes, I will be able to go to French class, too.

2. **Bilde aus den Satzbestandteilen vollständige Sätze. Verwende das *will future*, wenn möglich.**

the weather / be better / soon

____ .

they / can / go fishing / next week

____ .

Andy / must / be careful / with his leg

____ .

can / they / come back / before Sunday

____ ?

3. **Setze die Fragen ins *will future***

Where are you? _______________________________ ?

What do you need? _______________________________ ?

When must I be there? _______________________________ ?

Why can't you help me? _______________________________ ?

bearbeitet am: __________ erreichte Punktzahl: __________

Ab 7 erreichten Punkten kannst du mit Test 110 fortfahren.

Test 110 Bildung und Gebrauch des *will future*

Schwierigkeitsgrad: ● ● ○

1. **Fülle die Lücken.**

I hope Ms Hart ____________________ (not give) us too much homework

I think the weather ____________________ (be) fine in the afternoon.

Do you think the sun ____________________ (shine) later on?

Yes, I'm sure we ____________________ (have) lots of sunshine.

I ____________________ (play) football with you, if you like!

Yes, I ____________________ (like) that very much.

I've got an idea: Let's ask Ms Hart! She ____________________ (tell) us.

She ____________________ (know), how much homework we

____________________ (get).

2. **Wie können wir im Deutschen Sätze wiedergeben, die im Englischen das *will future* erfordern? Etwa: *She will be in Scotland next summer.* Kreuze an.**

durch das Präteritum ☐

durch das Perfekt ☐

durch das Präsens ☐

durch das Futur I ☐

3. **Gib zwei mögliche Übersetzungen für den Beispielsatz aus Aufgabe 2 an:**
She will be in Scotland next summer.

____

____

____

bearbeitet am: ______ erreichte Punktzahl: ______

Ab 11 erreichten Punkten kannst du mit Test 111 fortfahren.

Test 111 Bildung und Gebrauch des *will future*

Schwierigkeitsgrad: ● ● ●

1. **Wie siehst du dein Leben in 20 Jahren vor dir? Bilde eigene Sätze mit Vermutungen und Hoffnungen, für die du die folgenden Stichwörter benutzt. Schreibe mindestens vier Sätze.**

hope – think – believe – be happy – have a fine job – have money – look good – (not) be married

____

____

____

____

____

____

2. **Übersetze ins Englische.**

Viele Leute kommen zum Fußballspiel am Samstag.

______________________________.

Es wird schneien. Wir werden warme Sachen tragen müssen.

____

______________________________.

Ich glaube, Lucas, Andrew und Chris fahren nächstes Jahr zusammen in Urlaub.

____

______________________________.

3. **Was bezeichnen die Verben *be sure, believe, hope*? (mehrere Antworten gelten.)**

____

bearbeitet am: __________ erreichte Punktzahl: ______

Ab 7 erreichten Punkten kannst du mit Test 112 fortfahren.

Test 112 Bildung und Gebrauch des *going to future*

Schwierigkeitsgrad: ● ○ ○

1. Setze folgende kurze Sätze ins *going to future* (Kurzform).

I go to the concert. ______________________.

You come home. ______________________.

Dad cleans his car. ______________________.

Timmy calls Debbie. ______________________.

Noah doesn't help his mother.

______________________.

He goes to football practice instead.

______________________.

2. Fülle die Lücken mit den Verben im *going to future* (Langform).

I ______________________ (stay) home tomorrow.

Sophie ______________________ (bring) me our homework.

Anna ______________________ (clean) her bike.

We ______________________ (be) fine.

Darla ______________________ (play) the piano for you.

Mr Sheffield ______________________ (take) some days off work.

I ______________________ (not go) out tonight.

Hilary ______________________ (not feel) happy after that game.

______________________ (you / be) okay with that?

______________________ (she / come) with us?

bearbeitet am: __________ erreichte Punktzahl: __________

Ab 13 erreichten Punkten kannst du mit Test 113 fortfahren.

Test 113 Bildung und Gebrauch des *going to future*

Schwierigkeitsgrad: ● ● ○

1. **Hier siehst du den Wochenplaner der Familie Fleming. Jeder hat so seine Pläne! Bilde zu jedem Eintrag einen vollständigen Satz mit dem *going to future.***

Monday	Tuesday	Wednesday	Thursday	Friday	Saturday	Sunday
Dave play tennis		dad meet Paul		mum go to the movies	Alyssa visit aunt Betty	

On Monday Dave ______________________________.

______________________________.

______________________________.

______________________________.

2. **Fülle die Lücken und trage ein, um was für eine Art Satz (A oder B) es sich handelt.**

A. Pläne, Vorhaben **B.** wahrscheinliche Ereignisse

Dad ______________ (wash) the dishes after breakfast. ☐

You haven't done your homework? Mr Bark ______________ (notice). ☐

On the weekend I ______________ (run) a mile every morning. ☐

The door is unlocked. Someone ______________ (come in). ☐

3. **Bilde aus den Satzbestandteilen vollständige Sätze im *going to future.***

Ella / fall / down the stairs

______________________________.

Will and Robyn / come / to the party

______________________________?

I / can / see / my cousin / next summer

______________________________.

bearbeitet am: ______ erreichte Punktzahl: ______

Ab 9 erreichten Punkten kannst du mit Test 114 fortfahren.

Test 114 Bildung und Gebrauch des *going to future*

Schwierigkeitsgrad: ● ● ○

1. Beantworte die Fragen mit vollständigen Antworten.

Look at the boat! Is it going to sink? No, ______________________________.

Are you going to watch TV tonight? Yes, ______________________________.

Are we going to be in Hull soon? Yes, ______________________________.

Is Mike going to see Amy? No, ______________________________.

2. Stelle die zu den Antworten passenden Fragen.

______________________________? Yes, I'm going to cry.

______________________________? Yes, I'm going to spend a lot of money at the stores.

______________________________? No, I am not going to be nice to Mr Owen.

______________________________? Yes, my team is going to lose the match.

3. Übersetze ins Englische und verwende Kurzformen, wo möglich.

Wir besuchen Oma am Sonntag nicht.

______________________________.

Musst du morgen mit uns mitkommen?

____

Ich werde einen Kuchen für deinen Geburtstag nächste Woche backen.

____

______________________________.

bearbeitet am: ______________ erreichte Punktzahl: ______

Ab 9 erreichten Punkten kannst du mit Test 115 fortfahren.

Test 115 Grundlagen der Wortstellung

Schwierigkeitsgrad: ● ● ○

1. **Unterstreiche jeweils das Subjekt im Satz.**

   Ms Taylor gives her son a sandwich.

   He is very hungry.

   Children want tasty food.

2. **Unterstreiche jeweils das Prädikat (Hilfsverb gestrichelt und Vollverb ganz) im Satz.**

   Layla must do her homework at once.

   I will help her later.

   Her teacher can give her a good grade.

3. **Bilde jeweils aus Subjekt, Prädikat und Ergänzung einen korrekten Satz im *simple present*.**

   Janet – can – swim – our teacher – with its toy mouse – won't – us – any homework – give – very fast – the cat – play

   A. ____ .

   B. ____ .

   C. ____ .

4. **Welche Aussagen über die Wortstellung in englischen Aussagesätzen sind wahr? Kreuze an.**

	richtig	falsch
A. Das Subjekt steht in jedem Aussagesatz vor dem Verb.	☐	☐
B. Ergänzungen (Objekte, Orts- und Zeitangaben) usw. stehen im Allgemeinen vor dem Prädikat.	☐	☐
C. Auch in Nebensätzen steht das Subjekt immer vor dem Prädikat.	☐	☐
D. Zeitangaben folgen meist ganz hinten im Satz.	☐	☐

bearbeitet am: __________ erreichte Punktzahl: ______

Ab 13 erreichten Punkten kannst du mit Test 116 fortfahren.

Test 116 Bejahte Aussagesätze

Schwierigkeitsgrad: ● ● ○

1. **Bilde aus den Satzteilen korrekt geordnete vollständige Sätze in der angegebenen Zeitform.**

a car dealer / at an auction / sell / a new Ford / my brother

simple present:

____ .

present progressive:

____ .

simple past:

____ .

past progressive:

____ .

present perfect:

____ .

present perfect progressive:

____ .

will future:

____ .

going to future:

____ .

2. **Gib die richtige Reihenfolge folgender Satzteile in einem englischen Aussagesatz an und setze einen vollständigen Satz daraus zusammen.**

A. Prädikat	**B.** Subjekt	**C.** Zeitangabe	**D.** Objekt	**E.** Adverb der Art und Weise
answer	the man	last week	the questions	nervously

___ → ___ → ___ → ___ → ___

____ .

bearbeitet am: ________ erreichte Punktzahl: ____

Ab 8 erreichten Punkten kannst du mit Test 117 fortfahren.

Test 117 Bejahte Aussagesätze

Schwierigkeitsgrad: ● ● ●

1. **Ergänze die Tabelle mit den fehlenden Sätzen oder den Zeitformen mit Subjekt und Verb.**

Satz	Zeitform
I never walk to school.	*simple present*: I / walk
______________________	*simple past*: mum / come home / yesterday
Your friends have been staying with us.	______________________
______________________	*going to future*: I / work / a lot / tomorrow
He's just called me.	______________________
______________________	*past progressive*: she / read / all night
We'll have to leave soon.	______________________

2. **Ergänze den Nebensatz mit Hauptsätzen aus den Wörtern in der richtigen Reihenfolge.**

When they're on holiday, ...

at the beach / go surfing / often

... ____ .

all day / in the sun / lie

... ____ .

3. **Übersetze die Nebensätze und ergänze sie zum Hauptsatz.**

She will have fun, ...

weil sie die Sonne mag.

... ____ .

wenn sie genug Zeit haben wird.

... ____ .

bearbeitet am: __________ erreichte Punktzahl: ______

Ab 9 erreichten Punkten kannst du mit Test 118 fortfahren.

Test 118 Bejahte Aussagesätze

Schwierigkeitsgrad: ● ● ●

1. **Bilde aus den Satzbestandteilen vollständige Sätze. Achte darauf, die passende Zeitform zu verwenden und alle Bestandteile in die richtige Wortfolge zu bringen.**

Greg / last night / get sick

____.

Charly and Ted / tonight / Kim and Vicky / meet

____.

tennis lessons / have / in Hull / every Wednesday / I

____.

never / be / he / to Australia

____.

2. **Übersetze mit korrekter Wortstellung ins Englische.**

Jimmy macht manchmal den Abwasch.

____.

Ich komme nächstes Wochenende mit euch auf die Party.

____.

Micky gab ihr glücklich den Ring.

____.

3. **Was steht in englischen Aussagesätzen von allen Bestandteilen zuletzt? Kreuze an.**

- das Prädikat ☐
- das Objekt ☐
- die Zeitangabe ☐
- die Ortsangabe ☐

bearbeitet am: ____________ erreichte Punktzahl: ______

Ab 8 erreichten Punkten kannst du mit Test 119 fortfahren.

Test 119 Verneinte Aussagesätze

Schwierigkeitsgrad: ● ○ ○

1. **Bilde aus den Satzteilen vollständige Sätze in der angegebenen Zeitform (Langform).**

simple present: we / cannot go on holiday / to Greece / every year

____.

present progressive: the boy / not wait / at the bus stop

____.

simple past: Naomi / not call / her mum

____.

past progressive: Nicholas / not listen / to his teacher

____.

present perfect: Sarah / not be / to the hairdresser

____.

present perfect progressive: I / not stay up / all night

____.

will future: sun / not shine / tomorrow

____.

going to future: the baby / not sleep quietly / here

____.

2. **Welche Aussagen über Verneinungen im Englischen sind wahr? Kreuze an.**

	richtig	falsch
A. Verneinungen im *simple present* und *simple past* benötigen eine Form von *do* als Umschreibung.	☐	☐
B. Im *past progressive* wird mit *was/were* und *not* verneint.	☐	☐
C. Das *not* oder *n't* folgt direkt aufs Hilfsverb.	☐	☐

bearbeitet am: ____________ erreichte Punktzahl: ______

Ab 9 erreichten Punkten kannst du mit Test 120 fortfahren.

Test 120 Verneinte Aussagesätze

Schwierigkeitsgrad: ● ● ○

1. **Unterstreiche jeweils das Hilfsverb (gestrichelt) und das Verneinungselement (ganz).**

We do not sell flowers.

Tony didn't go to school yesterday.

They won't be in Europe next year.

She was not standing there with the others.

I cannot buy him a present.

2. **Ergänze den Nebensatz mit Hauptsätzen aus den Wörtern in der richtigen Reihenfolge.**

When we meet, ...

about school / not talk

... ____ .

in the house / for long / not stay

... ____ .

3. **Übersetze die Nebensätze und ergänze sie zum Hauptsatz.**

We are glad, ...

wenn wir nicht Unterricht haben.

... ____ .

weil wir nicht lernen müssen.

... ____ .

4. **Wo ist das Verneinungselement in englischen Aussagesätzen zu finden? Kreuze an.**

nach dem Hilfsverb	☐	nach dem Vollverb	☐
nach dem Subjekt	☐	am Satzende	☐

bearbeitet am: ______ erreichte Punktzahl: ______

Ab 12 erreichten Punkten kannst du mit Test 121 fortfahren.

Test 121 Verneinte Aussagesätze

Schwierigkeitsgrad: ● ● ○

1. **Bilde aus den passenden Satzbestandteilen jeweils einen korrekten verneinten Satz im *simple past*.**

play – the children – all day – I – in class – not tell – you – your parents – not sleep – not be allowed to – everything

A. ____ .

B. ____ .

C. ____ .

2. **Im Zoo war nicht alles wie erwartet! Dennis berichtet. Bilde aus den passenden Satzbestandteilen jeweils einen korrekten verneinten Satz im *past progressive*.**

the monkeys – not eat – bananas – the lions – not roar – loudly – the parrots – not talk – to the visitors

A. ____ .

B. ____ .

C. ____ .

3. **Ordne die Satzbestandteile zu verneinten Aussagesätzen an und notiere sie.**

going to future: not wash / the car / dad

____ .

simple past: their game / not stop / the boys

____ .

present perfect: for years / mum / to the movies / in London / not go

____

____ .

bearbeitet am: ____________ erreichte Punktzahl: ______

Ab 7 erreichten Punkten kannst du mit Test 122 fortfahren.

Test 122 Verneinte Aussagesätze

Schwierigkeitsgrad: ● ● ●

1. **Bilde aus den Satzbestandteilen vollständige Sätze und verneine sie. Notiere die verneinte Form. Achte darauf, die passende Zeitform und korrekte Wortfolge zu verwenden.**

may / children / in museums / run

____.

thunderstorms / tomorrow / there / be

____.

last year / more / Christmas decoration / put on / they

____.

pass / my test / I / have / yet

____.

since Christmas / her new book / Maya / read

____.

2. **Übersetze mit korrekter Wortstellung ins Englische. Verwende die Langform.**

Hannah nimmt nicht den Bus.

____.

Tina geht am Samstag nicht ins Kino.

____.

Ihr habt mir nie zugehört.

____.

Er schrieb gestern seinen Test nicht.

____.

bearbeitet am: __________ erreichte Punktzahl: ______

Ab 7 erreichten Punkten kannst du mit Test 123 fortfahren.

Test 123 Fragen ohne Fragewort

Schwierigkeitsgrad: ● ○ ○

1. **Unterstreiche jeweils das Subjekt in der Frage.**

Do you like mushrooms?

Can he play basketball?

Are they going to help us?

2. **Unterstreiche jeweils das Prädikat (Hilfsverb gestrichelt und Vollverb ganz) in der Frage.**

Did you know the answers?

Will Luke marry Lorelai?

Can't you see we're busy?

3. **Bilde jeweils aus Subjekt, Prädikat und Ergänzung eine korrekte Frage im *simple present*.**

can eat – Matt – live – on his bike – your hamster – in a cage – I – go – my lunch – to school

A. ____ ?

B. ____ ?

C. ____ ?

4. **Welche Aussagen über englische Fragesätze sind wahr? Kreuze an.**

	richtig	falsch
A. Fragen ohne Fragewort nennt man Entscheidungsfragen.	☐	☐
B. Das Hilfsverb steht bei Fragen immer ganz hinten.	☐	☐
C. Das Subjekt steht bei Fragen hinter dem Hilfsverb.	☐	☐
D. Mit *do* und *did* umschreibt man Fragen in simple present und simple past (wenn es kein anderes Hilfsverb gibt).	☐	☐

bearbeitet am: ________ erreichte Punktzahl: ________

Ab 13 erreichten Punkten kannst du mit Test 124 fortfahren.

Test 124 Fragen ohne Fragewort

Schwierigkeitsgrad: ● ● ○

1. Forme die Aussagen zu Fragesätzen um.

Newcastle lies in the North of England.

____?

You are doing your homework.

____?

Sylvia has lived in Canada.

____?

Gabrielle will arrive here soon.

____?

People can fly to London in an hour.

____?

Patrick had to clean the house.

____?

2. Formuliere aus den Satzbestandteilen höfliche Fragen mit *would like* oder *could*.

you / a glass of water

____?

you / go / to the movies / with me

____?

you / tell / me / the way to the train station

____?

bearbeitet am: ____________ erreichte Punktzahl: ______

Ab 7 erreichten Punkten kannst du mit Test 125 fortfahren.

Test 125 Fragen ohne Fragewort

Schwierigkeitsgrad: ● ● ○

1. **Stelle die zu den Antworten passenden Fragen.**

____ ? Yes, I am smiling.

____ ? Yes, you can go.

____ ? No, I won't be here tomorrow.

____ ?
No, she did not kiss the new girl.

____ ?
Yes, he has been allowed to watch the movie.

2. **Was passiert jedes Jahr? Bilde aus den passenden Satzbestandteilen jeweils einen korrekten Fragesatz im *simple present*.**

make – go – in summer – children – on holiday – snowballs – families – flowers – grow – in winter – in spring

A. ____ ?

B. ____ ?

C. ____ ?

3. **Was geht beim Fußballspiel im Stadion vor sich? Bilde aus den passenden Satzbestandteilen jeweils einen korrekten Fragesatz im *present progressive*.**

flags – wave – in the air – people – shout – loudly – the players – run – along the field

A. ____ ?

B. ____ ?

C. ____ ?

bearbeitet am: ______________ erreichte Punktzahl: ______

Ab 9 erreichten Punkten kannst du mit Test 126 fortfahren.

Test 126 Fragen ohne Fragewort

Schwierigkeitsgrad: ● ● ○

1. **Verbinde die Fragen mit den passenden Antworten.**

Does she have good maths grades?	You are next, aren't you?
Will the Jamesons come to the meeting?	He has, hasn't he?
Am I next in line?	She does, doesn't she?
Has she been sleeping enough?	She hasn't, has she?
Has Steve got a brother?	They won't, will they?
Are we going to win this match?	It didn't, did it?
Did the dog eat my shoe?	We are, aren't we?

2. **Ergänze die Fragen durch die richtigen Frageanhängsel (*question tags*).**

He often listens to pop music, ______________________________?

Teachers don't smoke in class, ______________________________?

Children cannot drive cars, ______________________________?

She will come with us, ______________________________?

You went to Turkey on holiday, ______________________________?

I don't have to wash the dishes now, ______________________________?

Clara hasn't cleaned her shirt yet, ______________________________?

3. **Was wird bei bejahten Aussagesätzen als *question tag* angehängt?**

eine Bejahung	☐	kein *question tag*	☐
eine Verneinung	☐	immer eine Form von *do*	☐

bearbeitet am: ____________ erreichte Punktzahl: ______

Ab 12 erreichten Punkten kannst du mit Test 127 fortfahren.

Test 127 Fragen ohne Fragewort

Schwierigkeitsgrad: ● ● ●

1. **Bilde aus den Satzbestandteilen vollständige Fragen. Achte darauf, die passende Zeitform und korrekte Wortfolge zu verwenden.**

rain / tomorrow / there be

____?

an e-mail / write / me / she / yesterday

____?

you / now / would like / a cup of tea

____?

Mia and Lily / their shoes / yet / put on

____?

paint / the walls / they / when you came in

____?

2. **Übersetze die Fragen ins Englische.**

Würdest du mir bitte das Salz reichen?

____?

Wirst du am Samstag fernsehen?

____?

Habt ihr euer Steak schon gegessen?

____?

Du magst Bella, nicht wahr?

____?

bearbeitet am: ______ erreichte Punktzahl: ______

Ab 7 erreichten Punkten kannst du mit Test 128 fortfahren.

Test 128 Fragen mit Fragewort

Schwierigkeitsgrad: ● ○ ○

1. Finde in dem Worträtsel sieben englische Fragewörter. Sie können auch schräg oder rückwärts buchstabiert sein.

W	F	G	P	T	H
O	H	W	M	A	C
W	H	E	N	H	E
T	O	L	R	W	H
W	W	H	Y	E	W
H	C	I	H	W	A

2. Bilde vollständige Fragesätze mit den vorgegebenen Fragewörtern.

The children go to school by bike today.

Who? ______________________________?

Where? ______________________________?

How? ______________________________?

When? ______________________________?

3. Stelle Fragen nach dem unterstrichenen Satzteil.

A new boy came to school.

______________________________?

He told us his name.

______________________________?

He came here, because his family had moved.

______________________________?

He sat down at a table next to Sally.

______________________________?

bearbeitet am: __________ erreichte Punktzahl: ______

Ab 12 erreichten Punkten kannst du mit Test 129 fortfahren.

Test 129 Fragen mit Fragewort

Schwierigkeitsgrad: ● ● ●

1. **Bilde aus den Satzbestandteilen Fragen in der korrekten Wortfolge und in der angegebenen Zeitform.**

simple present: when / I / go home / can

____ ?

present progressive: Kayla / for us / wait / where

____ ?

simple past: colour / Jeff / choose / which

____ ?

past progressive: you / why / not listen / to your mother

____ ?

2. ***How much* oder *how many*? Fülle die Lücken.**

____________________ pets have you got?

____________________ milk would you like?

____________________ stars can you count?

____________________ time do you need?

3. **Stelle die passenden Fragen und verwende dafür die Kurzform wie im Beispiel.**

Who's this?	This is Peter.
______________________________ ?	That is an airplane.
______________________________ ?	That's our new teacher.
______________________________ ?	My birthday's in May.

bearbeitet am: __________ erreichte Punktzahl: __________

Ab 9 erreichten Punkten kannst du mit Test 130 fortfahren.

Test 130 Fragen mit Fragewort

Schwierigkeitsgrad: ● ● ●

1. **Bilde aus den Satzbestandteilen vollständige Fragen mt Fragewort. Achte darauf, die passende Zeitform und korrekte Wortfolge zu verwenden.**

say / you / to her / last night / what

____?

why / answer / my question / she / never

____?

when / can / I / her / again / see

____?

meet / she and I / where / in future

____?

2. **Übersetze die Fragen ins Englische.**

Wo kann ich meine Jacke finden?

____?

Wie gelange ich von hier nach London?

____?

Wen werdet ihr zu eurer Party einladen?

____?

Wann kam Julian gestern nach Hause?

____?

Welchen Knopf muss ich drücken?

____?

bearbeitet am: erreichte Punktzahl:

Ab 8 erreichten Punkten kannst du mit Test 131 fortfahren.

Test 131 Befehlssätze bilden und verwenden

Schwierigkeitsgrad: ● ○ ○

1. **Erics Mum gibt ihm so einige Anweisungen. Setze die passende Befehlsform ein.**

sleep – stop – go – brush – help

____________________ upstairs.

____________________ your sister. ____________________ fighting.

____________________ your teeth. ____________________ well.

2. **Was musst du tun? Wandle die Aussagesätze in Befehlssätze um.**

You must wait for the green light.

____ .

You must take the bus to school.

____ .

You mustn't hurt other children.

____ .

You mustn't shout or talk in class.

____ .

3. **Welche Aussage über die englische Befehlsform ist wahr? Kreuze an.**

	richtig	falsch
A. Die Befehlsform entspricht immer der Grundform.	☐	☐
B. Hinter englischen Befehlssätzen steht immer ein Ausrufezeichen.	☐	☐

bearbeitet am: __________ erreichte Punktzahl: ______

Ab 9 erreichten Punkten kannst du mit Test 132 fortfahren.

Test 132 Befehlssätze bilden und verwenden

Schwierigkeitsgrad: ● ● ○

1. Welche Verben würden hier als Befehle passen? Fülle die Lücken mit eigenen Ideen.

_______________ your homework.

_______________ your breakfast.

_______________ your hands.

_______________ to me.

_______________ home before seven.

2. Bilde vollständige Befehlssätze. Wähle verneinte Befehlssätze, wo diese sinnvoll sind.

sit still _______________.

be late _______________.

make so much noise _______________.

go to bed _______________.

shout in class _______________.

3. Übersetze ins Englische. Vergiss das richtige Satzschlusszeichen nicht.

Komm bitte her!

____

Sei nicht dumm!

____

Kauft diese mp3-Player nicht!

____

bearbeitet am: __________ erreichte Punktzahl: __________

Ab 11 erreichten Punkten kannst du mit Test 133 fortfahren.

Test 133 Konjunktionen richtig verwenden

Schwierigkeitsgrad: ● ● ●

1. **Verbinde jeweils die Haupt- und Nebensätze, die zusammengehören. Achte besonders auf die Konjunktionen am Anfang jedes Nebensatzes.**

She is thirsty, ...	... before you could leave.
He didn't want to go to school, ...	... but he had to.
Ella got a good grade in her test ...	... because she didn't drink enough.
Dean arrived ...	... although she didn't study a lot.

2. **Unterstreiche in dem Text alle Konjunktionen am Anfang der Haupt- und Nebensätze.**

My friend Tammy and I were late for school, because we had an accident on the way. When we were crossing the street, a man on a bicycle came. He didn't stop fast enough and hit Tammy. I tried to hold her back, but she fell. It was a hard fall, so her arm was hurt. Although the man offered to take us to a hospital, Tammy got up. She said that her arm wasn't broken and went to school with me.

3. **Schreibe die unterstrichenen Konjunktionen mit ihren deutschen Bedeutungen heraus.**

______________________	______________________
______________________	______________________
______________________	______________________
______________________	______________________
______________________	______________________
______________________	______________________
______________________	______________________

bearbeitet am: __________ erreichte Punktzahl: ____

Ab 20 erreichten Punkten kannst du mit Test 134 fortfahren.

Test 134 Konjunktionen richtig verwenden

Schwierigkeitsgrad: ● ● ○

1. Kreuze alle Konjunktionen an, mit denen die Sätze sinnvoll werden. Manchmal passt mehr als eine Lösung.

I'm staying in bed today, ... I am ill.

☐ that ☐ because ☐ until

My stomach was aching, ... I went to bed last night.

☐ and ☐ when ☐ before

I had stomach pain, ... I fell asleep.

☐ because ☐ until ☐ that

Now I am ill ... I don't have to go to school

☐ so ☐ and ☐ although

I think ... I am going to be ill tomorrow, too.

☐ but ☐ before ☐ that

2. Wähle eine passende Konjunktion für jede Lücke aus und setze sie ein.

before – so – that – until – although – but

Ms Hunter tried to walk, ______________________ she couldn't with her broken foot.

My friends and I played football, ______________________ it got dark.

I'll do my homework, ______________________ I go to bed.

I know ______________________ she likes me.

He smiled at me, ______________________ I felt really good.

I had to go home early, ______________________ the match wasn't over.

bearbeitet am: __________ erreichte Punktzahl: __________

Ab 12 erreichten Punkten kannst du mit Test 135 fortfahren.

Test 135 Konjunktionen richtig verwenden

Schwierigkeitsgrad: ● ● ●

1. **Fülle die Lücken mit den passenden Konjunktionen.**

_______________ they came home, they sat down in front of the TV at once.

He did not stay, _______________ the match was over.

_______________ we got our new teacher, I've never understood maths.

Believe me _______________ I've never lied to you!

_______________ the kiss felt good, she stopped her friend.

I really wish I had more money, _______________ I haven't!

2. **Übersetze ins Deutsche.**

When he arrived, he said hello to everyone.

____

____.

I saw her at once, because she was wearing an orange jacket.

____

____.

Aaron will study for this test, until he knows every English word in it.

____

____.

Would you like to wear your green cap or would you like to take the blue one?

____

____?

bearbeitet am: __________ erreichte Punktzahl: __________

Ab 8 erreichten Punkten kannst du mit Test 136 fortfahren.

Test 136 Bedingungssätze

Schwierigkeitsgrad: ● ○ ○

1. **Füge die *if*-Sätze mit den jeweils passenden Hauptsätzen zusammen und notiere die vollständigen Sätze noch einmal auf den Linien.**

If she goes to bed now, ...

If you miss your piano lessons, ...

If your team wins the football match, ...

If Finn eats any more chocolate, ...

If Annie doesn't call Derek, ...

... he will be sick.

... you will have a party.

... you won't be able to play well.

... she won't be tired tomorrow.

... he will feel sad.

____ .

____ .

____ .

____ .

____ .

2. **Fülle die Lücken mit der richtigen Form der Verben in Klammern.**

If the weather ____________________ (stay) good,

we ____________________ (go) to the beach.

If the others ____________________ (come) too,

we ____________________ (have) lots of fun together.

If it ____________________ (be) very hot outside,

you ____________________ (have to bring) the sun screen.

bearbeitet am: __________ erreichte Punktzahl: __________

Ab 9 erreichten Punkten kannst du mit Test 137 fortfahren.

Test 137 Bedingungssätze

Schwierigkeitsgrad: ● ● ●

1. **Fülle die Lücken mit den passenden Verben aus der Reihe oben in der richtigen Zeitform.**

win – enjoy – tell – get – feed – visit

If we ask our neighbour, she ______________________ the cats, during our holidays.

If I ______________________ you what she said about you, you will be shocked.

Aunt Jane will be so happy, if her nieces ______________________ her some time.

If Carol and Paige are always late for class, they ______________________ awful grades.

My mum ______________________ her weekend, if I and my sisters sleep over at our friends' houses.

If Melissa doesn't play better than yesterday, Sammy ______________________ this tennis match.

2. **Bilde aus den Satzbestandteilen vollständige Bedingungssätze in der korrekten Form.**

if / my friend / like to → we / have / a long phone talk / tonight

____.

if / our teacher / let us go → school / finish / early / today

____.

if / Tim / have got / enough money → he / buy / a new fingerboard

____.

3. **Welche Zeitform hat das Verb in *if*-Sätzen niemals? Kreuze an.**

will future ☐ *present tense* ☐

bearbeitet am: ______ erreichte Punktzahl: ______

Ab 11 erreichten Punkten kannst du mit Test 138 fortfahren.

Test 138 Bedingungssätze

Schwierigkeitsgrad: ● ● ○

1. **Setze *if* oder *when* in die Lücken ein.**

My parents will get angry, ________________ I am not home by seven o'clock.

Can I open the window? ________________ it gets too cold, I'll close it again.

________________ the bus stops at the next stop, we'll have to get off.

We'll have tea, ________________ we come home.

________________ doesn't leave now, she'll miss her bus.

Please phone us, ________________ you arrive in Edinburgh.

________________ the weather is bad, we won't rent a boat.

2. **Setze *if* oder *when* in die Lücken ein und ergänze die Sätze dann mit den richtigen Formen der Verben in Klammern.**

Sam will be so happy, ________________ his girlfriend ____________________________ (come home) from her holidays in France.

________________ we do more sports, we ____________________________ (get) thinner.

________________ I win first prize at the running competition today,

I ____________________________ (have) a big party with all my friends.

________________ Lisa ____________________________ (not make) too many mistakes, she will pass her exam.

They won't leave, ______________ we ____________________________ (not ask) them to.

3. **Worum geht es bei Sätzen mit *when*? Kreuze an.**

um eine Bedingung ☐ um einen Zeitpunkt ☐

um eine Folge ☐ um eine Verneinung ☐

bearbeitet am: ________ erreichte Punktzahl: ________

Ab 15 erreichten Punkten kannst du mit Test 139 fortfahren.

Test 139 Bedingungssätze

Schwierigkeitsgrad: ● ● ●

1. **Was wirst du tun, wenn …? Führe die *if*-Sätze mit deinen eigenen Worten zu Ende. Hier gibt es natürlich viele mögliche Lösungen.**

If I get thirsty, …

____.

If I miss the bus home from school, …

____.

If I am late for class, …

____.

If I win 100 Euros in a lottery, …

____.

2. **Übersetze ins Englische.**

Jill wird ins Konzert gehen, wenn (falls) sie Karten bekommt.

____.

Ich gehe nach Hause, wenn (sobald) es dunkel wird.

____.

3. **Übersetze ins Deutsche.**

I will not go shopping, if you don't come with me.

____.

If there are no red boots in my size, I will buy brown ones.

____.

bearbeitet am: __________ erreichte Punktzahl: ______

Ab 7 erreichten Punkten kannst du mit Test 140 fortfahren.

Test 140 Relativsätze mit Relativpronomen

Schwierigkeitsgrad: ● ○ ○

1. **Englische Relativsätze können von vier Relativpronomen eingeleitet werden. Ordne die Buchstaben zu den korrekten Relativpronomen um und trage sie bei den Begriffen ein, auf die sie sich jeweils beziehen.**

W	I	H	H	C

W	O	H

W	S	E	O	H

T	T	H	A

W		

Personen

W				

Gegenstände und Tiere

T			

Personen, Gegenstände und Tiere

W				

Besitzverhältnis, Zugehörigkeit

2. **Unterstreiche die Relativsätze und kreise ihre Relativpronomen ein.**

These are the boys who helped us.

Minis are cars which are small.

Pupils who don't do their homework will get worse grades.

Airplanes which are too old are not safe.

Dogs that bark don't bite.

That is the cafe which I like to go to.

3. **Welche Aussagen über englische Relativsätze sind wahr? Kreuze „richtig" oder „falsch" an.**

	richtig	falsch
A. Bei Personen kann als Relativpronomen nur *who* stehen.	☐	☐
B. Präpositionen können im Relativsatz direkt vor dem Relativpronomen oder ganz am Satzende stehen.	☐	☐
D. Bei Gegenständen und Tieren kann als Relativpronomen wahlweise *which* oder *that* stehen.	☐	☐

bearbeitet am: ______ erreichte Punktzahl: ______

Ab 15 erreichten Punkten kannst du mit Test 141 fortfahren.

Test 141 Relativsätze mit Relativpronomen

Schwierigkeitsgrad: ● ● ●

1. **Beschreibe die unterstrichenen Personen näher, indem du einen Relativsatz bildest wie im Beispiel.**

customer / buy something in a store
A customer is someone who buys something in a store.

fisherman / catch fish

____ .

waiter / work in a restaurant

____ .

journalist / write for a newspaper

____ .

assistant / help his or her boss

____ .

2. **Setze das richtige Relativpronomen ein. Oft passen mehrere.**

Ms Harris is the teacher ______________ I like best.

There's Jennifer ______________ is my good friend.

Is love a feeling ______________ makes people happy?

That is the fountain pen ______________ I like to write with.

Mr Jenkins is the neighbour ______________ car has got the golden-coloured wheels.

Is this Jojo's friend Gina ______________ goes to school with her?

Is that the spotted dog ______________ you told me about?

bearbeitet am: ______________ erreichte Punktzahl: ______

Ab 9 erreichten Punkten kannst du mit Test 142 fortfahren, ab 10 mit Test 143.

Test 142 Relativsätze mit Relativpronomen

Schwierigkeitsgrad: ● ● ○

1. **Beschreibe die unterstrichenen Gegenstände näher, indem du einen Relativsatz bildest wie im Beispiel.**

coffee maker / make coffee
A coffee maker is something that makes coffee.

lipstick / colour your lips

____ .

toaster / roast bread

____ .

ruler / measure things

____ .

hose / water the garden

____ .

2. **Setze das richtige Relativpronomen ein. Oft passen mehrere.**

Can you give me that book ______________ is on the shelf?

Carol is watching the DVD ______________ Clara gave her.

Ms Grouse is mum's friend ______________ daughter lives in Ohio.

Can you see that boy ______________ is wearing the red shirt?

Do I have to clean the dishes ______________ are really dirty?

Can you repair the watch ______________ is broken?

Will they go to the lake ______________ is in Scotland?

bearbeitet am: ______________ erreichte Punktzahl: ______

Ab 9 erreichten Punkten kannst du mit Test 143 fortfahren.

Test 143 Relativsätze mit Relativpronomen

Schwierigkeitsgrad: ● ● ○

1. Setze das richtige Relativpronomen ein. Oft passen mehrere.

Vanessa doesn't like people ________________ talk too little.

Brandon likes movies ________________ show a lot of blood.

We won't go to a country ________________ everyone else goes to on holiday.

Haven't you always wanted that ice cream ________________ had chocolate chips in it?

He was a boy ________________ thought he knew everything.

Would you repeat this question ________________ I didn't understand?

Do you like books ________________ are not about witches and wizards?

2. Verbinde die Sätze so, dass aus einem der Hauptssätzte jeweils ein Relativsatz wird.

Taylor is a girl. Chad likes her.

____.

Gabriella likes a boy. His name is Troy.

____.

Basketball is a fast game. Chad and Troy like to play it.

____.

Sometimes there are musical shows. Everyone likes them.

____.

Gabriella sings with Troy. He also loves to sing.

____.

bearbeitet am: ____________ erreichte Punktzahl: ______

Ab 11 erreichten Punkten kannst du mit Test 144 fortfahren.

Test 144 Relativsätze mit Relativpronomen

Schwierigkeitsgrad: ● ● ○

1. Hier geht es um London. Finde den passenden Relativsatz, füge das richtige Relativpronomen ein und bilde aus den Teilen jeweils Haupt- und Relativsatz. Achte auf die korrekten Zeitformen!

... may rule from Buckingham Palace

... flow through the city

... be made out of wax

... be the capital of England

... be called Heathrow

... many tourists like

... write her books in London

There is a large airport near London ...

____.

The London Eye is an attraction ...

____.

The Queen is the only one ...

____.

The Thames is the river ...

____.

Virginia Woolf was a writer ...

____.

London has always been the city ...

____.

There's a museum for figures ...

____.

bearbeitet am: ____________ erreichte Punktzahl: ______

Ab 6 erreichten Punkten kannst du mit Test 145 fortfahren.

Test 145 Relativsätze mit Relativpronomen

Schwierigkeitsgrad: ● ● ●

1. **Finde immer zwei zueinander passende Sätze und verbinde sie so, dass aus einem Teil jeweils ein Relativsatz wird.**

I watched the movie.

Have you seen the pencil?

What's the name of the teacher?

Basketball is a popular game.

Younger and older people like to play it.

You've told me about the movie.

It was in my bag.

We will get her in Englisch next year.

____

____.

____

____.

____

____.

____

____.

2. **Übersetze ins Englische.**

Jenny kannte die Leute nicht, die ihre Eltern besuchten.

____.

Werden James und Ian das Fußballspiel sehen, das heute im Fernsehen ist?

____.

Kennt ihr den Schriftsteller, der so viel über London schrieb?

____.

bearbeitet am: __________ erreichte Punktzahl: ______

Ab 6 erreichten Punkten kannst du mit Test 146 fortfahren.

Test 146 Relativsätze ohne Relativpronomen

Schwierigkeitsgrad: ● ● ○

1. Finde heraus, ob das Relativpronomen als Objekt im Relativsatz steht. In dem Fall kann man es weglassen. Kreuze die richtige Aussage an und notiere den Satz ohne Relativpronomen, wenn dies möglich ist.

That is the young man **who** helped carry our furniture.
Who helped carry our furniture? –„**Wer** hat uns beim Möbeltragen geholfen?"

A. Mit *who* wird das Subjekt bezeichnet. Es kann nicht weggelassen werden. ☐

B. Mit *who* wird das Objekt bezeichnet. Es kann weggelassen werden. ☐

Ohne Relativpronomen könnte der Satz heißen:

____ .

Isn't that the girl who we met last week?
Who did we meet last week? –„**Wen** haben wir letzte Woche getroffen?"

A. Mit *who* wird das Subjekt bezeichnet. Es kann nicht weggelassen werden. ☐

B. Mit *who* wird das Objekt bezeichnet. Es kann weggelassen werden. ☐

Ohne Relativpronomen könnte der Satz heißen:

____ .

2. Steht das Relativpronomen als Objekt im Relativsatz und kann somit weggelassen werden? Streiche das Relativpronomen aus allen Sätzen, in denen es verzichtbar ist.

I liked the horse that had the silvery mane.

They caught the thief who stole all the purses.

Where is that DVD that we wanted to watch?

Ben helped his grandma whose knees hurt very much.

I bought the book which you told me about.

Isn't that the pen that I bought for you?

bearbeitet am: __________ erreichte Punktzahl: _____

Ab 11 erreichten Punkten kannst du mit Test 147 fortfahren.

Test 147 Relativsätze ohne Relativpronomen

Schwierigkeitsgrad: ● ● ○

1. **Setze die richtigen Relativpronomen überall dort ein, wo sie stehen müssen. Dort, wo sie gestrichen werden können, lässt du sie weg.**

Anita comes from a country _______________ is very far from England.

Have you seen the picture _______________ Anthony gave to me?

I think she is the most beautiful girl _______________ I have ever met.

Art was the subject _______________ Cedric was best at.

Nina did not like the comedy show _______________ was on TV last night.

I've got the CD _______________ they were looking for.

Did you spend all the money _______________ grandma gave you yesterday?

Will they show the film _______________ was already on TV?

2. **Übersetze ins Englische. Lasse alle nicht erforderlichen Relativpronomen weg.**

Hast du den Hund gesehen, den Al kaufte?

____?

Ich mag die Schuhe nicht, die Nicky trug.

____.

Gib das Buch dem Jungen, der dort steht!

____.

Ich habe eine neue Freundin, deren Schwester nicht sehr nett zu mir ist.

____

____.

bearbeitet am: ______ erreichte Punktzahl: ______

Ab 10 erreichten Punkten kannst du mit Test 148 fortfahren.

Test 148 Grundzahlen

Schwierigkeitsgrad: ● ○ ○

1. Verbinde die Telefonnummern mit den entsprechenden Zahlwörtern. Lies dir jede Nummer dann noch einmal laut vor. Achtung: 0 spricht man als „Oh".

244978	one-four-two-five-three-six
895210	double-six-double-three-double-nine
125567	eight-nine-five-two-one-oh
663399	two-four-four-nine-seven-eight
142536	one-two-double-five-six-seven

2. Schreibe die Zahlen auf den Linien aus.

8 ____________	17 ____________	21 ____________
55 ____________	12 ____________	48 ____________
67 ____________	13 ____________	96 ____________

3. Bringe die Buchstaben in die richtige Reihenfolge. Welche Zahlen über zehn verbergen sich hinter dem Buchstabensalat?

weyntt ____________________

nnniteee ____________________

eentffi ____________________

ytriht ____________________

bearbeitet am: ____________ erreichte Punktzahl: ______

Ab 15 erreichten Punkten kannst du mit Test 149 fortfahren.

Test 149 Grundzahlen

Schwierigkeitsgrad: ● ● ○

1. **Schreibe die Zahlen auf den Linien aus.**

100 ______________________

345 ______________________

777 ______________________

1 000 ______________________

4 000 ______________________

33 000 ______________________

200 000 ______________________

1 000 000 ______________________

2. **Zähle jede Zahlenreihe im gleichen Abstand weiter und ergänze die fehlenden Zahlwörter.**

five, ten, fifteen, ______________________ thirty-five

twelve, twenty-two, ______________________ sixty-two

three, six, ______________________ twenty-one

fifty, one hundred, ______________________ two hundred and fifty

3. **Löse die Rechenaufgaben und trage die Ergebnisse erst als Ziffern, dann als Zahlwörter ein.**

2 + 16 + 42 = 60 sixty

78 – 8 – 6 = ______ ______________________

33 – 4 + 2 = ______ ______________________

2 + 16 + 23 = ______ ______________________

bearbeitet am: ______ erreichte Punktzahl: ______

Ab 12 erreichten Punkten kannst du mit Test 150 fortfahren.

Test 150 Ordnungszahlen

Schwierigkeitsgrad: ● ○ ○

1. Schreibe die Zahlen auf den Linien aus.

1st ________	5th ________
42nd ________	12th ________
83rd ________	9th ________
24th ________	30th ________
15th ________	11th ________
13th ________	8th ________
6th ________	17th ________

21. Bringe die Buchstaben in die richtige Reihenfolge. Welche Ordnungszahlen verbergen sich hinter dem Buchstabensalat?

teensixth ________

ftyro-thfuro ________

gheiethti ________

bearbeitet am: ________ erreichte Punktzahl: ________

Ab 14 erreichten Punkten kannst du mit Test 151 fortfahren.

Test 151 Ordnungszahlen

Schwierigkeitsgrad: ● ● ○

1. Ergänze die Sätze. Schreibe alle Ordnungszahlen, die vorkommen, als Wörter aus.

The first day of the week is ______________________________ .

May is the ______________________________ month of the year.

Christmas day is on the ______________________________ of December.

The third day of the week is ______________________________ .

Nine is the ______________________________ number.

Thursday is the ______________________________ day of the week.

Their parents are usually the ______________________________ people that babies see in their lives.

This coat is really old. I bought it ______________________________-hand.

I liked this bike best of all. It was my ______________________________ choice.

2. Übersetze ins Englische. Notiere dabei alle Ordnungszahlen, die vorkommen, als Ziffern.

Charlene ist meine zweite Freundin.

____ .

Wird diese Band den ersten Preis gewinnen?

____ ?

Nick war Sechzehnter in der Warteschlange.

____ .

Das war dein dritter Versuch!

____ !

bearbeitet am: ______________ erreichte Punktzahl: ______

Ab 11 erreichten Punkten kannst du mit Test 152 fortfahren.

Test 152 Uhrzeit

Schwierigkeitsgrad:

1. Wie spät ist es hier? Schreibe die Uhrzeit in Worten aus.

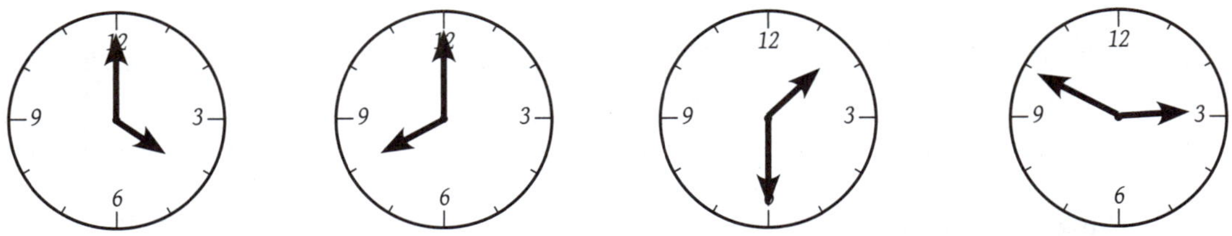

It's ______________ o'clock.

It's ______________ ______________ .

It's ______________ past ______________ .

It's ______________ to ______________ .

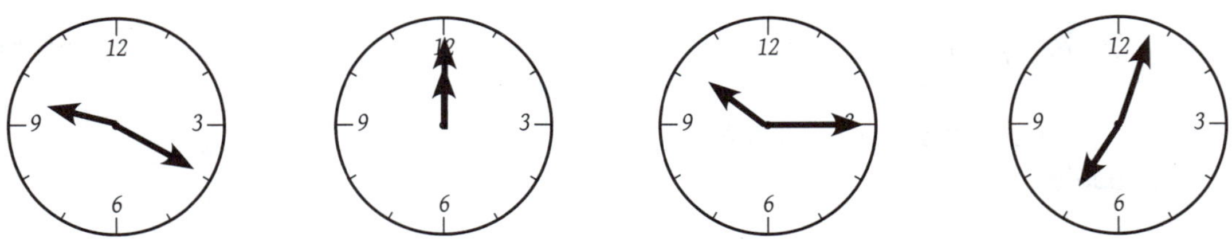

______________ ______________ .

______________ ______________ .

______________ ______________ .

______________ ______________ .

2. Zeichne die fehlenden Zeiger in die Uhren ein.

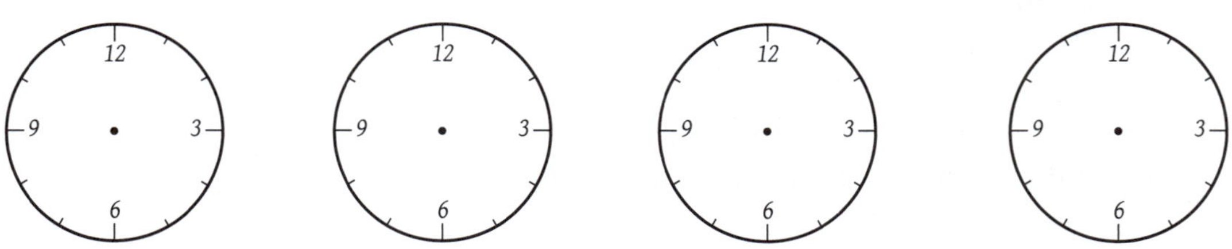

It's a quarter to eight.

It's five past nine.

It's ten to five.

It's twelve minutes past eleven.

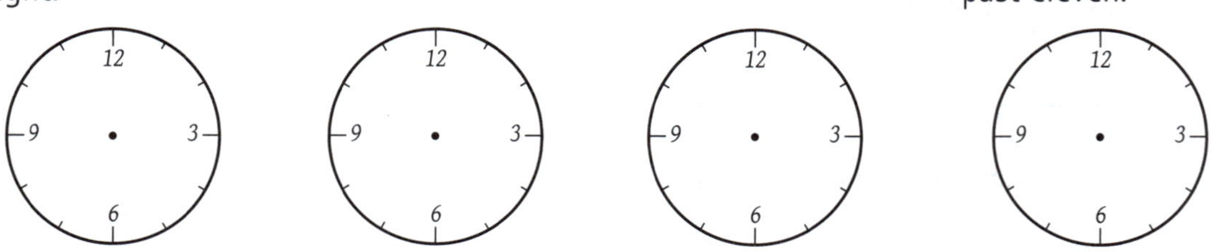

It's half past six.

It's twenty-five to one.

It's a quarter past ten.

It's two minutes to four.

bearbeitet am: ______________ erreichte Punktzahl: ______

Ab 13 erreichten Punkten kannst du mit Test 153 fortfahren.

Test 153 Uhrzeit

Schwierigkeitsgrad: ● ● ○

1. Auf dem Stundenplan hier siehst du, wie ein normaler Schultag für Lizzy verläuft. Gib Lizzys Stundenplan unten in ganzen Sätzen mit ausgeschriebener Uhrzeit wieder.

1. 8.50–9.40	2. 9.45–10.35	10.35–10.50	3. 10.55–11.45
maths	English	first break	history

4. 11.50–12.40	12.40–13.40	5. 13.45–14.30
PE	lunch break	music

Lizzy has maths from ______________________________ to ______________________________ . Lizzy has English from ______________________________ to ______________________________ .

The first break is from ______________________________ to ______________________________ . History is from ______________________________ to ______________________________ .

Lizzy has PE from ______________________________ to ______________________________ . Lunch break is from ______________________________ to ______________________________ .

Lizzy has music from ______________________________ to ______________________________ .

2. Gib die Uhrzeitangaben in der englischen Schreibweise mit Ziffern plus *a.m.* und *p.m.* an.

07.10	7 a.m.	11.27	____________
09.19	____________	19.10	____________
21.30	____________	17.15	____________

bearbeitet am: ____________ erreichte Punktzahl: ____________

Ab 15 erreichten Punkten kannst du mit Test 154 fortfahren.

Test 154 Jahreszahlen

Schwierigkeitsgrad: ● ● ○

1. Schreibe die folgenden Jahreszahlen als Wörter aus und lies sie laut mit.

1600 ______________________________

1998 ______________________________

2000 ______________________________

2011 ______________________________

1794 ______________________________

1566 ______________________________

1986 ______________________________

1882 ______________________________

2034 ______________________________

2. Übersetze ins Englische und schreibe die Jahreszahlen aus.

1789 war ein wichtiges Jahr.

______________________________.

1945 endete der Krieg.

______________________________.

Du wirst die Schule 2018 verlassen.

______________________________.

3. Mit welcher Präposition werden Jahreszahlen angegeben? Kreuze an.

at ☐ of ☐

on ☐ in ☐

bearbeitet am: ________ erreichte Punktzahl: ________

Ab 11 erreichten Punkten kannst du mit Test 155 fortfahren.

Test 155 Daten und Feiertage

Schwierigkeitsgrad: ● ● ●

1. **Im Englischunterricht werden die Kinder gefragt, wann sie Geburtstag haben. Schreibe ihre Antworten in ganzen Sätzen mit ausführlicher Datumsangabe auf.**

Neill: July11th
Neill's birthday is on the eleventh of July

Maya: May 2nd
Maya's birthday is on the ______________________________.

Jonas: April 1st

______________________________.

Julian: September 23rd

______________________________.

Connie: October 16th

______________________________.

2. **Man kann ein Datum auch kürzer ausdrücken. Notiere folgende Daten in der kürzeren Schreibweise mit Ziffern und gib dahinter an, wie diese ausgeprochen wird.**

14/09/2010: September 14th, 2010 – September the fourteenth, two thousand (and) ten

20/05/1998:

____

01/03/2011:

____

10/08/2018:

____

12/06/2002:

____

bearbeitet am: ____________ erreichte Punktzahl: ______

Ab 7 erreichten Punkten kannst du mit Test 156 fortfahren.

Test 156 Daten und Feiertage

Schwierigkeitsgrad: ● ○ ○

1. Kennst du die Feiertage auf Englisch? Übersetze ihre Namen.

Easter ______________________

Christmas ______________________

New Year's Eve ______________________

New Year's Day ______________________

2. Trage ein, in welchem Monat die Feiertage jeweils liegen.

Halloween is in ______________________ .

Christmas is in ______________________ .

Easter is in ______________________ or in

______________________ .

New Year's Eve is in ______________________ .

New Year's Day is in ______________________ .

3. Ordne die britischen Feiertage den Daten aus der Reihe oben zu und fülle die Lücken mit den passenden Daten in ausführlicher Form.

January 1st – May 1st – December 25th – December 26th

Christmas Day is on the ______________________ .

Boxing Day is on ______________________ .

May Day is on ______________________ .

New Year's Day is on ______________________ .

bearbeitet am: ________ erreichte Punktzahl: ________

Ab 11 erreichten Punkten kannst du mit Test 157 fortfahren.

Test 157 Mengenangaben mit Genitiv

Schwierigkeitsgrad: ● ● ○

1. Verbinde die Mengenangaben mit *of* und einem jeweils passenden Substantiv.

a	pound	of	tea
	pair		soup
	spoonful		crisps
	piece		apple juice
	pot		children
	glass		cake
	bag		carrots
	bowl		sugar
	group		socks

2. Suche aus der Reihe oben die richtige Mengenangabe für jedes Substantiv und verbinde die beiden mit *of*.

~~bar~~ – cup – slice – kilo – bottle – box – pack

a bar of chocolate

a ______________________________ of water

______________________________ coffee

______________________________ cookies

______________________________ oranges

______________________________ tissues

______________________________ bread

bearbeitet am: ________ erreichte Punktzahl: ________

Ab 12 erreichten Punkten kannst du mit Test 158 fortfahren.

Test 158 Mengenangaben mit Zahlen

Schwierigkeitsgrad: ● ● ○

1. **Beantworte die Fragen in ganzen Sätzen. Schreibe die Zahlenangaben in Worten aus.**

How many toes have you got?

I have got ______________________________ .

How many hours are there in a day?

______________________________ .

How many shoes are a pair?

______________________________ .

How many feet has a pig got?

______________________________ .

How many legs has a spider got?

______________________________ .

2. **Suche die passenden Mengenangaben plus Substantiv und trage sie in die Lücken ein. Schreibe die Ziffern dabei als Zahlwörter aus.**

| 12 years | 1 minute | 8 seconds | 2 shirts | 50 metres | 60 minutes |

There are ______________________________ in an hour.

She ran the distance of ______________________________ in

______________________________ .

He was so cold that he wore ______________________________ and a pullover.

I can hold my breath for ______________________________ .

Her older brother is ______________________________ old.

bearbeitet am: ____________ erreichte Punktzahl: ____________

Ab 9 erreichten Punkten kannst du mit Test 159 fortfahren.

Test 159 Mengenangaben mit Mengenwörtern

Schwierigkeitsgrad: ● ○ ○

1. Setze *much* oder *many* vor die Substantive.

____________ food	____________ sugar
____________ dogs	____________ women
____________ milk	____________ birthdays
____________ pictures	____________ pens
____________ cups	____________ rice
____________ numbers	____________ bananas
____________ peas	____________ fingers
____________ money	____________ hair
____________ coins	____________ noise

2. Ergänze die Fragen durch *much* oder *many.*

How ____________ windows are there in the classroom?

How ____________ time have we got?

How ____________ money have you got?

How ____________ children are in that room?

How ____________ does that game cost?

How ____________ water will we need?

How ____________ apples are there in the bag?

How ____________ subjects do you have at school?

bearbeitet am: ____________ erreichte Punktzahl: ____________

Ab 17 erreichten Punkten kannst du mit Test 160 fortfahren.

Test 160 Mengenangaben mit Mengenwörtern

Schwierigkeitsgrad:

1. **Übersetze ins Englische und verwende dabei *much* oder *many*.**

Sie gingen auf viele Partys.

____.

Sie hatten viel Spaß.

____.

2. **Setze *much*, *many*, *a lot of* oder *lots of* passend ein. Hier sind teilsweise mehrere Lösungen möglich.**

How ____________ eggs are there in the fridge?

Jane hasn't got ____________ time.

Do you know ____________ English words?

There was too ____________ wood in the fireplace.

How ____________ lessons do you have on Friday?

You cannot see ____________ stars tonight.

There is too ____________ water in the bucket.

How ____________ brothers has Timmy got?

There were ____________ ships at the harbour.

He put too ____________ salt in the food.

Grandpa hasn't got ____________ hair.

I have never seen so ____________ cats before.

There are too ____________ poor people in the world.

bearbeitet am: ____________ erreichte Punktzahl: ____________

Ab 12 erreichten Punkten kannst du mit Test 161 fortfahren.

Test 161 Mengenangaben mit Mengenwörtern

Schwierigkeitsgrad: ● ● ○

1. **Fülle die Lücken mit *some* oder *any.***

There aren't ________________ sweets left.

Why aren't there ________________ flowers on the table?

Jamie went to the movies with ________________ friends.

We will need water and ________________ glasses.

She doesn't need ________________ help.

Do you know ________________ actors?

Cindy doesn't own ________________ pets.

Do you need ________________ nails with that hammer?

Here are ________________ grapes for you.

Has Matthew got ________________ sisters?

Linda doesn't want ________________ presents for her birthday.

2. **Suche aus der Reihe oben die passenden Substantive zum Ergänzen der Sätze und fülle die Lücken davor mit *some* oder *any.***

time – presents – meat – sugar – fun

Sue is a vegetarian. She does not eat ________________ ________________ .

I've been working all week. Now I want to have ________________ ________________ .

Here is your coffee. Only I haven't got ________________ ________________ .

Tomorrow is mum's birthday. Have you bought ________________ ________________ yet?

Sorry, I can't stay. I haven't got ________________ ________________ .

bearbeitet am: ________ erreichte Punktzahl: ________

Ab 17 erreichten Punkten kannst du mit Test 162 fortfahren.

Test 162 Mengenangaben mit Mengenwörtern

Schwierigkeitsgrad:

1. **Übersetze nur die unterstrichenen Begriffe ins Deutsche.**

There were <u>some plates</u> on the table, but there was<u>n't any food</u>! I also could <u>not</u> see <u>any milk</u> for the coffee. Was there <u>any sugar</u>? There was <u>some jam</u>, but there were <u>no spoons</u>. There were<u>n't any knives</u> and <u>not many napkins</u>.

____

____

____

____

____

____

____

____

2. **Welche Aussagen über *some* und *any* sind wahr? Kreuze „richtig" oder „falsch" an.**

	richtig	falsch
A. *Some* bedeutet vor einem Substantiv im Singular „etwas", vor einem Substantiv im Plural bedeutet es „einige".	☐	☐
B. *Some* lässt sich in der Bedeutung von „einige" auch durch *many* ersetzen.	☐	☐
C. *Any* wird in verneinten Aussagesätzen verwendet.	☐	☐
D. *Some* wird immer in Fragen verwendet.	☐	☐
E. *not any* ... bedeutet „kein/e".	☐	☐
F. Diese Regeln gelten nicht für zusammengesetzte Begriffe wie *somebody* oder *something*.	☐	☐

bearbeitet am: __________ erreichte Punktzahl: ______

Ab 11 erreichten Punkten kannst du mit Test 163 fortfahren.

Test 163 Mengenangaben mit Mengenwörtern

Schwierigkeitsgrad:

1. **Setze die englischen Begriffe richtig zusammen und trage sie dann unter den passenden deutschen Begriffen ein.**

some- -thing -one -body -where

etwas

____

jemand

____

____

irgendwo

____

2. **Trage *some*, *any* oder die jeweils passende Zusammensetzung ein.**

We need to paint the kitchen. Can ______________________ please help me?

I really need ______________________ help.

Does she need ______________________ help?

Yes, we really must do ______________________ to help her.

Are there ______________________ cookies left? I can't find them ______________________.

I cannot find ______________________ cookies either.

______________________ must have eaten them all.

Okay, let's bake ______________________ new ones then!

Dad, may I have ______________________ money for new shoes, please?

No, I won't give you ______________________ more money. Go and ask ______________________ else.

bearbeitet am: erreichte Punktzahl:

Ab 13 erreichten Punkten kannst du mit Test 164 fortfahren.

Test 164 Mengenangaben mit Mengenwörtern

Schwierigkeitsgrad: ● ● ○

1. **Trage die die fehlenden Zusammensetzungen von *any* ein.**

Our neighbour has gone. Did ______________________ know her?

Did ______________________ talk to her?

Did she do ______________________ wrong?

Did she go ______________________ ?

2. **Trage die passenden Mengenwörter ein. Manchmal passt mehr als eines.**

– I need ____________ glue. Can you give me ____________ glue?

– No, I haven't got ____________ . Go and ask Emma. She may have ____________ glue left from last week.

– I already asked her. She hasn't got ____________ glue either.

– Oh, poor you! You're not having ____________ luck today, are you?

– Is there ____________ good party in town tonight?

– Yes, but I haven't got ____________ money. Have you got ____________ other ideas?

– Perhaps Sally can lend us ____________ money. I think she has got ____________ .

– Let me ask you ____________ questions. You haven't read your newspaper for days now. Don't you need to know ____________ news?

– I didn't want to read so ____________ . I don't need ____________ information.

bearbeitet am: ____________ erreichte Punktzahl: ______

Ab 15 erreichten Punkten kannst du mit Test 165 fortfahren.

Test 165 Nützliche Formulierungen

Schwierigkeitsgrad: ● ● ○

1. **Hier findest du einige im Englischunterricht besonders nützliche Fragen und Wendungen. Merk sie dir gut und notiere ihre deutsche Bedeutung.**

I have a question / May I ask a question?

____________________ .

____________________ ?

I don't understand this.

____________________ .

Can you write that on the blackboard, please?

____________________ ?

Is that right?

____________________ ?

What's for homework?

____________________ ?

May I go to the toilet, please?

____________________ ?

I agree / I disagree.

__________ . / __________ .

I am not feeling well.

____________________ .

How do you spell this word?

____________________ ?

I think this is interesting / boring.

__________ . / __________ .

bearbeitet am: __________ erreichte Punktzahl: __________

Ab 11 erreichten Punkten kannst du mit Test 166 fortfahren.

Test 166 Das Wörterbuch

Schwierigkeitsgrad: ● ● ○

1. Um Vokabeln in deinem Wörterbuch zu finden, musst du vor allem das Alphabet sehr gut beherrschen. Trage bei den folgenden Buchstaben immer diejenigen zwei Buchstaben ein, die im Alphabet davor und danach kommen.

_____ T _____ _____ D _____ _____ U _____ _____ M _____ _____ B _____

_____ W _____ _____ Q _____ _____ P _____ _____ I _____ _____ E _____

_____ K _____ _____ F _____ _____ N _____ _____ L _____ _____ Y _____

2. Trage hier den jeweils übernächsten Buchstaben im Alphabet ein.

A _____ U _____ F _____ W _____ K _____ H _____

V _____ T _____ J _____ R _____ M _____ D _____

C _____ O _____ X _____ E _____ S _____ G _____

3. Streiche alle Wörter aus, die alphabetisch nicht zwischen die zwei roten Leitwörter passen, welche darüber angegeben sind.

helpful – his

her – hectic – herring – honey – hidden – holy – hen – highlight – hit – hay – human – hippo

miss – month

mistake – mixer – mind – modern – menu – must – money – moan – my – mission – mouth

4. Finde die englische Übersetzung folgender deutscher Wörter in deinem Wörterbuch. Als Nachschlaghilfe findest du den englischen Oberbegriff vorweg.

paper: Taschenbuch _____________________ Büroklammer _____________________

back: Hintergrund _____________________ Rückenschmerz _____________________

come: zurückkommen _____________________ zur Sprache kommen _____________________

bearbeitet am: __________ erreichte Punktzahl: __________

Ab 54 erreichten Punkten kannst du mit dem Abschlusstest fortfahren.

1 Teste nochmals dein Können – Wortarten

1. **Setze diese Substantive in den Plural und unterstreiche alle Lösungen, deren Endung wie [iz] ausgesprochen wird.**

boy ______________	church ______________
goose ______________	lady ______________
bridge ______________	mouse ______________
wife ______________	nose ______________
foot ______________	fox ______________

2. **Welche der folgenden Substantive lassen sich zählen und welche nicht? Trage sie in die richtige Spalte der Tabelle ein.**

information	milk	food	foot	honey
bread	wood	egg	mouse	phone

zählbar (*countable*)	**nicht zählbar** (*uncountable*)

3. **Verbinde diese Substantive mit dem s-Genitiv.**

Nina/bicycle ______________

my brother/shirt ______________

my parents/house ______________

the children/pencils ______________

the baby/hair ______________

bearbeitet am: ______ erreichte Punktzahl: ______

Maximale Punktzahl: 29 Punkte

2 Teste nochmals dein Können – Wortarten

1. **Bilde aus den Substantiven und Adjektiven sinnvolle Vergleichssätze mit dem Komparativ oder mit *not as ... as ...***

loud: rock concerts / flute players

____ .

high: the Alps / hills of Shropshire

____ .

beautiful: Cambridge / Manchester

____ .

2. **Fülle die Lücken mit den richtigen Grund- oder Steigerungsformenen der Adjektive und Adverbien in Klammern.**

Does Jen feel ____________________ (good) today than yesterday?

Watch out, children! Don't run on the street so ____________________ (careless)!

Oh no, this must be the ____________________ (bad) movie that I ever watched!

John smiled at me ____________________ (happy).

He had ____________________ (nice) eyes.

Aunt Dora is a ____________________ (careful) driver. She never goes

____________________ (fast) than she is allowed.

3. **Fülle die Lücken mit den passenden Pronomen oder Possessivbegleitern.**

Where is Victoria? I can't see ____________________ . Is ____________________ not here?

I still have ____________________ keys. ____________________ will need them.

What about the others? Can you find ____________________ ? ____________________

train will leave soon. I must go too, and I haven't got ____________________ bags yet.

bearbeitet am: ____________ **erreichte Punktzahl:** ______

Maximale Punktzahl: 17 Punkte

3 Teste nochmals dein Können – Wortarten/Zeiten

1. Füge die Satzteile in der richtigen Reihenfolge zu vollständigen Sätzen zusammen. Bilde Fragesätze, wo Fragezeichen stehen, verwende die passende Zeitform und achte besonders auf die korrekte Form und ggf. Umschreibung der modalen Hilfsverben.

all the time / you / watch television

____ ?

may / leave / I / the classroom / now

____ ?

not shine / the sun / last year / a lot

____ .

cannot / you two / have / sweets / every day

____ !

just / finish / cleaning his room / Sebastian

____ .

must not / in museums / touch / people / the paintings

____ !

yesterday / Julia / not be able to / find / her umbrella

____ .

Our car / get / next year / must / some new tires

____

____ ?

Milly and Pete / their homework / cannot / yet / do

____

____ .

bearbeitet am: ________ erreichte Punktzahl: ____

Maximale Punktzahl: 9 Punkte

4 Teste nochmals dein Können – Zeiten

1. **Bilde aus den Satzbestandteilen vollständige Sätze. Beachte den richtigen Gebrauch von *simple present* und *present progressive.***

look here! / bus / come

____ .

Anne / usually / go for a walk / on weekends

____ .

I / do / my homework / right now

____ .

2. ***Simple past, past progressive* oder *present perfect*? Setze die fehlende Zeitform ein.**

When I ____________________ (sit) on the sofa last night, the cat ____________________ (jump) on my lap.

Evie ____________________ (learn) three new dances since last week.

Josh ____________________ (ride) his bike, when it suddenly ____________________ (start) to rain.

Our class ____________________________ (already / read) two stories by Roald Dahl.

Last summer I and two friends ____________________ (go) on holiday to a cottage in Denmark. Our parents ____________________ (drive) us there.

3. **Übersetze ins Englische. Beachte den richtigen Gebrauch von *will future* und *going to future.***

Kylies Geburtstag ist diesen Oktober an einem Samstag.

____ .

Werden Nathan und Wyatt dieses Wochenende Tina treffen?

____ ?

bearbeitet am: __________ erreichte Punktzahl: ______

Maximale Punktzahl: 13 Punkte

5 Teste nochmals dein Können – Sätze

1. **Wandle die Aussagesätze in eine Frage um und umgekehrt.**

Kayla went shopping. She spent a lot of money.

_______________________? _______________________?

Can Sam come home early tonight?

____.

2. **Suche oben die passende Konjunktion und das passende Satzende und verbinde alles zu vollständigen Sätzen. Achte auch auf die passende Zeitform.**

although – because – but

scare – go ice skating – be cheap

I will not buy these boots, ______________ they ______________.

I often went skiing, ______________ I never ______________.

I don't like horror movies, ______________ they ______________ me.

3. **Bilde aus den zwei Sätzen jeweils einen Haupt- und einen Relativsatz. Setze das Relativpronomen in Klammern, wo es nicht notwendig ist.**

Marlon is a good friend. You can trust him.

____.

That's my aunt. Her name is Susie.

____.

4. **Übersetze ins Englische mit *if* oder *when.* Beachte die richtige Zeitform für Bedingungssätze.**

Wenn (sobald) die Schule aus ist, gehe ich sofort nach Hause.

____.

Falls es schneit, bauen wir einen Schneemann.

____.

bearbeitet am: __________ erreichte Punktzahl: __________

Maximale Punktzahl: 12 Punkte

6 Teste nochmals dein Können – Zahlen, Zeit, Mengen

1. **Notiere die Geburtstagsdaten in ganzen Sätzen mit ausführlicher Datumsangabe.**

Mira: September 3rd, 2000
Mira's birthday is on the ______________________________________.

Noah: February 1st, 2001

______________________________________.

Sophie: October 9th, 1998

______________________________________.

2. **Setze *much*, *many*, *some* oder *any* passend ein. Hier sind teils mehrere Lösungen möglich.**

How ____________ teeth are there in your mouth?

Dylan cannot buy this CD, he hasn't got so ____________ money.

Does he know ____________ famous people?

Although it was noon, they couldn't see ____________ people in the streets.

My soup doesn't taste good, I need ____________ salt.

Have you got ____________ cats or dogs at home?

Ms Jordan would like ____________ cream in her coffee.

Is there ____________ cake left?

3. **Suche die richtige Mengenangabe für jedes Substantiv und verbinde die beiden mit *of*.**

bottle – pound – minute – cup

a ______________________________ hot chocolate

a ______________________________ orange juice

a ______________________________ meat

a ______________________________ silence

bearbeitet am: ____________ erreichte Punktzahl: ____________

Maximale Punktzahl: 15 Punkte

Lösungen zu Test 1

1 (10 Punkte):

tree – trees	glass – glasses
question – questions	house – houses
nose – noses	window – windows
pen – pens	bush – bushes
banana – bananas	fox – foxes

2 (10 Punkte):

ladies – lady	days – day
bees – bee	hobbies – hobby
halves – half	dresses – dress
toys – toy	lives – life
diaries – diary	countries – country

3 (6 Punkte):

a bus and a car – buses and cars
a pear and a plum – pears and plums
a plane and a bike – planes and bikes
a girl and a baby – girls and babies
a box and a pan – boxes and pans
a minute and a second – minutes and seconds

Regel:
Die meisten englischen Wörter bilden ihren Plural durch ein angehängtes *-s*.
Wörter, die auf *-y* enden, bilden ihren Plural auf *-ies*. Wörter, die auf *-s*, *-x*, *-ch* oder *-sh* enden, bilden ihren Plural auf *-es*.
Wörter auf *-f* oder *-fe* bilden ihren Plural auf *-ves*.

Lösungen zu Test 2

1 (14 Punkte):

wife – wives	sandwich – sandwiches
shelf – shelves	house – houses
daisy – daisies	window – windows
party – parties	fly – flies
witch – witches	church – churches
star – stars	orange – oranges
hand – hands	brush – brushes

2 (9 Punkte):

In my room, my books are on the shelves on the wall.
My mother and my father are my parents.
I don't have any brothers, but two sisters.
On a farm, there are lots of animals beginning with "c": chickens and cows and often cats.

3 (9 Punkte):

flakes	<u>faces</u>	apples	brakes	tomatoes
<u>noses</u>	<u>pages</u>	candles	toes	<u>bridges</u>
<u>hedges</u>	shoes	<u>mazes</u>	<u>cases</u>	tables
ropes	centres	clothes	<u>braces</u>	<u>spices</u>

Regel:
Bei Wörtern, die auf *-ce*, *-ge*, *-se* und *-ze* enden, wird das im Singular stumme *e* mit dem Plural *-s* wie [iz] ausgesprochen.

Lösungen zu Test 3

1 (6 Punkte):

woman – women	foot – feet
mouse – mice	man – men
tooth – teeth	child – children

2 (2 Punkte):

sheep – sheep geese – goose

3 (6 Punkte):

one woman and one child	two women and four children
one man's foot	two men's feet
one bad tooth	two bad teeth
one cat and one mouse	two cats and eight mice
one glass of water	three glasses of water
one country and one man	many countries and many men

4 (3 Punkte):

Ladies and gentlemen, your dinner is ready.
Water, wine and other drinks are served at the bar.
I have one nose, one mouth, two eyes, two ears and 32 teeth.

Lösungen zu Test 4

1 (7 Punkte):

trousers☒, glasses☒, tongs☒, scissors☒, shorts☒, jeans☒, lungs☒

3 (5 Punkte):

I cannot read well, I have lost my glasses.
I like to go to sleep dressed in my red pyjamas
We should drink eight glasses of water every day.
Your clothes are torn. You need a new pair of trousers.

2 (7 Punkte):

zählbar (*countable*): glass, cup, peach
nicht zählbar (*uncountable*): water, tea, news, sugar

Regel:
Paarwörter (*pair nouns*) bezeichnen Dinge, die aus zwei gleichen Teilen bestehen (wie etwa zwei Brillengläsern). Sie werden nur im Plural verwendet. Nicht zählbare Substantive (*uncountable nouns*) lassen sich nicht in einzelne Elemente aufteilen. Es gibt sie nur im Singular. Du musst diese Wörter (*food, water, homework*, etc.) auswendig lernen.

Lösungen zu Test 5

1 (6 Punkte):

Sarah has got four dresses.
She has got five pairs of shoes.
She has got three pyjamas.
She has got four pairs of jeans
She has got two pairs of sunglasses.
She has got eight T-shirts.

3 (4 Punkte):

The milk is cold. My jeans are new.
The scissors are sharp. The music is loud.

2 (3 Punkte):

Where are the scissors?
She likes my new (pair of) glasses.
I am looking for my (pair of) trousers. Are they here?

Regel:
Um Paarwörter zählbar zu machen, braucht man die Umschreibung *a pair of ...* bzw. *two, three* etc. *pairs of ....*

Lösungen zu Test 6

1 (10 Punkte):

Jerry's sister
your mother's car
Mr Frazer's dogs
the horse's colour
the dentist's chair
our teacher's glasses
Anne's book
our neighbour's newspaper
my grandmother's TV set
aunt Susie's friend

2 (8 Punkte):

Whose pen is this? It's Alice's pen.
Is this your house? No, it's Muriel's house.
Is this your cap? No, it's Timmy's cap.
Is this your brother's car? No, it's my mother's car.
Whose birthday is it? It's Fran's birthday.
Are these Ms Jenson's CDs? No, they are Mr Clay's CDs.
Are those your trainers? No, they are Philip's trainers.
Is this my drink? No, it's Jennifer's drink.

Regel:
Etwas oder jemand, das oder der zu einer Person oder einem Tier gehört, bekommt im Genitiv einen Apostroph plus *s* (*'s*) angehängt.

Lösungen zu Test 7

1 (5 Punkte):

the pupils' classroom
the policemen's motorbikes
the houses' roofs
her colleagues' haircuts
your doctors' orders

2 (4 Punkte):

my sisters' shoes
my aunts' presents
her cats' food
the children's toys

Lösungen zu Test 7 (fortgesetzt)

3 (7 Punkte):

Whose party is it?
Whose hammer is it?
Whose game is it?
Whose chips are those?
Whose computer is it?
Whose stickers are these?
Whose business is that?

Regel:
Etwas, das zu mehreren Personen oder Tieren gehört, bekommt an die Pluralform nur einen Apostroph ohne zusätzliches *s*. Aber bei unregelmäßigen Pluralformen wird wieder Apostroph plus *s* (*'s*) angehängt.

Lösungen zu Test 8

1 (10 Punkte):

the roof of the house
the handle of the door
the size of the garden
the top of the mountain
the taste of the wine
the spelling of the word
the beginning of our lesson
the quality of your photos
the legs of their chair
the colour of his plane model

2 (7 Punkte):

the boys' toys
the families' dogs
the walls of the room
the doors of the closets
the colour of his teeth
their parents' houses
the women's skirts

Regel:
Etwas, das zu einer unbelebten Sache gehört, bildet den Genitiv mit der Präposition *of*.

Lösungen zu Test 9

1 (5 Punkte):

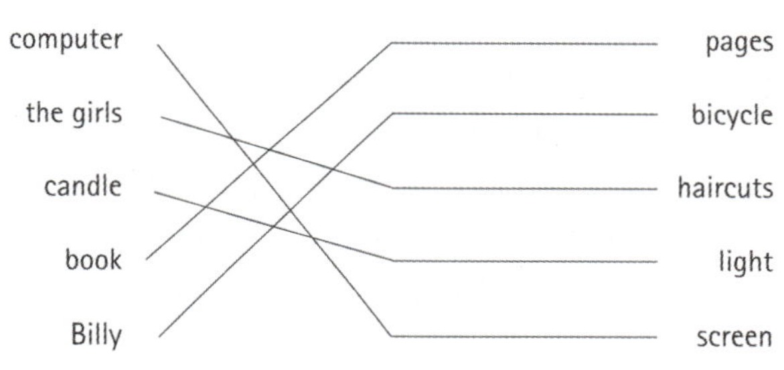

the screen of the computer
the girls' haircuts
the light of the candle
the book's pages
Billy's bicycle

2 (3 Punkte):

The pupils' teacher is (comes) from London.
What's (What is) at the end of the month?
The colour of his eyes is green.

Lösungen zu Test 10

1 (12 Punkte):

angekreuzt werden:
the alligator, the apple, the exercise, the ears, the end

2 (8 Punkte):

an aunt
a question
a father
an eternity
a mother
an answer
an uncle
a year

Regel:
Die im Deutschen als „der/die/das" bekannten bestimmten Artikel gibt es im Englischen nur als eine Form: *the*. Beginnt das Wort nach dem Artikel mit einem Vokal, sprechen wir *the* wie [ði] aus.

Regel:
Der unbestimmte Artikel „ein/eine" wird im Englischen mit *a* oder *an* ausgedrückt. Beginnt das Wort nach dem unbestimmten Artikel mit einem Konsonanten, verwenden wir *a*. Beginnt es aber mit einem Vokal, muss es *an* heißen.

Lösungen zu Test 10 (fortgesetzt)

3 (10 Punkte):

a camel	Konsonant
an elephant	Vokal
a monkey	Konsonant
a beautiful girl	Konsonant
an ugly doll	Vokal

Lösungen zu Test 11

1 (16 Punkte):

a young kitten	an old horse
a happy pupil	an unhappy teacher
an easy test	a difficult exercise
a cheap earring	an expensive scarf
a stupid mistake	an intelligent answer
an interesting story	a boring book
a hard start	a soft landing
a happy pupil	an unhappy teacher

2 (14 Punkte):

– I have a sore throat today, and a fever, and a headache, too. I think I caught a cold. Can you bring me a large orange and a ripe banana?
– Yes, but I'm in a hurry. I must leave the house in a minute.
– Just bring me an orange then. I will eat an apple later, I know we have some left in the kitchen.
– I'm afraid you can't go to the theatre tomorrow night.
– You're right, that's a pity.

Lösungen zu Test 12

1 (3 Punkte):

Jackie plays the guitar.
Vanessa plays the violin.
Her brother plays the trumpet.

2 (3Punkte):

My mother is a baker.
Your father is a hairdresser.
Dr Johnson is a doctor.

3 (3 Punkte):

Timmy can play the piano.
Mr Black is a farmer.
I often play the guitar.

Regel:
Im Englischen gibt es Ausdrücke, die den bestimmten Artikel erfordern, obwohl er im Deutschen nicht steht. Dazu gehören Musikinstrumente. Berufsbezeichnungen wie „Ich bin Koch" stehen im Englischen mit dem unbestimmten Artikel: *I'm a cook.*

Lösungen zu Test 13

1 (11 Punkte):

– I got a remote-controlled helicopter and an airplane for my birthday. They go very fast, and you must have a lot of practice to fly them.
– Well, I got / interesting new computer games and an expensive new mp3 player for my birthday. My old one was broken, but / mp3 players are not cheap, so I was really surprised I got a new one.
– Yes, I'd love to have a player, too! Did you have an enormous party?
– Of course! It wouldn't be a birthday without a party!

2 (17 Punkte):

Dear Vicky, how are you? Here in Spain everything is fine, the weather is great, and the sun is shining a lot. Before breakfast I go for a swim in the hotel pool, and after / lunch at the beach I go swimming in the sea. The shops down there sell the best ice cream ever. After / supper in the evening, we play / card games, or sometimes I play the guitar. My mother says she never wants to get back to / work, but I will like to be back in / school soon. I miss you and the others from our class. Love, Lynn

Regel:
Auch kennt das Englische Substantive in Redewendungen, vor denen kein bestimmter Artikel stehen darf, obwohl wir ihn im Deutschen verwenden, u. a. Straßennamen, vor, nach oder zu Mahlzeiten, in der Schule und bei der Arbeit.

Lösungen zu Test 14

1 (25 Punkte):

on	window	tomato	red	run
new	car	take	eggs	rich
like	donkey	after	reason	table
milk	above	now	interesting	fine
hide	throw	hat	dark	off

Regel:
Mit Adjektiven *(adjectives)* werden Lebewesen, Gegenstände oder Ereignisse näher beschrieben. Wir drücken damit aus, **wie** etwas ist.

2 (11Punkte):

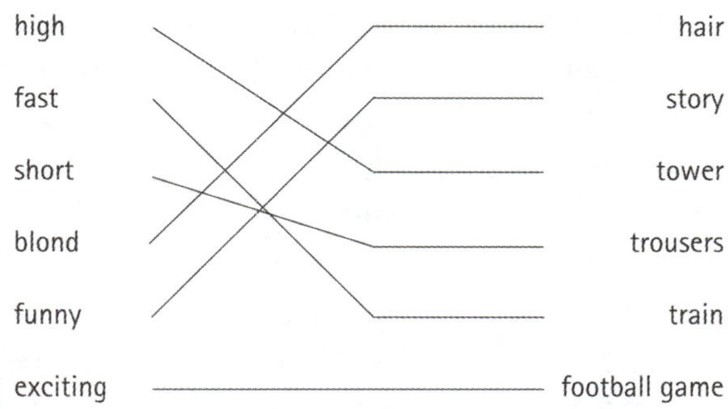

a high tower
short trousers
a funny story
a fast train
blond hair
an exciting football game

Lösungen zu Test 15

1 (8 Punkte):

a red fire engine
a cold winter
a hot summer
a soft pillow
a dark night
an orange carrot
an easy lesson
a little baby

2 (4 Punkte):

The children are wearing colourful summer clothes.
My friend's parents are nice.
A white dog is running after a small cat.
Your new glasses look good.

Lösungen zu Test 16

1 (6 Punkte):

an expensive jacket
a stupid boy
an empty cup
a poor woman
a cold day
a boring movie

2 (8 Punkte):

Antworten können hier variieren. Möglich wären folgende Wörter (aber auch andere):
cars: fast, quick, cool, great / loud, expensive, smelly
school: interesting, exciting, easy / boring, dull, hard
comic books: funny, interesting, colourful, cool, fine, great, nice / stupid, boring, dull
fresh fruit: healthy, tasty, important

3 (5 Punkte):

Richtig sind nur folgende zwei Antworten:
Adjektive geben stets Eigenschaften wieder.
Adjektive beziehen sich auch auf Pronomen.
Der Rest muss mit „falsch" angekreuzt werden.

Lösungen zu Test 17

1 (8 Punkte):

attributiv: A, B, D, F, G, H
prädikativ: C, E

2 (6 Punkte):

Beverly has a pair of green socks.	A
Lunch tastes good.	P
Anne feels bad.	P

Regel:
Wenn ein Adjektiv ein Substantiv beschreibt, steht es direkt **vor** seinem Bezugswort. Das nennt man **attributiven Gebrauch.**
Steht es **nach** einem **Verb der Wahrnehmung,** nämlich nach *feel, look, smell, sound* oder taste, dann sprechen wir von **prädikativem Gebrauch.**

Lösungen zu Test 18

1 (22 Punkte):

small	smaller	smallest
warm	warmer	warmest
great	greater	greatest
large	larger	largest
fine	finer	finest
fat	fatter	fattest
lucky	luckier	luckiest
busy	busier	busiest
pretty	prettier	prettiest
tired	more tired	most tired
interesting	more interesting	most interesting

2 (3 Punkte):

Benny is more carful.
Your car is the fastest.
Today the weather is hotter.

Regel:
Die Steigerungsformen der Adjektive (Komparativ und Superlativ) brauchen wir für Vergleiche. Durch Anhängen der Endungen *-er* und *-est* werden einsilbige Adjektive sowie zweisilbige auf *-y* gesteigert. Fast alle anderen werden mit Hilfe von *more* und *most* vor dem Adjektiv gesteigert. Bei der Steigerung wird aus einem *-y* am Ende ein *-i* vor dem *-er*/*-est*. Endkonsonanten können sich verdoppeln.

Lösungen zu Test 19

1 (8 Punkte):

far	further	furthest
bad	worse	worst
good	better	best
quiet	quieter	quietest

Regel:
Die **unregelmäßigen** Steigerungsformen (siehe Aufgabe 1) musst du auswendig lernen. Es gibt zum Glück nicht so viele davon!

2 (6 Punkte):

Superman is stronger than Spiderman.
Snow White's hair is darker than Cinderella's hair.
Tower Bridge is more famous than London Eye.
Sherlock Holmes is taller than Miss Marple.
Marge Simpson is thinner than Homer Simpson.
Avatar is more successful than *Titanic*.

Lösungen zu Test 20

1 (20 Punkte):

lazy	lazier	laziest
hard	harder	hardest
boring	more boring	most boring
busy	busier	busiest
great	greater	greatest
bad	worse	worst
happy	happier	happiest
good	better	best
funny	funnier	funniest
terrible	more terrible	most terrible

2 (6 Punkte):

I am tall. Lena is taller. Kimmy is the tallest .
My hair is long. Selina's hair is longer. Kimmy's hair is the longest.
My shoes are expensive. Janine's shoes are more expensive. Kimmy's shoes are the most expensive.

Lösungen zu Test 21

1 (12 Punkte):

Chips are tastier than soup.
Soup is not as tasty as chips.

The Eiffel Tower is higher than the Tower of London.
The Tower of London is not as high as the Eiffel tower.

French cafés are more elegant than Irish pubs.
Irish pubs are not as elegant as French cafés.

The Sahara desert is hotter than the North Sea.
The North Sea is hotter than the Sahara desert.

A stop watch is more exact than a grandfather clock.
A grandfather clock is not as exact as a stop watch.

A movie is better than football.
Football is not as good as a movie.
(Oder: Football is better than a movie.
A movie is not as good as football.)

Regel:
Im Vergleich steht der Komparativ immer mit *than.* Das Gegenteil („weniger ...") übersetzen wir mit dem Ausdruck *not as ... as.*

Lösungen zu Test 22

1 (14 Punkte):

clear	clearly	gentle	gently
funny	funnily	clever	cleverly
horrible	horribly	hopeful	hopefully
fantastic	fantastically	secret	secretly
simple	simply	exciting	excitingly
sweet	sweetly	basic	basically
nice	nicely	heavy	heavily

Regel:
Adverbien beschreiben Tätigkeiten, also Verben. Sie werden gebildet, indem man ein *-ly* ans Adjektiv anhängt. Aber Achtung: Endet das Adjektiv auf *-y*, wird das Adverb zu *-ily*, ein stummes *-e* am Ende des Adjektivs fällt weg, und bei Adjektiven auf *-ic* wird die Adverbendung zu *-ically.*

2 (5 Punkte):

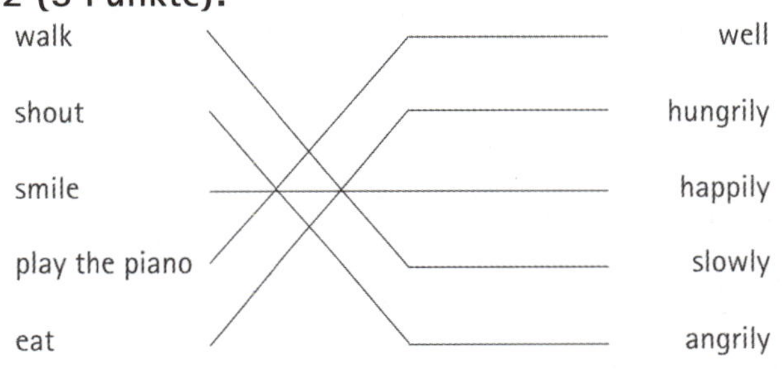

walk slowly
shout angrily
smile happily
play the piano well
eat hungrily

Lösungen zu Test 23

1 (15 Punkte):

good	well	bad	badly
warm	warmly	cold	coldly
hard	hard	soft	softly
late	late	early	early
slow	slowly	fast	fast
loud	loudly	quiet	quietly
sad	sadly	happy	happily

Regel:
Achtung, bei einigen Adverbien trügt der Schein. *Nearly* bedeutet z. B. „fast" und *hardly* „kaum".

2 (10 Punkte):

She is quick.	She comes quickly.
This is a good joke.	You tell it well.
He is a loud boy.	He often talks loudly .
He has a slow car.	He drives it slowly.
She is a careful mother.	She watches her children carefully.

Regel:
Die Formen der unregelmäßigen Adverbien musst du wieder lernen. Dazu gehören etwa *well* (von *good*) sowie einige identische Adjektiv-/Adverbformen wie *fast, hard, late, long, high, fine, early.*

Lösungen zu Test 24

1 (5 Punkte):

Jason is a good football player.
He practices hard.
Melissa swims very fast.
She is a fast swimmer.
It's late already. Nearly midnight!

2 (10 Punkte):

Hi Jenny, I am your new pen-pal from Germany. First I want to tell you something about me, then I would like to learn some interesting things about you. My name is Lea. I can dance and sing well and I like riding horses. I have a big pony called Lisa. Lisa looks really pretty. She can run very fast and jump very high. So tell me about you – are you a good dancer or singer, too? Dou you like long pony rides? Write back quickly please! Your friend, Lea

Lösungen zu Test 25

1 (14 Punkte):

lazily	more lazily	most lazily
hard	harder	hardest
boringly	more boringly	most boringly
busily	more busily	most busily
great	greater	greatest
badly	worse	worst
simply	more simply	most simply
happy	happier	happiest

Regel:
Die weitaus meisten Adverbien werden mit *more* und *most* gesteigert. Ausnahmen sind unregelmäßige Adverbien wie *well – better – best* und *badly – worse – worst* und die identischen Formen (s. Test 23).

2 (8 Punkte):

Beverly feels better than last week.
My aunt Susan drives faster than my dad. Dad is a much more carfeul driver than his sister.
I think that was a good play. They all acted very well.
When Philip came into the room, Joanna started to talk more nervously than before.
Can you please be a little quicker? We're all waiting here!

Lösungen zu Test 26

1 (14 Punkte):

I had the worst day of the year.
I woke up with a terrible headache, and then someone stole my newest „Green Day" CD at school. That was even worse than the pain.

Tim's sister is older than him, but nevertheless he is taller than her. Their little brother is the smallest of the whole family. But he grows faster than any baby I know.

My dad eats more healthily than me and my brothers, but my mom eats most healthily of us all. We children cannot stand all this healthy food.

Can Max not jump higher than Ben? He said he were the best jumper of the class. And I believed him so easily!

Lösungen zu Test 27

1 (22 Punkte):

<u>She</u> is coming home.	sie
<u>We</u> are on our way to school.	wir
<u>It</u> takes some time.	es
Must <u>I</u> go to school today?	ich
<u>He</u> is on the phone.	er
<u>You</u> are late again, Stephen.	du
<u>It</u>'s finished!	es
<u>You,</u> Viv and Anne, sit down!	ihr
<u>I</u> can call again later.	ich
Now <u>they</u> are listening.	sie
Do <u>they</u> know <u>we</u> live here?	sie / wir

Lösungen zu Test 27 (fortgesetzt)

2 (6 Punkte):

Where is your Jacket?	It is on the chair.
Where is your exercise book?	It is in my schoolbag.
Where are your glasses?	They are on the table.
Where is your lunch money?	It is in my pocket.
Where are your keys?	They are in my jacket.
Where is the bus?	It is outside at the bus stop.

Regel:
Durch die Personalpronmomen (*personal pronouns*) können Substantive ersetzt werden. Stehen sie im Satz für Subjekte, dann lauten sie der Reihe nach:
I – you – she/he/it – we – you – they

Lösungen zu Test 28

1 (7 Punkte):

Personalpronomen	she	he	it
the carpet			X
Ms O'Casey	X		
the cow			X
Robert		X	
our cat Jinx			X
your sister	X		
my uncle		X	

2 (10 Punkte):

"Hello Lucy. It's good to see you!"
"Good morning, Sandy. How are you?"
"I'm fine, and you? How is Christopher, is he feeling better?"
"Yes, he is well again. How about little Ella, is she okay?"
"Yes, she is fine, thank you. All three children are fine, they are taking piano lessons now."
"Good. Well, I have to hurry."
"Okay, see you!"

Regel:
Personen und Haustiere mit Eigennamen werden mit *she* oder *he* bezeichnet. Bei Gegenständen und anderen Tieren heißt es *it*. Das gilt völlig einheitlich, ohne grammatikalische Geschlechter zu unterscheiden – viel leichter als im Deutschen, oder?

Lösungen zu Test 29

1 (8 Punkte):

I	→	me	it	→	it
you	→	you	we	→	us
she	→	her	you	→	you
he	→	him	they	→	them

Regel:
Stehen die Personalpronmomen im Satz für Objekte (egal, ob Dativ- oder Akkusativobjekte), dann lauten sie der Reihe nach:
me– you – her/him/it – us – you – them

2 (10 Punkte):

You have two dogs, Emily, right?	du
Do you want to go, dear?	du
You must excuse me, Mr Lawson.	Sie
See you later, boys!	euch
May I see you after class, Ms Mifflin?	Sie
Can I help you, sir?	Ihnen
I love you, darling!	dich
I give you the bags, Ethan!	dir
I trust you, Uncle Stephen.	dir
Where are you going on holiday, children?	ihr

Lösungen zu Test 30

1 (7 Punkte):

Where is my red model plane?	I can't find it.
Where are my Chucks?	I can't find them.
Where is mum?	I can't find her.
Where is my homework?	I can't find it.
Where are you, dad?	I can't find you.
Where is my friend Danny?	I can't find him.
Where are you going?	Wait for me!

Lösungen zu Test 30 (fortgesetzt)

2 (12 Punkte):

What would you like to do, girls? – Let us play some volleyball!
Where is Alex? I can't see him anywhere. Perhaps he is in the garden.
Hey, dad, let us play football! – Sorry, Jacob I can't. I've hurt my foot. It hurts terribly.
Mr and Ms Miller are at not home now. But they will come back tonight.
Poor Mia! She forgot to do some grocery shopping, and now her freezer is completely empty. It is a pity!
Come here, sweetheart, and give me a kiss!

Lösungen zu Test 31

1 (6 Punkte):

her boyfriend
his shop
their books
his boots
her toothbrush
its tree

Regel:
Durch Possessivbegleiter (*possessive determiners*) erkennen wir, zu wem oder zu was etwas gehört. Sie stehen direkt vor ihrem Bezugssubstantiv. Der Reihe nach lauten sie:
my – you – her/his/its – our – your – their

2 (7 Punkte):

There is dad with his car.
There is Ms Honeychurch with her roses.
There are Michael and Andy with their bikes.
There are some dogs with their bones.
There is Emma with her cat.
There is grandpa with his slippers.
There are three girls with their bags.
There are two parents with their baby.

Lösungen zu Test 32

1 (13 Punkte):

Lily is looking for her glasses. Her sister is helping her look. They are looking in the living room and in Lily's room and in her closet, also in their parents' bedroom – nothing! Lily calls up to her mother: "We can't find my glasses, where are they?" Her mother says: "Call your dad, he's at his office. Perhaps he knows, where you put your glasses." Lily calls her father, but he doesn't know, where they are, either. Finally, her sister finds Lily's glasses on the garden table in their garden.

3 (1 Punkt + 1 Bonus für die Nennung)

Es gibt 5 Möglichkeiten, „sie/Sie" auszudrücken: *she, her, they, them* und *you* (Höflichkeitsanrede).

2 (8 Punkte):

my	→	mine	our	→	ours
your	→	yours	your	→	yours
her	→	hers	their	→	theirs
his	→	his			

Regel:
Possessivpronomen (*possessive determiners*) zeigen ebenso den Besitz an, ersetzen aber Substantive und können allein stehen. Der Reihe nach lauten sie:
mine – yours –hers/his – ours – yours – theirs

Lösungen zu Test 33

1 (14 Punkte):

This chair is useless. Its leg is broken. It's a pity!
Have you lost your watch? You're late again!
I think you're very clever! Your plan sounds great.
It's five o'clock already! The dog needs its food.
This shirt is beautiful, it's true. Its colour looks good.
You're feeling cold? No wonder, your coat is ...
Your bus is leaving soon. Don't forget your bag!

Regel:
Oft verwechselt werden die Formen *its* und *it's*. Wenn die Kurzform von *it is* gemeint, heißt es richtig *it's*. Ist aber der Possessivbegleiter „sein" gemeint, heißt es *its*. Ähnliche Verwechslungsgefahr besteht zwischen der Kurzform *you're* („du bist") und dem Possessivbegleiter *your* („dein").

2 (12 Punkte):

I am looking for my seat. I don't think this one is mine, because it isn't my seat row number. Perhaps it's over there, next to your seat, Alyssa! Is yours in row number 13?
Escuse me, madam, is this your suitcase? I took it by mistake, because it looks just like mine. I'm sorry, I will go find my own luggage right away.
Let me see your passport, sir. And open your bags for us, please. What about that backpack over there? Is it yours, too?
I don't think he is sleeping enough. His eyes look very tired.

Lösungen zu Test 34

1 (15 Punkte):

This here is a mouse, and that over there is a rat.
These here are my cookies, and those over there are yours.
These potatoes here and those green beans over there are too old, I won't buy them.
This is my plate, and that one at the other end of the table is your plate.
These are my Magic cards, and those on the table are yours.
That was your idea last week, and this is my idea today!
Is this white dog yours? Mine is that black one on the lawn.
That girl on the chair in the back is my girlfriend.

2 (9 Punkte):

this hat	–	these hats
that child	–	those children
that woman	–	those women
this plane	–	these planes
this orange	–	these oranges
this lady	–	these ladies
that page	–	those pages
that house	–	those houses
this family	–	these families

Regel:
Mit den Demonstrativpronomen (demonstrative pronouns) *this* (Sg.) und *these* (Pl.) verweisen wir auf Personen oder Dinge in der Nähe. *That* (Sg.) und *those* (Pl.) verweisen auf weiter entfernte Dinge oder Personen.

Lösungen zu Test 35

1 (7 Punkte):

Carlos: What do you call this room here?
Carlos: And what are these things here called?
Carlos: What is that thing on the hook?
Carlos: What is that room where you cook?
Carlos: And what are those things you eat with?
Carlos: Whose room is that one over there?
Carlos: What's that book on your bed?

2 (13 Punkte):

– Look at this shirt! I think it's nice. But that shirt on the left looks nice, too. Do you like this shirt better than that one on the left?
– I'm not sure. But I really like those trousers over there.
– Would you like to buy these two cheap DVDs here, or that one expensive DVD?
– I think I'll buy that DVD of *Avatar*. It' on sale in the back.
– Just look at this mess here! Put those dirty socks in the washing and that jumper on the floor, too!
– Mum, this is my room. I live here ...
– O stop it! Just put them on that chair in the corner ...

Lösungen zu Test 36

1 (5 Punkte):

Which one would you like?
this DVD or that one?
this street to the left, or that one to the right?
paprika-flavoured crisps, or salted ones?
where can I find very ripe ones?

Regel:
Die Wörter *one* (Sg.) oder *ones* (Pl.) brauchen wir anstelle eines Substantivs, wenn wir es nicht noch einmal benennen wollen.

2 (5 Punkte):

– Can I try on that bikini?	
– Which bikini?	one
– That yellow bikini in the window.	one
– It's a little too large, isn't it? Have you got a smaller yellow bikini?	
– No, I don't think so. We have no other yellow bikinis.	ones
– Can I try on the orange bikini on that rack there?	one
– Oh, this bikini fits perfectly. I will take it.	one

Lösungen zu Test 37

1 (19 Punkte):

Which dress should she wear? The green one or the black one?
You don't need all of your old toys! Let's keep only the ones you really play with.
You can eat these carrots. The other ones are bad.
He has got many T-shirts, but he wears only the black ones.
There are two crayons in her pencil case: a hard one and a soft one.
Which movie should we watch? The one at the Rex, or the one at the Metropol?
Here's your Halloween candy: the sweets on the left are Tristan's and the ones on the right are Leah's.
I know all the books on your shelf, but I don't know the ones next to your bed.
No, the small car in front of the shop window isn't mine. It's the big black one next to it.
There are three rules: two old ones and a new one.
I like going to the movies, but I don't like all films – there are some good ones and there are some bad ones.
You don't like that kind of pie? Come on, try this one!
Not all pupils wear glasses – only the ones with weak eyes.
Can you give me one of your balloons? I'd like the green one!

Lösungen zu Test 38

1 (17 Punkte):

Unterstrichen werden:
have, find, call, can, open, eat, is, have, cannot, sleep, think, must, wait, arrives, is, like, build

2 (15 Punkte):

can, tell, is, do, need, is, must, do, can, do, need, go, can, help, look, is ('s)

Regel:
Verben sind Tunwörter, die angeben, was jemand tut oder was geschieht. Ihre Grundform (*infinitive*) wird durch Beugen/Konjugieren zur Personalform. Im Englischen gibt es dabei im Präsens vor allem das Anhängen von *–s* an die Form von *she/he/it* zu beachten, z. B. *she finds.*

3 (6 Punkte):

Our English teacher is a nice lady.
I never forget my homework for her.
My brother likes his maths teacher best.
She does not give them much homework.
School starts at nine.

Lösungen zu Test 39

1 (21 Punkte):

nouns	adjectives	adverbs	verbs
jam	purple	totally	swim
leg	grey	quickly	remember

2 (16 Punkte):

infinitive	simple past	past participle
turn	turned	turned
jump	jumped	jumped

Lösungen zu Test 39 (fortgesetzt)

nouns	adjectives	adverbs	verbs
knee	quiet	well	run
idea	strong	wildly	forget
mistake	bitter		feel
dolphin			make

infinitive	simple past	past participle
play	played	played
paint	painted	painted
wave	waved	waved
enjoy	enjoyed	enjoyed
walk	walked	walked
promise	promised	promised

Regel:
Um englische Verben in allen Zeiten (*tenses*) richtig zu verwenden, müssen wir jeweils ihre drei Stammformen kennen: die Grundform *infinitive*, die Vergangenheitsform *simple past* und das Partizip Perfekt *past participle*. Es gibt regelmäßige und unregelmäßige Verben. Die regelmäßigen Verben bilden ihre Stammformen durch Anhängen von *-ed* an den Wortstamm. Das stumme *-e* vom Wortende entfällt dabei.

Lösungen zu Test 40

1 (36 Punkte):

infinitive	simple past	past participle
be	was, were	been
become	became	become
begin	began	begun
bind	bound	bound
bite	bit	bitten
blow	blew	blown
break	broke	broken
bring	brought	brought
build	built	built
burn	burnt	burnt
buy	bought	bought
catch	caught	caught
choose	chose	chosen
come	came	come
cost	cost	cost
creep	crept	crept
cut	cut	cut
do	did	done

Regel:
Die unregelmäßigen Verben haben abweichende Stammformen. Du musst jeweils alle drei Formen auswendig lernen. Daher ist es wichtig, alle vier Tabellenübungen von Test 40–43 abzuschließen.

Lösungen zu Test 41

1 (36 Punkte):

infinitive	simple past	past participle
draw	drew	drawn
dream	dreamt/dreamed	dreamt/dreamed
drink	drank	drunk
drive	drove	driven
eat	ate	eaten
fall	fell	fallen
feel	felt	felt
fight	fought	fought
find	found	found
fly	flew	flown
forbid	forbade	forbidden
forget	forgot	forgotten
get	got	got/gotten
give	gave	given
go	went	gone
grow	grew	grown
have	had	had
hear	heard	heard

Lösungen zu Test 42

1 (36 Punkte):

infinitive	simple past	past participle	infinitive	simple past	past participle
hold	held	held	meet	met	met
hurt	hurt	hurt	pay	paid	paid
keep	kept	kept	put	put	put
know	knew	known	read	read [red]	read [red]
learn	learnt/learned	learnt/learned	ride	rode	ridden
leave	left	left	say	said	said
let	let	let	see	saw	seen
lose	lost	lost	send	sent	sent
make	made	made	show	showed	shown

Lösungen zu Test 43

1 (36 Punkte):

infinitive	simple past	past participle	infinitive	simple past	past participle
sing	sang	sung	teach	taught	taught
sit	sat	sat	tell	told	told
sleep	slept	slept	think	thought	thought
speak	spoke	spoken	throw	threw	thrown
spend	spent	spent	understand	understood	understood
stand	stood	stood	wake	woke	woken
steal	stole	stolen	wear	wore	worn
swim	swam	swum	win	won	won
take	took	taken	write	wrote	written

Lösungen zu Test 44

1 (14 Punkte):

I am	I'm	I am not	I'm not
you are	you're	you are not	you aren't
she is	she's	she is not	she isn't
he is	he's	he is not	he isn't
it is	it's	it is not	it isn't
we are	we're	we are not	we aren't
they are	they're	they are not	they aren't

2 (10 Punkte):

Dear Alina, my name is Julia. I am in fifth grade and live in a town in the North of England called Newcastle. I am 11 years old and have two brothers. They are both older than me, and we are a nice family. But still I am happy to have a girl as a a penfriend now. How old are you? What is your hobby? My hobbies are books and horses. I put in a photo of myself. It is a pity that I haven't got a picture of you yet. Please send me one! Yours, Julia

Regel:
Das englische Verb *be* bedeutet „sein". Im Präsens gibt es eine Lang- und eine Kurzform: *I am – I'm, you are – you're, she/he/it is – she's/he's/it's.* Verneint werden Sätze mit *not*, Kurzformen: *aren't, isn't.* (Aber: *I'm not)*

Lösungen zu Test 45

1 (8 Punkte):

- No, I'm not from Scotland, I'm from Wales.
- No, he isn't my brother, he is my cousin.
- No, they aren't teachers, they are sales people.
- No, we aren't in the tennis team, we're in the chess club.

2 (4 Punkte):

My name is Susan.
That is / that's my sister over there.
She is not / she's not alone.
And you are / you're with some friends, too.

Lösungen zu Test 46

1 (9 Punkte):
No, I'm not.
No, he isn't.
Yes, I am.
No, she isn't.
Yes, it is.
No, you aren't.
No, we aren't / you aren't.
Yes, they are.
No, she isn't.

Regel:
Bei bejahten Kurzantworten können wir keine Kurzform verwenden: *No, we aren't,* aber: *Yes, we are.*

2 (8 Punkte):
Are you at school now?
Is he in the kitchen?
Is she in the hospital?
Are they at the movies?
Are you on holiday?
Am I a good reader?
Is that my scarf?
Are you the worst singer of the class?

Lösungen zu Test 47

1 (8 Punkte):

Are Gabriel and Dylan late for school?	Yes, the are.
Is this test difficult?	No, it isn't.
Are you a pop music fan?	Yes, I am.
Is Hannah happy?	No, she isn't.

2 (4 Punkte):
Is your name Henry?
Are we at the same school?
Is the party on Saturday?
Are you a guest at that party, too?

Lösungen zu Test 48

1 (9 Punkte):
At home, there are carpets in all rooms.
At home, there is a fireplace in the living room.
At home, there are two bathrooms.
At home, there is a swing set in the garden.
At home, there are chairs around the tables.
At home, there is a grandfather clock in the hall.
At home, there are four bedrooms.
At home, there is a carport in the front.
At home, there are lots of books on the shelves.

2 (4 Punkte):
Yes, there is sugar in the corn flakes.
No, there isn't milk in the fridge.
Yes, there are chocolate cookies in my bag.
Yes, there is an alarm system in his expensive new car.

Regel:
Der englische Ausdruck *there is/there* are bedeutet nicht dasselbe wie „da ist/sind". Übersetzen müssen wir diese häufige Wendung mit „es gibt" oder „es ist/sind".

Lösungen zu Test 49

1 (6 Punkte):
Is there a rhino?
Are there bunnies?
Are there snakes?
Is there a polar bear?
Is there a whale?
Are there penguins?

2 (7 Punkte):
There are six windows in the classroom.
There is one door in the classroom.
There are many chairs in the classroom.
There are a lot of desks in the classroom.
There are three posters in the classroom.
There are two lamps in the classroom.
There is one sponge in the classroom.

Lösungen zu Test 50

1 (6 Punkte):

Luke has got a computer in his room.
Luke's sister Betsy has got two hamsters.
Luke's mum and dad have got 400 DVDs.
Luke and Betsy have got a red and a green bicycle.
The family has got a dog named Lassie.
The dog has got a new leash.

Regel:
Das englische Verb *have got* bedeutet als ganzer Ausdruck „haben" im Sinn von „besitzen". Im Präsens wird bei *she/he/it has* verwendet. Verneint werden Sätze mit *not*, die Kurzformen sind: *haven't, hasn't.*

2 (12 Punkte):

Josh has got a brother but he hasn't got a sister.
He has got a father and a mother.
Sam hasn't got a father, but he has got three uncles.
Nell hasn't got a brother but she has got a sister.
She has got two fathers!
Josh has got two uncles, but he hasn't got an aunt.
Sam hasn't got a sister, but he has got two aunts.

Lösungen zu Test 51

1 (10 Punkte):

No, I haven't.
Yes, I am.
Yes, I have.
Yes, it is.
No, I'm not.
Yes, I have.
Yes, I am.
No, I haven't.
Yes, I have.
No, he isn't.

2 (3 Punkte):

Angekreuzt werden müssen:
besitzen
das *got*
bejahenden Kurzantworten

Regel:
Die Kurzformen lauten: *I've got, she's/he's/it's got.* Bei bejahten Kurzantworten können wir keine Kurzform verwenden: *No, I haven't*, aber: *Yes, I have.*

Lösungen zu Test 52

1 (6 Punkte):

Ms Peters has got a good job.
Jonathan and Olivia have got new school bags.
Cornwall has got a lot of beaches.
Mark's dog has got a bone to chew.
London has got four big airports.
The new girl in class has got a nice hair band.

2 (3 Punkte):

I've got good grades in English.
You've got a bigger garden.
He's got a very small car.

Lösungen zu Test 53

1 (8 Punkte):

No, he hasn't.
Yes, he has.
Yes, she has.
No, she hasn't.
No, he hasn't.
No, he hasn't.
Yes, he has.
Yes, she has.

2 (10 Punkte):

Has Nell got two fathers?
Has Sam got a brother?
Has Josh got two uncles?
Has Josh got an aunt?
Has Nell got an uncle?
Has Sam got a mother?
Has Nell got a mother, too?
Has Sam got a father?
Has Nell got an aunt?
Has Josh got a brother?

Lösungen zu Test 54

1 (10 Punkte):

Has Tony got 100 CDs? Yes, he has.
Has Zoey got a twin sister? No, she hasn't.
Have the brothers got a TV set? No, they haven't.
Have we got time? Yes, we have / you have.
Have you got sunglasses? Yes, I have / you have.

2 (8 Punkte):

Deine Antwort sollte bei jeder Frage einer dieser zwei Möglichkeiten entsprechen:
Yes, I have. / No, I haven't.

Lösungen zu Test 55

1 (4 Punkte):

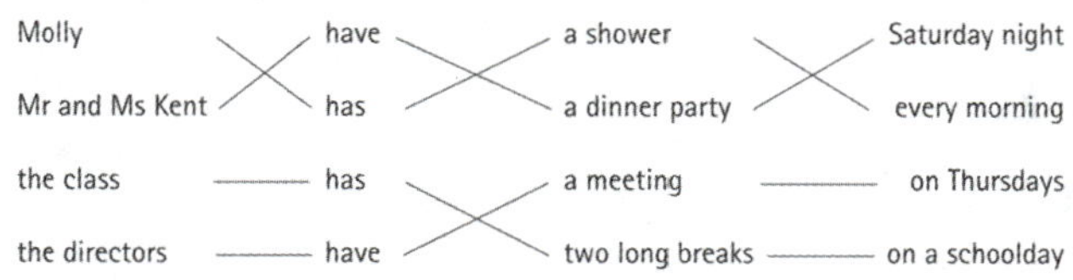

Molly has a shower every morning.
Mr and Ms Kent have a dinner party Saturday night.
The class has two long breaks on a schoolday.
The directors have a meeting on Thursdays.

2 (3 Punkte):

Do we have breakfast together?
You have fun in front of your computer.
Does Nicholas have football practice every Wednesday?

Regel:
Wenn „haben" nicht „besitzen" bedeutet, sondern z. B. ein Vorhaben oder eine Tätigkeit bezeichnet, verwenden wir *have* allein als Verb. Fragen und Verneinungen werden regelmäßig mit *do* umschrieben.

Lösungen zu Test 56

1 (11 Punkte):

Dear Rachel, I really have fun here at summer camp. My days are so busy that I haven't got much time to write, sorry. Let me tell you about my day: We get up at seven o'clock and have breakfast. I usually have toast and a glass of orange juice. Then we go outside and have a little football match. I haven't got my own football here with me, so we take Brandon's ball. Then we have lunch. In the afternoon, we play games or build things or have swimming lessons. I have quiet nights, because I've got (I have got) a bed for myself here. That's all for now. I hope you have a lot of fun, too! Yours, Matt

2 (3 Punkte):

I have basketball practice today.
Do you have a bath on Saturday?
My grandparents haven't got a car.

Lösungen zu Test 57

1 (5 Punkte):

My brothers do a lot of sports.
Linda does her shopping after lunch.
Lucas does his homework every day.
I do the washing, and you do the ironing.

2 (3 Punkte):

No, I do not live in East Berlin.
No he does not go to school on Saturdays.
No, they do not like Italian food.

3 (5 Punkte):

No, she doesn't.
No, I don't.
No, they don't.
No, it doesn't.
No, we don't.

Regel:
Als Vollverb gebraucht bedeutet do „tun" oder „erledigen". Als Hilfsverb brauchen wir es für die Verneinung und für Fragen. Das *-s* bei *she/he/it* wird dann ans Hilfsverb *do* anghängt zu *does*. Die Kurzformen für die Verneinung lauten: *don't/doesn't*.

Lösungen zu Test 58

1 (4 Punkte):

I don't live in Manchester.
My friends don't like football.
He doesn't do his homework.
Our cat doesn't eat fish.

Regel:
Verneinte Befehlssätze, also Verbote, bilden wir mit dem Hilfsverb *don't: Don't shout!*

2 (6 Punkte):

Don't eat sweets!
Don't have a party!
Don't forget to water the flowers!
Don't leave the door open!
Don't watch TV late!
Don't drink Coke!

Lösungen zu Test 59

1 (6 Punkte):

Do you like cheese cake?
Does she eat meat?
Do they serve tea here?
Do we have coffee?
Do you want to pay?
Do they take credit cards?

2 (4 Punkte):

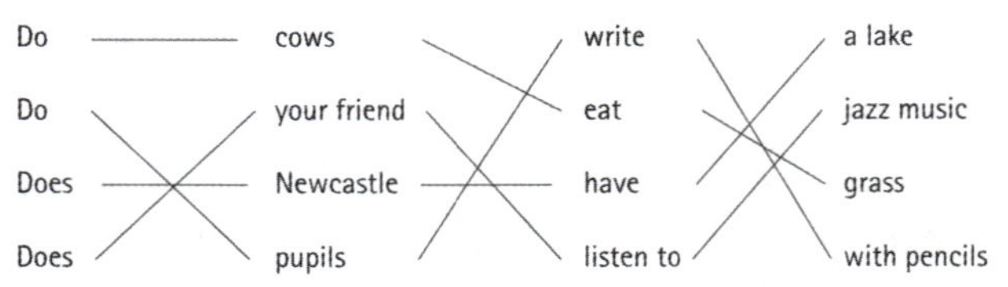

Do cows eat grass?
Do pupils write with pencils?
Does your friend listen to jazz music?
Does Newcastle have a lake?

Lösungen zu Test 60

1 (6 Punkte):

Does he watch television before bedtime?
Does she like going on holiday in Italy?
Do they always do their homework on time?
Do I speak too loudly in class?
Do Jen and Nick come home early on weekdays?
Do you like swimming in the lake in the morning?

Lösungen zu Test 61

1 (8 Punkte):

I can swim in the sea.
I cannot/can't swim in the soup.
I cannot/can't repair a space ship.
I can repair a bike.
I cannot/can't visit planet Mars.
I can visit Great Britain.
I can drink lemon water.
I cannot/can't drink motor oil.

Regel:
Das Hilfsverb (*auxiliary verb*) *can* bedeutet „können" und bezeichnet eine Fähigkeit, Möglichkeit, Erlaubnis oder Bitte. Es steht immer in Verbindung mit einem Vollverb. Verneint wird mit *cannot* bzw. der Kurzform *can't*.

2 (5 Punkte):

Sorry, no I can't.
Yes, she/he can.
No, she can't.
No, they can't.
Yes, you can.

Lösungen zu Test 62

1 (7 Punkte):
Can you play the piano?
Can Jim play the guitar?
Can Angie sing well?
Can Chris play the drums?
Can Payton play the bass?
Can you rock?
Can I join you?

Regel:
Die Vergangenheitsform von *can* lautet *could*, verneint wird mit *could not* bzw. *couldn't. Could* steht außerdem für „könnte", etwa in höflichen Fragen.

2 (10 Punkte):
Can/Could you pass me the salt, please?
Your sisters can do a lot of magic tricks, that's great!
When I was a boy, I could stand on my hands.
You can use my old computer, but you can't have the new one, I need it myself!
Last summer, I couldn't swim, but now I've been to swimming class and now I can swim.
I can/could buy the red bathing suit, but I also can/could buy the blue one. I couldn't/cannot/can't buy both suits, because I don't have enough money.

Lösungen zu Test 63

1 (9 Punkte):
Last year Anna couldn't/could not/wasn't able to go to Boston as an exchange student, because she was ill. But this year she can/is able to go.
When he was one year old, Brian couldn't/could not/wasn't able to speak clearly. But now he is three and can/is able to speak very well.
Jenny couldn't/could not/wasn't able to run 800 m before. But she practiced and this time she can/is able to run 800 m really fast.
Right now Charles can't/cannot/isn't able to play the piano very well yet. But he has a new teacher and can/is able to play much better than he could/was able to last year.

2 (4 Punkte):
The baby can't/cannot/isn't able to walk yet.
Sophia couldn't eat meat.
Can you/Are you able to repair my car?
Can you help me?

Regel:
Umschrieben wird *can* mit dem Ersatzausdruck *be able to.* Diesen verwendet man auch für alle anderen Zeiten außer *simple present* und *simple past.*

Lösungen zu Test 64

1 (4 Punkte):
A. May/Can I come in, please?
B. Yes, you may /can use our toilet.
C. After hospital Ms Sweetly can walk again now.
D. No, you mustn't/can't play in the street ...

2 (4 Punkte):
A. Bitte
B. Erlaubnis
C. Fähigkeit
D. Verbot

3 (3 Punkte):
No, you may not/must not/mustn't!
No, you may not/must not/mustn't!
No, you may not/must not/mustn't!

4 (3 Punkte):
May we smoke in school?
May he talk in class?
May they fight in the halls?

Regel:
Das Hilfsverb *may* wird im Sinn von „dürfen", also als Erlaubnis oder verneint als Verbot verwendet. Es kann auch eine Vermutung ausdrücken. Verneint wird als strenges Verbot mit *must not* oder *mustn't.* Dies gilt ausschließlich für Sätze im *simple present.*

Lösungen zu Test 64

1 (4 Punkte):

Now that he is twelve, my brother can/may/is allowed to go to school on his bike.
When I was smaller, I wasn't allowed to go out to play, because it was too dangerous.
Don't go, Sid! You know, we mustn't/aren't allowed to leave the house, when mum is gone!
Not too long ago, French children were allowed to drink wine with their meals.

2 (5 Punkte):

When I was nine, I couldn't/wasn't allowed to stay up after nine o'clock. Now I can /may/am allowed to stay up until eleven.
Alice couldn't/wasn't allowed to go out after school last year. Now she can/may/is allowed to stay out until five o'clock, if there is no homework.

3 (2 Punkte):

Children can/may/are allowed to play on the grass.
Dogs couldn't/weren't allowed to go to the beach.

Regel:
Umschrieben wird *may* mit dem Ersatzausdruck *be allowed to.* Damit lassen sich Erlaubnisse und Verbote in allen Zeiten ausdrücken.

Lösungen zu Test 66

1 (5 Punkte):

Eric, you must wash your hands.
Oliver must be at home by four.
Kat, you must drink your tea.
Eric must buy some catfood.
You all must show me your homework.

2 (6 Punkte):

Maya must take her medicine.
She must stay in bed.
She needn't go to school or do her homework.
She must let a doctor examine her.
She mustn't play outside.
She needn't do any housework.

3 (1 Punkt):

I needn't get up early for school.

Regel:
Das Hilfsverb *must* für „müssen", bezeichnet eine Notwendigkeit, Verpflichtung oder Aufforderung. Verneint wird mit *need not* oder *needn't.* Dies gilt ausschließlich für Sätze im *simple present.*

Lösungen zu Test 67

1 (3 Punkte):

Did they have to help me?
Must he?/Does he have listen to her?
I must wait here/I have to wait here.

2 (5 Punkte):

"I had to go to bed early yesterday, I felt so tired."
"Then you must/have to hear what happened later."
"Oh no! You mustn't/needn't tell me that,
I needn't know all that right now. Come on, we must/have to hurry!"
"Okay, you're right. I mustn't be late for school again, I must/have to get good grades this year!"

3 (2 Punkte):

Did you have to wait (for) long?
We must/have to sit in the bus.

Regel:
Umschrieben wird *must* mit dem Ersatzausdruck *have to.* Damit lassen sich Notwendigkeiten, Aufforderungen, Verpflichtungen sowie deren Verneinungen und Fragen in allen Zeiten ausdrücken.

Lösungen zu Test 68

1 (6 Punkte):

Ned had to walk the dog. B
May I have the sugar, please? F
You must be there on time! A
You can watch TV tonight. C
Visitors mustn't touch the paintings. D
After a year of piano lessons Anna could play ... E

2 (6 Punkte):

can ↔ can't
must ↔ needn't
may ↔ mustn't

3 (3 Punkte):

Stop! You mustn't feed the zoo animals, they could get sick. D
Adam is cool, he can hold his breath for two full minutes! E
Mr Jones is a baker, he must go to work at 4 a.m. every day. B

4 (3 Punkte):

can ↔ be able to
may ↔ be allowed to
must ↔ have to

Lösungen zu Test 69

1 (16 Punkte):

In February	at lunch
On August, 10th	in summer
at Christmas	on your birthday
in the morning	at two o'clock
in the afternoon	after midnight
in the evening	before next week
at night	until/by next
in 2011	by day

Regel:
Präpositionen der Zeit geben an, wann etwas geschieht. Welches Wort man wo gebraucht, musst du auswendig lernen. Einige Richtlinien: Bei Uhrzeiten oder Mahlzeiten steht *at*, bei Wochentagen und Daten steht *on* und bei längeren Abschnitten wie Jahren, Monaten, Jahreszeiten *in*.

2 (13 Punkte):

Sandy wakes up at seven o'clock in the morning.
She has breakfast at eight and then leaves the house after breakfast.
School ends at four o'clock in the afternoon.
Sandy doesn't come home from school before five o'clock.
At dinner she tells her family about her day.
In the evening she reads a little or watches TV.
On weekends her days are different, of course.
On Sundays she can sleep until ten o'clock or even after ten, if she wants to.

Lösungen zu Test 70

1 (13 Punkte):

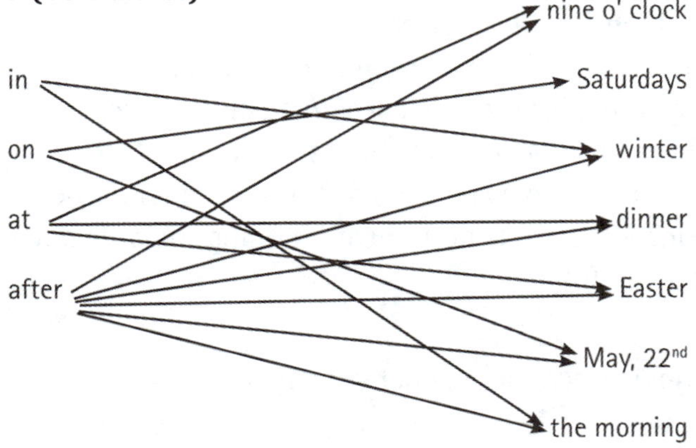

2 (11 Punkte):

Jonas was born in 2004.
His birthday is on April, 1st.
His grandma's birthday is in the same month.
What's the weather like in April?
In spring there is a lot of wind, but mostly at night.
It helps to start the party early, at two o'clock.
The children can eat birthday cake and play until five in the afternoon.
Then everyone goes home and must be in bed before ten, so they will not be tired in the morning.

Lösungen zu Test 71

1 (8 Punkte):

on the left
in the room
in front of the mirror
next to the TV set
under the roof
above the table
behind the sofa
through the passage

2 (5 Punkte):

above the clouds
on the right
behind the house
into the garden
up the street
under the clouds
on the left
in front of the house
out of the garden
down the street

3 (11 Punkte):

On the right there is Caroline's desk with a chair in front of/behind/next to it. On the left there is her bed with a little lamp next to/behind it. There are two windows in her room, one on the left-hand wall, and one on the right-hand wall. Posters are hanging on all the walls. Caroline likes her room tidy. She puts her shoes neatly under/in front of her bed and has no clothes lying around on the floor. Her bed is made, and the covers are on it.

Regel:
Präpositionen des Ortes geben an, wo etwas geschieht oder wo es sich befindet. Auch hier hilft es am meisten, wenn du die wichtigsten Wendungen wie Vokabeln auswendig lernst.

Lösungen zu Test 72

1 (17 Punkte):

I can't find my keys. They are not in my bedroom and not in the kitchen. They're not on the shelves or on/in the fridge, either.
Did you look under your bed or on the TV set? And what about under the magazines on the living room table?
Where is your brother? Is he not at home? He's not in his room or in the garden.
Did you look in the living room in front of the TV?
Gina wants to leave for school, but all her things are still in her room. Her pencil case is on her desk, and her books are on her bed. Some pens are still lying in front of her computer.

2 (5 Punkte):

into
in
in front of
next to
above

Lösungen zu Test 73

1 (10 Punkte):

Sue tries
we dance
Tim walks
I sleep
the car stops
people write
the girl watches
Jane buys
he learns
she knows

Regel:
Das *simple present* ist eine der beiden Zeiten, die im Englischen die Gegenwart ausdrücken. Seine Form entspricht der Grundform des Verbs plus angehängtem *-s* bei *she/he/it*. An Zischlaute [ʃ, tʃ, s] wird *-es* angehängt, aus *-y* wird *-ies*.

2 (12 Punkte):

At night most people sleep.
I've got a dog. He likes to run and play.
Do you watch television often?
When she's at school, she doesn't lie in her bed.
I have got three brothers. We live in a small house, so we fight a lot. My teacher thinks I'm lazy.
You play soccer very well. Does she go to school in the afternoon? My parents don't hear anything if I walk down the stairs carefully.

Regel:
Das *simple present* bezeichnet vor allem gewohnheitsmäßige oder wiederholte Vorgänge und Tatsachen.

Lösungen zu Test 74

1 (8 Punkte):

always	usually	every weekend	often
seldom	sometimes	every August	never

2 (8 Punkte):

Ich spiele jeden Montag Fußball.
Sie gehen selten ins Kino.
Schläfst du nachts?
Meine Mutter sieht nie fern.
Ich esse immer Reis mit Ketchup.
Manchmal hasse ich meine Schwester.
Du bist oft gelangweilt.
Normalerweise trinke ich morgens Tee.

Lösungen zu Test 75

1 (6 Punkte):

Does Mia like her sister?
Do you eat meat?
Are my eyes brown?
Do they watch TV on Sundays?
Does she play table tennis?
Have you got two cars?

2 (9 Punkte):

Snails don't go faster than horses.
Kids don't drive their own cars.
Trucks aren't/are not smaller than bikes.
Animals don't talk to people.
The sun doesn't shine at night.
Donald Duck doesn't love his uncle.
Most old people don't love computers.
The police don't rob a bank when they need money.
Babies don't walk and talk right after birth.

Lösungen zu Test 76

1 (6 Punkte):

Sue has Sandwiches for breakfast in the morning.
At night the moon shines into her bedroom.
She sometimes goes swimming with her sister in the afternoon.
Every year she goes on holiday with her grandparents.
She sleeps late on Sundays.
She never goes out without her purse.

2 (5 Punkte):

You are never late.
I always forget my homework.
You never read a book.
They usually play together./Usually they play together.
We ride our bikes sometimes./Sometimes we ride our bikes.

Lösungen zu Test 77

1 (12 Punkte):

We are having a party.
The music is playing.
My cat is purring.
My friends are eating crisps.
Tina is having some cake.
We are making fun of her.
But she is laughing, too.
Now we are dancing.
Everyone is joining in!
We are doing a funny dance.
The dancers are putting their hands up in the air.
All my friends are having fun!

2 (12 Punkte):

writing	meeting
lying	letting
putting	seeing
swimming	running
waking	carrying
hitting	coming

Regel:
Das *present progressive* ist die Verlaufsform der Gegenwart, die für momentan stattfindende Tätigkeiten oder Verläufe über eine gewisse Dauer benutzt wird. Seine Form entspricht der Grundform des Verbs plus angehängtem *-ing*. Endet ein Verb auf *-ie* wird *-ying* daraus. Ein stummes -e am Wortende fällt weg, und Endkonsonanten nach kurzem Vokal werden verdoppelt.

Lösungen zu Test 78

1 (7 Punkte):
Are you working?
Is she going home?
Are we meeting at school?
Is he asking for help?
Are they playing games?
Are you looking at me?
Is she doing this on purpose?

2 (4 Punkte):
Yes, I am planning a dancing career.
Yes, I am stretching my muscles.
Yes, my lesson is starting now.
Well, no, you are not getting on my nerves.

Lösungen zu Test 79

1 (6 Punkte):
~~go~~: I'm coming home now.
~~later~~: He is running on the lawn.
~~can~~: They are riding their bikes.
~~tomorrow~~: The teacher is listening to you.
~~always~~: We are eating Pizza right now.
~~usually~~: I'm doing my homework now.

2 (12 Punkte):
7 a.m.: I'm getting up.
7.15: I'm taking a shower and brushing my teeth.
7.30: I'm having breakfast. My mother is reading the newspaper.
7.45: I'm walking to the bus station.
7.55: I'm sitting on the bus. The bus is driving me to school.
8.10: I'm leaving the bus. I'm talking to my friends.
8.15 We're entering our classroom. We're waiting for the teacher.

Lösungen zu Test 80

1 (3 Punkte):
Angekreuzt werden müssen: always, a month ago, yesterday

2 (14 Punkte):

Der Junge läuft und schläft gleichzeitig.	Das geht nicht.
Der Hund spielt und bellt gleichzeitig.	Das geht.
Es regnet und der Boden ist trocken.	Das geht nicht.
Ich lese und höre meiner Mutter nicht zu.	Das geht.
Der Mann fährt Auto und sieht einen Film.	Das geht nicht!
Sie spielt Klavier und Gitarre gleichzeitig.	Das geht nicht.
Die Katze frisst und schnurrt dabei.	Das geht.

Lösungen zu Test 81

1 (8 Punkte):
Ich lese gerade.
Ich lese (grundsätzlich gern).
Kate spielt gerade jetzt Basketball.
Kate spielt Basketball (z.B. in einem Verein).
Er isst gerade jetzt Fisch.
Er isst im Allgemeinen Fisch. (Er mag Fisch.)
Du redest gerade viel.
Du redest (immer) viel.

2 (13 Punkte):
I like to ride my bike every day. Do you want to know what I'm doing at this moment? I'm cycling to the shop. I need new brakes. I'm waiting now, because the mechanic is talking to another customer. The mechanic knows a lot about bikes. And he likes me. Sometimes I get smaller parts for free. Now the customer is leaving, but the mechanic is talking on the phone! Is he ignoring me? Ah no, he's coming over. Okay, I have to go, bye!

Lösungen zu Test 82

1 (5 Punkte):

I usually like vegetables.
I'm writing an e-mail just/right now./
Just/right now I'm writing an e-mail.
Sometimes I get angry with my parents./
I get angry with my parents sometimes.
Look, the dog is sleeping on the couch! It usually sleeps on the floor.
Every Sunday I visit my grandma./
I visit my grandma every Sunday.

2 (10 Punkte):

Hi, Leo. – Hi!? Are you talking to me?
Yes, I am. We go to the same dancing class.
Oh, I see! What is your name?
I'm Nina. Do you have a mobile phone?
Yes, I have. Why?
I want to call my mother, I am late.
Look, my mother is coming! We can take you with us.

Lösungen zu Test 83

1 (14 Punkte):

Is Ron at home? No, I'm sorry. He is playing soccer at school.
Look, are Paul and Sue wearing the same cardigan?
Yes, they are. I wonder if they know each other.
Do cats eat fruit? No, cats don't eat fruit. They prefer meat.
Oh, you are reading a book. Do you read a lot?
Yes, I do.
What are you doing? I'm cleaning my desk.
Is Sarah arguing with her friend? Yes, she is.
Unfortunately, they argue a lot.

2 (5 Punkte):

want
like
need
love
know

Lösungen zu Test 84

1 (16 Punkte):

sleep – slept	laugh – laughed
talk – talked	send – sent
walk – walked	keep – kept
drive – drove	put – put
get – got	read – read [red]
go – went	buy – bought
see – saw	play – played
look – looked	feel – felt

Angekreuzt werden:
talk, walk, look, laugh, play

Regel:
Die einfache Vergangenheit *simple past* wird bei regelmäßigen Verben durch ein an die Grundform angehängtes *-ed* gebildet. Ein *-y* am Ende wird zu *-ied*, ein stummes *-e* am Ende entfällt. Endkonsonanten nach einfachem Vokal werden verdoppelt. Die unregelmäßigen Formen musst du auswendig lernen (siehe Test 40–43).

2 (12 Punkte):

simple present	simple past
tell	told
stand	stood
sing	sang
build	built
write	wrote
catch	caught

Lösungen zu Test 85

1 (10 Punkte):
Grace was tired this morning.
We were very worried.
Were you at school yesterday?
My dog was in its basket.
Last year, I was much smaller.
My teachers were on holiday.
My brother was ill.
There was an accident on the road.
Many people were there to watch.
You were at the swimming pool.

2 (11 Punkte):
Last year, Tobias visited a British school. The other kids asked him a lot of questions. Were the questions hard for Tobias? No, they weren't. The teachers explained everything to him. When Tobias answered a question, he said something wrong. But nobody laughed. A girl even smiled at him. Then the teacher finished the lesson, and Tobias played soccer with the others.

Regel:
Das *simple past* bezeichnet abgeschlossene Vorgänge, die in der Vergangenheit stattfanden.

Lösungen zu Test 86

1 (6 Punkte):
No, they didn't.
Yes, I did.
No, it didn't.
Yes, he did.
Yes, they were both at home.
Yes, I went to the movies on Sunday.

Regel:
Bei Fragen und Verneinungen gebrauchen wir im *simple past* die Formen *did* und *did not* oder die Kurzform *didn't.*

2 (7 Punkte):
Did you go on holiday with your parents?
Did you drive?
Did you spend all your pocket money?
Did you make some friends?
Did you eat special food?
Did you see any wild animals?
Did you like it there?

Lösungen zu Test 87

1 (5 Punkte):
When did you get up?
Why did you throw away my bag?
What did you have for lunch?
Why did you take my shirt?
Where was Mom?

2 (8 Punkte):
feel
keep
get
break
draw
hit
leave
drink

3 (11 Punkte):
Yesterday I went to a concert. It was great. I saw my favourite singer. He is much smaller than I thought. But I like him anyway. I stayed until he left the stage. After the concert my mom came to get me, so I arrived at home safely.

Lösungen zu Test 88

1 (1 Punkt):
next year

Regel:
Bei Fragen mit Fragewörtern wird kein umschreibendes *did* gebraucht.

2 (8 Punkte):
Where did Tim go with his parents?
When did the family arrive at the hotel?
Who slept in a single bed room?
What wasn't far away from the hotel?
Who did Tim meet at the beach?
Who did the man try to impress?
Why did the kids laugh?
How did Tim feel at the end of the day?

Lösungen zu Test 89

1 (8 Punkte):

doing	riding
carrying	having
swimming	running
waking	driving

Regel:
Das *past progressive* ist die Verlaufsform der Vergangenheit, die für Abläufe über einen früheren Zeitraum benutzt wird oder für solche Handlungen, die abliefen, während eine andere einsetzte. Gebildet wird das *past progressive* aus *was/were* plus der Verlaufsform mit *-ing.*

2 (1 Punkt):
Antwort C ist richtig: Aus der Vergangenheit von *be* und der Verlaufsform

3 (7 Punkte):
I was writing an e-mail to my friend Frida, when my sister called.
I was having dinner and watching TV, when the doorbell rang.
They were singing and dancing along to the music, when it stopped.
We were walking along the beach, when the rain started.
She was doing her homework, when she remembered her basketball lesson.

Lösungen zu Test 90

1 (10 Punkte):
I was doing my homework. I was chatting on the internet. I was reading a book. I was writing an e-mail. I was having dinner with my parents. I was dancing with my friend. I was walking the dog. I was playing the piano. I was riding my bike. I was talking to my friend on the phone.

2 (5 Punkte):
Was the cat lying on the sofa?
Was her father listening to music?
Were the flowers blooming in the garden?
Was her grandma baking a cake?
Were the bees humming in the bushes?

Lösungen zu Test 91

1 (6 Punkte):
No, I wasn't enjoying the trip.
No, I wasn't eating right.
No, Pauline wasn't talking to me.
Yes, I was arguing with her.
No, I wasn't getting along well with the others.
No, the teachers weren't paying attention.

2 (12 Punkte):
Were you sleeping at 10 o'clock? No, I wasn't.
Was your dog lying in your bed? Yes, it was.
Was I writing a test, when you knocked? Yes, you were.
Were you and Eli listening to music? No, we weren't.
Were the Hendersons playing table tennis yesterday? No, they weren't.
Was Samantha playing the guitar when her brother called? Yes, she was.

Lösungen zu Test 92

1 (5 Punkte):

Ben was reading.
Sarah was talking to her friend.
Birds were flying in the sky.
The woman was driving to Brussels.
Christmas was coming.

2 (9 Punkte):

It was raining, while Lisa was running through the fields.
She was practising for her first marathon run.
She was dreaming about her success, so she wasn't watching her steps.
Suddenly she tripped and fell. Oh! Her ankle was aching!
She was holding her leg, when she saw she didn't have her phone.
While she was waiting, she suddenly heard a noise.
Someone was coming!

Lösungen zu Test 93

1 (8 Punkte):

Last night, Sarah was hiking in the mountains.
Suddenly, she met a bear.
The bear was growling.
Sarah was screaming.
The bear was looking into her eyes.
It was showing her its teeth.
Sarah was shivering.
Then Sarah woke up!

2 (4 Punkte):

I was playing the piano all day.
I was eating, when you called.
What were you doing last night?
While I was reading, you suddenly came in.

Lösungen zu Test 94

1 (20 Punkte):

steal	stole	was/were stealing
move	moved	was/were moving
climb	climbed	was/were climbing
think	thought	was/were thinking
do	did	was/were doing
speak	spoke	was/were speaking
lose	lost	was/were losing
wear	wore	was/were wearing
choose	chose	was/were choosing
burn	burnt	was/were burning

2 (5 Punkte):

A. falsch
B. richtig
C. falsch
D. richtig
E. richtig

Lösungen zu Test 95

1 (12 Punkte):

Last week, me and my parents went on holiday. While we were sitting in a restaurant, our car was stolen. We were very shocked! While one policeman was taking notes, another one tried to be nice. He offered me tea. While I was drinking, another policeman came in. The policemen were talking for a while, and my mother was getting nervous. But then they promised to look for our car very soon.

2 (4 Punkte):

While I was watching my favourite programme, the TV set exploded.
When my mother came back from work, I was cooking dinner.
When the accident happened, you were sitting in a café.
We got angry, because he was making fun of us all day.

Lösungen zu Test 96

1 (6 Punkte):

Were you waiting all day?
Did he go to the soccer game?
When did you go to sleep?
What were you doing, when I came home?
Was the music playing very loud?
Were they running to school?

2 (4 Punkte):

Suddenly someone knocked at the window. I opened it.
My friend stood there. He was laughing all the time.
I asked: "Were you here last night?"
He said: "Yes, while you were sleeping."

Lösungen zu Test 97

1 (4 Punkte):

A. richtig
B. falsch
C. falsch
D. richtig

Regel:
Das Perfekt *present perfect* wird gebildet durch *have/has* plus *past participle*. Bei regelmäßigen Verben wird für Letzteres nur ein *-ed* angehängt, die unregelmäßigen Formen musst du auswendig lernen (siehe Test 40–43). Die Verneinung bilden wir mit *not*, das immer nach *have/has* steht. Fragen setzen sich aus *have/has* plus Subjekt plus *past participle* zusammen.

2 (24 Punkte):

spend	have spent	draw	have drawn
buy	have bought	tell	have told
look	have looked	ring	have rung
talk	have talked	arrive	have arrived
watch	have watched	run	have run
go	have gone	hit	have hit
say	have said	be	have been
ask	have asked	ride	have ridden
laugh	have laughed	fly	have flown
cry	have cried	write	have written
meet	have met	do	have done
read	have read	have	have had

Lösungen zu Test 98

1 (6 Punkte):

I have missed her ever since.
We have been on holiday for three weeks.
I have forgotten to write him.
You have just eaten all my pancakes.
They have already painted the house.
Paul has never slept late.

Regel:
Das *present perfect* verwenden wir für Ereignisse, die bis in die Gegenwart hinein andauern oder sich auswirken. Zu den Signalwörtern für das *present perfect* gehören *just, since/for, ever, never, already, not yet.*

2 (3 Punkte):

I'm tired, because I've stayed up too long.
You're happy, because you've slept long.
He's sick, because he's eaten too much.

Regel:
Auch im *present perfect* kann *has/have* wie gewohnt zu *'s/'ve* abgekürzt werden.

Lösungen zu Test 99

1 (6 Punkte):

Oops! Sorry, I haven't noticed you.
Have you been to London before?
No, I haven't. What about you?
I've been here four times already.
Wow! Have you seen all the sights yet?
I've never visited the Tower.

2 (6 Punkte):

Ich hab den neuen Computer gesehen und überlege jetzt, ob ich ihn kaufen soll.
Ich habe das Geschirr gespült. Es ist jetzt sauber.
Ich bin seit drei Jahren mit Pam befreundet.
Ich war/bin die ganze Woche schon krank.
Ich habe John gebeten, zur Apotheke zu gehen, aber er ist noch nicht hingegangen/war noch nicht dort.
Ich habe dich nie um Hilfe gebeten.

Lösungen zu Test 100

1 (6 Punkte):

Have you ever heard an Australian talk? No, I haven't.
Has this dog ever spoken English? No, it hasn't.
Have trees ever grown 100 m tall? No, they haven't.
Have you ever drunk blood? No, I haven't.
Has anyone ever flown to the sun? No, no one has.
Has the earth ever exploded before? No, it hasn't.
Has she ever paid with stones at the supermarket? No, she hasn't.

2 (6 Punkte):

They have just caught a lot of fish.
He has not done his homework yet.
We have never gone on holiday without our dog.
Have you spent all your pocket money already?

Lösungen zu Test 101

1 (6 Punkte):

Have you been at home yet?
No, I haven't been there yet.
Have you ever been able to/allowed to go to Italy?
No, I've never been able to/allowed to go.
Have you had to wait for me?
Yes, I've had to wait, but now you're here.

Regel:
Die *present perfect*-Form für das modale Hilfsverb „müssen" lässt sich im Englischen nur mit *has/have had to* umschreiben, die für „können" lautet *has/have been able to* oder *has/have been allowed to.*

2 (7 Punkte):

Folgende Sätze gehören zusammen:
My little sister has been tired. Now she's asleep.
Mum has told him to stay home. But he doesn't want to.
They have/They've left the house. They are standing outside now.
She has/She's eaten all her sandwiches. She's full now.
We have/We've studied a lot for the exam. Our grades are good.
You have/You've seen my diary. Now you know that I like you.
I have/I've worked too hard. Now I'm tired.

Lösungen zu Test 102

1 (3 Punkte):

A. falsch
B. richtig
C. richtig

Regel:
Das *present perfect progressive* bezeichnet Abläufe über einen bestimmten Zeitraum, die zu einem früheren Zeitpunkt begannen, aber noch bis zur Gegenwart andauern oder noch immer Wirkung zeigen (z. B. *Karen has been learning English for two years*). Gebildet wird das *present perfect progressive* aus *has/have been* plus der Verlaufsform mit *-ing.*

Lösungen zu Test 102 (fortgesetzt)
2 (13 Punkte):
I've been waiting.
He's been diving.
She's been running.
You've been reading.
We've been talking.
Sam's been smiling.
She's been watching.
I've been drinking.
It's been raining.
We've been drawing.
You've been playing.
They've been whispering.
Sandy's been swimming.

Lösungen zu Test 103
1 (14 Punkte):

has done	has been doing
have written	have been writing
has thought	has been thinking
have given	have been giving
has ridden	has been riding
have thought	have been thinking
has enjoyed	has been enjoying
have chosen	have been choosing
has gone	has been going
have had	have been having
has said	has been saying
have lead	have been leading
has left	has been leaving
have sung	have been singing

2 (8 Punkte):
I have finished my homework quickly.
We have been shopping all day, and
I have spent a lot of money.
My dad has been watching TV for three hours.
The cat has been trying to catch a mouse all day.
The cake has been cooling down for two hours,
but it's still warm.
She has known him for a long time, but she still can't stand him.
I have brought you the newspaper, so now you can tell me the news.

Lösungen zu Test 104
1 (14 Punkte):
I've been a member of the chess club for three years.
Since eight o'clock this morning, she's been studying for the exam.
We've been talking for three hours now.
Hey, I've been waiting for you since two o'clock!
She's been lying in bed for a few days.
They've been driving, since they left London.
I haven't been able to talk to you for a while.

Regel:
Die Präposition *for* steht bei Handlungen zu einem bestimmten Zeit**punkt**, *since* bezeichnet einen Zeit**raum**. Beide werden übersetzt mit „seit".

2 (4 Punkte):
She has been playing computer games for three hours./
For three hours she has been playing computer games.
He has been sitting at his desk since 10 o'clock./
Since 10 o'clock he has been sitting at his desk.
The dog has been barking for half an hour!/
For half an hour the dog has been barking!
You've been reading your book for more than two hours now./
For more than two hours now you've been reading your book.

Lösungen zu Test 105
1 (6 Punkte):
Anne has been studying her books all day.
Robbie hasn't eaten since 8 o'clock.
We've just written a letter to grandma.
Have they been dancing all night?
You've been looking at me for five minutes now. Please stop!
Has she been walking around the store since 10 o'clock?

2 (3 Punkte):
I've never seen this animal.
Have you ever been to France?
I've been waiting here for hours!

Regel:
Das englische *present perfect* wird im Deutschen oft auch im Präteritum („Warst du schon mal ...?") oder im Präsens („Ich warte hier schon ...") wiedergegeben.

Lösungen zu Test 106
1 (6 Punkte):
Alexa will go to town.
Zach will go with her.
They will have breakfast.
I will make them a sandwich.
Mr Anderson will work for a big phone company.
Me and my family will like our new summer cottage.

2 (6 Punkte):
You will eat your sandwiches.
You will not stay hungry all morning.
I will take care that you will have regular meals.
They will know that you all will be okay.

Regel:
Die Zukunft lässt sich im Englischen vielfältig ausdrücken. Eine Möglichkeit dafür ist das *will future*. Es wird mit *will* plus Infinitiv gebildet, verneint wird mit *will not* plus Infinitiv. Kurzformen sind *'ll* und *won't*.

3 (5 Punkte):
I'm sure I'll marry, when I'm older.
Will you marry one day?
No, I won't marry. I'll live on my own and I'll mind my own business!

Lösungen zu Test 107
1 (5 Punkte):
The weather will get worse tomorrow. There will be a lot of clouds, and there will not be any sunshine. At night, it will rain a lot. I don't think we will have it very warm.

2 (8 Punkte):

You're hungry? I'll cook some pancakes.	C
I hope my friends won't forget me.	A
He'll love his presents, I'm sure.	B
Don't be afraid, I'll help you.	C

Regel:
Das *will future* wird bei sicheren Ereignissen der Zukunft, bei Hoffnungen, Vermutungen oder Vorhersagen, die ohne eigenes Zutun geschehen werden, oder bei raschen Entscheidungen für die nahe Zukunft eingesetzt.

3 (3 Punkte):
He thinks, Ashley will/'ll come next week.
On Saturday you will/'ll perhaps meet my girlfriend/friend.
I will not/won't go to the party later.

Regel:
Das *will future* wird im Deutschen oft als Präsens übersetzt, z. B. *I'll do the shopping later* – „Ich gehe später einkaufen".

Lösungen zu Test 108

1 (4 Punkte):
Ms Howe will have a new job next month.
She will prepare files for a lawyer.
Will he ask her to answer his phone calls?
Will she get better payment later?

2 (4 Punkte):
Yes, they will go.
No, they won't live there.
Yes, they will.
No, there won't be rain.

3 (3 Punkte):
Will you go on holiday to Spain?
Will you enjoy the long journey?
Will you love to be out in the sun all day?

Lösungen zu Test 109

1 (3 Punkte):
WIll you be in seventh form next year?
Will you have to take more maths lessons?
Will you be able to go to French class, too?

2 (4 Punkte):
The weather will be better soon.
They will be able to go fishing next week.
Andy will have to be careful with his leg.
Will they be able to come back before Sunday?

3 (4 Punkte):
Where will you be?
What will you need?
When will I have to be there?
Why won't you/will you not be able to help me?

Regel:
Sämtliche Formen der Zukunft lassen sich für modale Hilfsverben nur durch Umschreibungen mit *has/have to, be able to, be allowed to* ausdrücken.

Lösungen zu Test 110

1 (9 Punkte):
I hope Ms Hart won't/will not give us too much homework.
I think the weather'll/will be fine in the afternoon.
Do you think the sun'll/will shine later on?
Yes, I'm sure we'll/will have lots of sunshine.
I'll/will play football with you, if you like!
Yes, I'll/will like that very much.
I've got an idea: Let's ask Ms Hart!
She'll/will tell us.
She'll/will know, how much homework we'll/will get.

2 (2 Punkte):
Angekreuzt werden müssen:
durch das Präsens
durch das Futur I

3 (2 Punkte):
Sie ist nächsten Sommer in Schottland.
Sie wird nächsten Sommer in Schottland sein.

Lösungen zu Test 111

1 (4 Punkte):
Mögliche Sätze sind hier:
I hope/think/believe I will be happy.
I hope/think/believe I will have a fine job
I hope/think/believe I will have money.
I hope/think/believe I will look good.
I hope/think/believe I will/won't be married.

2 (4 Punkte):
Many/a lot of people will come to the football game on Saturday.
It will snow. We'll/will have to wear warm clothes.
I believe/think Lucas, Andrew and Chris will go on holiday together next year.

3 (1 Punkt):
mögliche Antworten:
Sie bezeichnen eine Hoffnung.
Sie bezeichnen eine Vermutung oder Vorhersage.

Lösungen zu Test 112

1 (6 Punkte):
I'm going to go to the concert.
You're going to come home.
Dad is going to clean his car.
Timmy is going to call Debbie.
Noah isn't going to help his mother.
He's going to go to football practice instead.

Regel:
Eine andere Möglichkeit, Zukünftiges auszudrücken, ist das *going to future*. Es wird mit einer Form von *be* plus *going to* plus Infinitiv gebildet, verneint wird mit *not*. Bei Fragen steht *be* vor dem Subjekt.

2 (10 Punkte):
I am going to stay home tomorrow.
Sophie is going to bring me our homework.
Anna is going to clean her bike.
We are going to be fine.
Darla is going to play the piano for you.
Mr Sheffield is going to take some days off work.
I am not going to go out tonight.
Hilary is not going to feel happy after that game.
Are you going to be okay with that?
Is she going to come with us?

Lösungen zu Test 113

1 (4 Punkte):
On Monday Dave's/is going to play tennis.
On Wednesday dad's/is going to meet Paul.
On Friday mum's/is going to go to the movies.
On Saturday Alyssa's/is going to visit aunt Betty.

2 (8 Punkte):
Dad's/is going to wash the dishes after breakfast. A
You haven't done your homework? Mr Bark is going to notice! B
On the weekend I'm/am going to run a mile every morning. A
The door is unlocked. Someone's/is going to come in. B

3 (3 Punkte):
Ella is going to fall down the stairs.
Are Will and Robyn going to come to the party?
I am going to see my cousin next summer.

Regel:
Das *going to future* wird vor allem für willentlich gefasste Pläne, Vorhaben, Absichten und Verabredungen verwendet sowie für wahrscheinliche oder absehbare Ereignisse.

Lösungen zu Test 114

1 (4 Punkte):
No, it is not going to sink.
Yes, I am going to watch TV tonight.
Yes, we are going to be in Hull soon.
No, Mike is not going to see Amy.

2 (4 Punkte):
Are you going to cry?
Are you going to spend a lot of money at the stores?
Are you going to be nice to Mr Owen?
Is your team going to lose the match?

3 (3 Punkte):
We're not/We aren't going to visit/see grandma on Sunday.
Are you going to have to come with us tomorrow?
I'm going to bake/make a cake for your birthday next week.

Lösungen zu Test 115

1 (3 Punkte):
Ms Taylor gives her son a sandwich.
He is very hungry.
Children want tasty food.

2 (6 Punkte):
Layla must do her homework at once.
I will help her later.
Her teacher can give her a good grade.

3 (3 Punkte):
A. Janet can swim very fast.
B. Our teacher won't give us any homework.
C. The cat plays with its toy mouse.

Regel:
Anders als im Deutschen steht in englischen Aussagesätzen immer das Subjekt vor dem Prädikat (aus Hilfsverb plus Vollverb), und das vor Ergänzungen (wie Objekten, Orts- und Zeitangaben) hintereinander. Das gilt auch für Nebensätze.

4 (4 Punkte):
A. richtig
B. falsch
C. richtig
D. richtig

Lösungen zu Test 116

1 (8 Punkte):
simple present: A car dealer sells my brother a new Ford at an auction.
present progressive: A car dealer is selling my brother a new Ford at an auction.
simple past: A car dealer sold my brother a new Ford at an auction.
past progressive: A car dealer was selling my brother a new Ford at an auction.
present perfect: A car dealer has sold my brother a new Ford at an auction.
present perfect progressive: A car dealer has been selling my brother a new Ford at an auction.
will future: A car dealer will sell my brother a new Ford at an auction.
going to future: A car dealer is going to sell my brother a new Ford at an auction.

Regel:
Im Englischen finden sich Ortsangaben immer vor Zeitangaben. Adverbien der Häufigkeit (*often, sometimes, always* usw.) stehen meist vor dem Vollverb, z. B. *You have never helped me.* Adverbien der Art und Weise stehen meist hinter dem Objekt: *She smiled happily.*

Lösungen zu Test 116 (fortgesetzt)

2 (5 Punkte):

B → A → D → E → C

The man answered the questions nervously last week.

Lösungen zu Test 117

1 (7 Punkte):

Mum came home yesterday.
present perfect progressive: Your friends / stay
I'm/I am going to work a lot tomorrow.
present perfect: he / call
She's/has been reading all night.
will future: we / must leave oder: we / have to leave

2 (2 Punkte):

When they're on holiday, they'll/will often go surfing at the beach.
When they're on holiday, they'll/will lie in the sun all day.

3 (2 Punkte):

She will have fun, because she likes the sun.
She will have fun, when she will have enough time.

Lösungen zu Test 118

1 (4 Punkte):

Greg got sick last night.
Charly and Ted are going to meet Kim and Vicky tonight. / Kim and Vicky are going to meet Charly and Ted tonight.
I have tennis lessons in Hull every Wednesday.
He's/has never been to Australia.

2 (3 Punkte):

Jimmy sometimes does the washing up.
I'm going to come with you to the party next weekend.
Micky gave her the ring happily.

3 (1 Punkt):

Angekreuzt werden muss:
die Zeitangabe

Lösungen zu Test 119

1 (8 Punkte):

We cannot go on holiday to Greece every year.
The boy is not waiting at the bus stop.
Naomi didn't call her mum.
Nicholas wasn't listening to his teacher.
Sarah has not been to the hairdresser.
I have not stayed up all night.
The sun will not shine tomorrow.
The baby is not going to sleep quietly here.

2 (3 Punkte):

A. richtig
B. richtig
C. richtig

Regel:
Der verneinende Teil *not* (Kurzform *n't*) steht in Aussagesätzen nach dem Hilfsverb in der Reihenfolge: Subjekt plus Hilfsverb plus *not* plus Vollverb plus Ergänzungen. Im *simple present* und *simple past* wird mit *do/does not* bzw. *don't/doesn't* als Hilfsverb umschrieben, im *simple past* mit *did not/didn't*.

Lösungen zu Test 120

1 (10 Punkte):
We do not sell flowers.
Tony didn't go to school yesterday.
They won't be in Europe next year.
She was not standing there with the others.
I cannot buy him a present.

2 (2 Punkte):
When we meet, we won't/will not talk about school.
When we meet, we won't/will not stay in the house for long.

3 (2 Punkte):
We are glad, when we don't/do not have lessons.
We are glad, because we don't/do not have to learn/study. (*nicht*: must not!!)

4 (1 Punkt):
Angekreuzt werden muss:
nach dem Hilfsverb

Lösungen zu Test 121

1 (3 Punkte):
The children weren't/were not allowed to play all day.
I didn't/did not sleep in class.
You didn't/did not tell your parents everything.

2 (3 Punkte):
The monkeys weren't/were not eating bananas.
The lions weren't/were not roaring loudly.
The parrots weren't/were not talking to visitors.

3 (3 Punkte):
Dad isn't/is not going to wash the car.
The boys didn't/did not stop their game.
Mum hasn't/has not gone to the movies in London for years.

Lösungen zu Test 122

1 (5 Punkte):
Children may not/must not/mustn't run in museums.
There won't/will not be thunderstorms tomorrow.
They didn't/did not put on more Christmas decoration last year.
I haven't/have not passed my test yet.
Maya hasn't/has not been reading her new book since Christmas.

2 (4 Punkte):
Hannah does not take the bus.
Tina is not going to go to the movies on Saturday.
You have never listened to me.
He did not write his test yesterday.

Regel:
Das modale Hilfsverb must kann nur durch Umschreibung mit *have to* verneint werden: *She must wash the dishes. – She doesn't have to wash the dishes.*

Lösungen zu Test 123

1 (3 Punkte):
Do you like mushrooms?
Can he play basketball?
Are they going to help us?

Regel:
Sogenannte Entscheidungsfragen ohne Fragewort, die nur bejaht oder verneint werden können, stehen immer in derselben Wortstellung: Hilfsverb plus Subjekt plus Vollverb plus Erweiterungen. Fehlt das Hilfsverb, wird mit einer Form von *do* umschrieben.

2 (6 Punkte):
Did you know the answers?
Will Luke marry Lorelai?
Can't you see we're busy?

Lösungen zu Test 123 (fortgesetzt)

3 (3 Punkte):
Can I eat my lunch?
Does Matt go to school on his bike?
Does your hamster live in a cage?

4 (4 Punkte):
A. richtig
B. falsch
C. richtig
D. richtig

Lösungen zu Test 124

1 (6 Punkte):
Does Newcastle lie in the North of England?
Are you doing your homework?
Has Sylvia lived in Canada?
Will Gabrielle arrive here soon?
Can People fly to London in an hour?
Did Patrick have to clean the house?

2 (3 Punkte):
Would you like a glass of water?
Would you like to go to the movies with me?
Could you tell me the way to the train station?

Regel:
Auf Englisch stellen wir Fragen höflicher und freundlicher, wenn wir *Would you like ... ?* verwenden, anstatt mit *do* zu fragen. Statt *can* klingt *could* netter, z. B. *Could you help me?*

Lösungen zu Test 125

1 (5 Punkte):
Are you smiling?
Can I go?
Will you be here tomorrow?
Did she kiss the new girl?
Has he been allowed to watch the movie?

2 (3 Punkte):
Do children make snowballs in winter?
Do families go on holiday in summer?
Do flowers grow in spring?

3 (3 Punkte):
Are flags waving in the air?
Are people shouting loudly?
Are the players running along the field?

Lösungen zu Test 126

1 (7 Punkte):

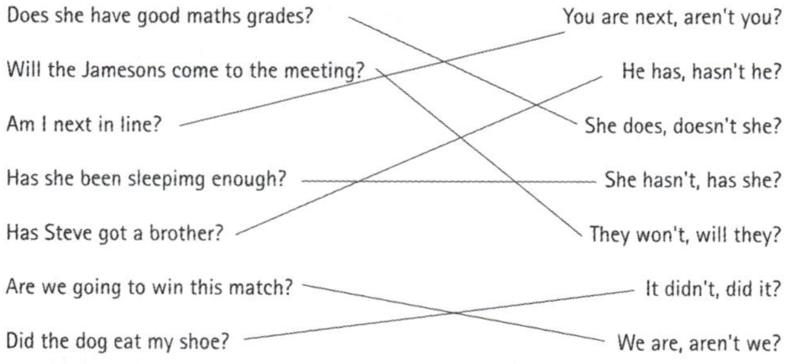

Regel:
Im Englischen werden an Aussagesätze in der gesprochenen Sprache zur Bekräftigung häufig sogenannte Frageanhängsel (*question tags*) gehängt. Inhaltlich bedeuten sie etwa dasselbe wie ein „..., nicht wahr?" im Deutschen. Gebildet werden sie bei Vollverbsätzen mit der passenden Form von *do* (*You like me, don't you?*), bei Sätzen mit Hilfsverben wird das Hilfsverb wiederholt (*She will, won't she?*) Ganz wichtig: Bejahte Sätze bekommen verneinte Frageanhängsel, Verneinungen bekommen bejahte Anhängsel!

Lösungen zu Test 126 (fortgesetzt)
2 (7 Punkte):
He often listens to pop music, doesn't he?
Teachers don't smoke in class, do they?
Children cannot drive cars, can they?
She will come with us, won't she?
You went to Turkey on holiday, didn't you?
I don't have to wash the dishes now, do you?
Clara hasn't cleaned her shirt yet, has she?

3 (1 Punkt):
Angekreuzt werden muss:
eine Verneinung

Lösungen zu Test 127
1 (5 Punkte):
Will there be rain tomorrow?
Did she write me an e-mail yesterday?
Would you like a cup of tea now?
Have Mia and Lily put on their shoes yet?
Were they painting the walls, when you came in?

2 (4 Punkte):
Would you pass me the salt, please?
Are you going to watch TV on Saturday?
Have you eaten your steak yet?
You like Bella, don't you?

Lösungen zu Test 128
1 (7 Punkte):

W	F	G	P	T	H
O	H	W	M	A	C
W	H	E	N	H	E
T	O	L	R	W	H
W	W	H	Y	E	W
H	C	I	H	W	A

2 (4 Punkte):
Who goes to school by bike today?
Where do the children go by bike today?
How do the children go to school today?
When do the children go to school by bike?

3 (4 Punkte):
Who came to school?
What did he tell us?
Why did he come here?
Where did he sit down?

Regel:
Bei Fragen mit Fragewörtern stehen diese ganz vorn im Fragesatz. Wie auch im Deutschen steht das Vollverb hinter dem Fragewort, wenn mit *who* oder *which* nach dem Subjekt eines Satzes gefragt wird, z. B.: *Who needs this?* Auch das Hilfsverb steht nach dem Fragewort: *Who can help me?* Wird nach etwas anderem gefragt, etwa nach dem Objekt (*what*), der Zeit (*when*), dem Ort (*where*), der Art und Weise (*how*) oder dem Grund (*why*), muss mit dem Hilfsverb *do* umschrieben werden, z. B.: *Why do you ask?*

Lösungen zu Test 129

1 (4 Punkte):
When can I go home?
Where is Kayla waiting for us?
Which colour did Jeff choose?
Why weren't you listening to your mother?

2 (4 Punkte):
How many pets have you got?
How much milk would you like?
How many stars can you count?
How much time do you need?

Regel:
Mit *how many ...?* wird nach einer genauen Anzahl gefragt, mit *how much ...?* fragen wir nach nicht zählbaren Dingen und Mengen.

3 (3 Punkte):
What's that?
Who's that?
When's your birthday?

Regel:
Bei Fragen mit Fragewort plus *is* wird sehr häufig die verkürzte Form *'s* verwendet.

Lösungen zu Test 130

1 (5 Punkte):
What did you say to her last night?
Why has she never answered my question?
When can I see her again?
Where are she and I going to meet in future?/
Where will she and I meet in future?

2 (5 Punkte):
Where can I find my jacket?
How do I get from here to London?
Who are you going to invite to your party?/
Whom are you going to invite to your party?
When did Julian come home last night?
Which button must I press?/
Which button do I have to press?

Lösungen zu Test 131

1 (5 Punkte):
Go upstairs.
Help your sister.
Stop fighting.
Brush your teeth.
Sleep well.

2 (4 Punkte):
Wait for the green light.
Take the bus to school.
Don't hurt other children.
Don't shout or talk in class.

Regel:
Mit der Befehlsform (*imperative*) werden nicht nur Befehle, sondern auch Bitten oder Aufforderungen ausgedrückt. Sie entspricht im Englischen immer der Grundform, egal ob im Singular oder Plural. Verneint wird mit *don't* plus Grundform. Im Englischen ist oft kein Ausrufezeichen, sondern ein Punkt hinter einem Befehlssatz zu finden.

3 (2 Punkte):
A. richtig
B. falsch

Lösungen zu Test 132

1 (5 Punkte):
Folgende Befehle sind möglich:
Do/finish/take out/put away your homework.
Eat/finish your breakfast.
Wash/clean/clap your hands.
Listen/Come to me.
Be/Come home before seven.

2 (4 Punkte):
Sit still.
Don't be late.
Don't make so much noise.
Go to bed.
Don't shout in class.

3 (3 Punkte):
Come here please.
Don't be stupid.
Don't buy these mp3 players.

Lösungen zu Test 133

1 (4 Punkte):

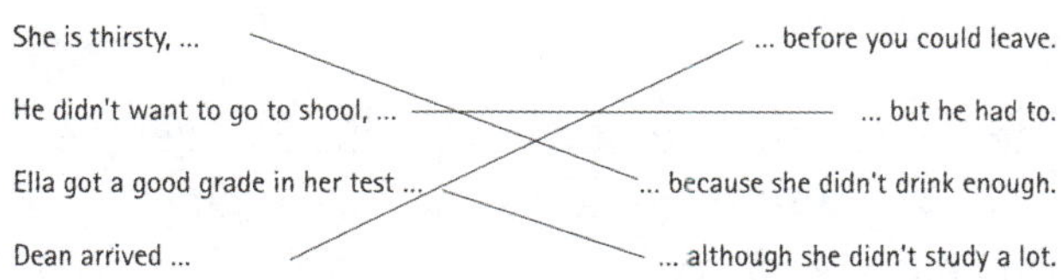

2 (7 Punkte):
My friend Tammy and I were late for school, because we had an accident on the way. When we were crossing the street, a man on a bicycle came. He didn't stop fast enough and hit Tammy. I tried to hold her back, but she fell. It was a hard fall, so her arm was hurt. Although the man offered to take us to a hospital, Tammy got up. She said that her arm wasn't broken and went to school with me.

3 (14 Punkte):

because	weil
when	als
and	und
but	aber
so	also
although	obwohl
that	dass

Regel:
Konjunktionen (*connectives*) sind Bindewörter. Sie stehen am Anfang von Neben- oder Hauptsätzen und verdeutlichen dort den inhaltlichen Bezug. Zum Beispiel bei Nebensätzen des Grundes: *She couldn't eat, because she was ill.* – „Sie konnte nicht essen, weil sie krank war." Die Bedeutung der englischen Konjunktionen musst du lernen wie andere Vokabeln.

Lösungen zu Test 134

1 (4 Punkte):

I'm staying in bed today, ... I am ill.
☐ that ☒ because ☐ until

My stomach was aching, ... I went to bed last night.
☒ and ☒ when ☒ before

I had stomach pain, ... I fell asleep.
☐ because ☒ until ☐ that

Now I am ill ... I don't have to go to school
☒ so ☒ and ☐ although

I think ... I am going to be ill tomorrow, too.
☐ but ☐ before ☒ that

2 (6 Punkte):
Folgende Konjunktionen sind hier möglich:
Ms Hunter tried to walk, but/although she couldn't with her broken foot.
My friends and I played football, until/although/but it got dark.
I'll do my homework, before/until I go to bed.
I know that/but she likes me.
He smiled at me, so/until I felt really good.
I had to go home early, although the match wasn't over.

Lösungen zu Test 135

1 (6 Punkte):

When they came home, they sat down in front of the TV at once.
He did not stay, until the match was over.
Before/until we got our new teacher, I've never understood maths.
Believe me that/because I've never lied to you!
Although the kiss felt good, she stopped her friend.
I really wish I had more money, but I haven't.

2 (4 Punkte):

Als er ankam, sagte er allen hallo/guten Tag/begrüßte er alle.
Ich sah sie sofort, weil sie eine orange Jacke anhatte/trug.
Aaron wird für diesen Test lernen, bis er jedes englische Wort darin kennt.
Möchtest du/Willst du/Würdest du gern deine grüne Kappe/Mütze aufsetzen/tragen, oder möchtest/willst/würdest du gerne die blaue nehmen?

Lösungen zu Test 136

1 (5 Punkte):

If she goes to bed now, she won't be tired tomorrow.
If you miss your piano lessons, you won't be able to play well.
If your team wins the football match, you will have a party.
If Finn eats any more chocolate, he will be sick.
If Annie doesn't call Derek, he will feel sad.

2 (6 Punkte):

If the weather stays good, we will go to the beach.
If the others come too, we will have lots of fun together.
If it is very hot outside, you will have to bring the sun screen.

Regel:
Bedingungs- oder *if*-Sätze (*if clauses*) sind Satzgefüge aus *if*- und Hauptsatz, die jeweils eine Bedingung und deren Folge bezeichnen. Der *if*-Satz steht im *simple present*, der zugehörige Hauptsatz immer im *will future*. Im Deutschen stehen diese Satzgefüge hingegen oft mit beiden Teilen im Präsens, z. B. „Wenn er nicht kommt, geht sie." – *If he doesn't come, she will leave.*

Lösungen zu Test 137

1 (6 Punkte):

If we ask our neighbour, she'll/will feed the cats, during our holidays.
If I tell you what she said about you, you will be shocked.
Aunt Jane will be so happy, if her nieces visit her some time.
If Carol and Paige are always late for class, they'll/will get awful grades.
My mum'll/will enjoy her weekend, if I and my sisters sleep over at our friends' houses.
If Melissa doesn't play better than yesterday, Sammy'll/will win this tennis match.

2 (6 Punkte):

If my friend likes to, we will have a long phone talk tonight.
If our teacher lets us go, school will finish early today.
If Tim has got enough money, he will buy a new fingerboard.

3 (1 Punkt):

Angekreuzt werden muss:
will future

Lösungen zu Test 138

1 (7 Punkte):

My parents will get angry, if I am not home by seven o'clock.
Can I open the window? If it gets too cold, I'll close it again.
When the bus stops at the next stop, we'll have to get off.
We'll have tea, when we come home.
If she doesn't leave now, she'll miss her bus.
Please phone us, when you arrive in Edinburgh.
If the weather is bad, we won't rent a boat.

3 (1 Punkt):

Angekreuzt werden muss:
um einen Zeitpunkt

2 (10 Punkte):

Sam will be so happy, when his girlfriend comes home from her holidays in France.
If we do more sports, we'll/will get thinner.
If I win first prize at the running competition today, I'll/will have a big party with all my friends.
If Lisa doesn't/does not make too many mistakes, she will pass her exam.
They won't leave, if we don't/do not ask them to.

Regel:
When kann ebenso wie *if* auch „wenn" bedeuten. Bei *when* ist jedoch ein Zeitpunkt gemeint, zu dem etwas geschieht, etwa im Sinn von „sobald". *If* lässt sich hingegen durch „falls" ersetzen – eine gute Probe, wenn du dir nicht sicher bist, welche Konjunktion die richtige ist.

Lösungen zu Test 139

1 (4 Punkte):

Mögliche Beispiellösungen wären:
If I get thirsty, I'll have a glass of water.
If I miss the bus home from school, I'll call my parents.
If I am late for class, I'll apologize.
If I win 100 Euros in a lottery, I'll buy 10 DVDs.

Hier sind aber auch sehr viele andere Antworten möglich. Um einen Punkt zu erhalten, müssen deine Lösungssätze *'ll, will, will not* oder *won't* enthalten und eine inhaltliche Folge der jeweiligen *if*-Sätze schildern.

2 (2 Punkte):

Jill will go to the concert, if she gets tickets.
I will go home, when it gets dark.

3 (2 Punkte):

Ich gehe nicht einkaufen/Ich werde nicht einkaufen gehen, wenn du nicht (mit mir) mitkommst.
Wenn es keine roten Stiefel in meiner Größe gibt, kaufe ich braune/werde ich braune kaufen.

Lösungen zu Test 140

1 (4 Punkte):

WHO Personen	WHICH Gegenstände und Tiere
THAT Personen, Gegenstände und Tiere	WHOSE Besitzverhältnis, Zugehörigkeit

Regel:
Relativsätze (*relative clauses*) sind Nebensätze, die Personen, Tiere oder Dinge näher beschreiben, z. B. *The girl who left.* Sie werden durch Relativpronomen eingeleitet, die immer direkt nach ihrem Bezugswort stehen. *Who* und *that* beziehen sich dabei auf Personen, *which* und *that* auf Dinge oder Tiere. *Whose* verdeutlicht ein Zugehörigkeitsverhältnis, z. B. *The girl whose dog ran away.* Alle Relativpronomen werden im Plural ebenso verwendet. Präpositionen stehen im Relativsatz vor dem Relativpronomen oder ganz hinten.

Lösungen zu Test 140 (fortgesetzt)

2 (12 Punkte):

These are the boys who helped us.

Minis are cars which are small.

Pupils who don't do their homework will get worse grades.

Airplanes which are too old are not safe.

Dogs that bark don't bite.

That is the cafe which I like to go to.

3 (3 Punkte):

A. falsch
B. richtig
C. richtig

Lösungen zu Test 141

1 (7 Punkte):

A fisherman is someone who/that catches fish.
A waiter is someone who/that works in a restaurant.
A journalist is someone who/that writes for a newspaper.
An assistant is someone who/that helps his or her boss.

Regel:
Relativsätze, die für das Verständnis des gesamten Satzes gebraucht werden, nennt man notwendige Relativsätze, z. B. „Das Mädchen, das nebenan wohnt, ist schüchtern." – *The girl who lives next door is shy.* In ihnen wird im Englischen **kein** Komma gesetzt.

2 (7 Punkte):

Ms Harris is the teacher who/that I like best.
There's Jennifer who/that is my good friend.
Is love a feeling which/that makes people happy?
That is the fountain pen which/that I like to write with.
Mr Jenkins is the neighbour whose car has got the golden-coloured wheels.
Is this Jojo's friend Gina who/that goes to school with her?
Is that the spotted dog which/that you told me about?

Lösungen zu Test 142

1 (4 Punkte):

A lipstick is something that/which colours your lips.
A toaster is something that/which roasts bread.
A ruler is something that/which measures things.
A hose is something that/which waters the garden.

2 (7 Punkte):

Can you give me that book that/which is on the shelf?
Carol is watching the DVD that/which Clara gave her.
Ms Grouse is mum's friend whose daughter lives in Ohio.
Can you see that boy who/that is wearing the red shirt?
Do I have to clean the dishes that/which are really dirty?
Can you repair this watch that/which is broken?
Will they go to the lake that/which is in Scotland?

Lösungen zu Test 143

1 (7 Punkte):

Vanessa doesn't like people who/that talk too little.
Brandon likes movies which/that show a lot of blood.
We won't go to a country which/that everyone else goes to on holiday.
Haven't you always wanted that ice cream which/that had chocolate chips in it?
He was a boy who/that thought he knew everything.
Would you repeat this question which/that I didn't understand?
Do you like books which/that are not about witches and wizards?

2 (5 Punkte):

Taylor is a girl who/that Chad likes.
Gabriella likes a boy whose name is Troy.
Basketball is a fast game which/that Chad and Troy like to play.
Sometimes there are musical shows which/that everyone likes.
Gabriella sings with Troy who/that also loves to sing.

Lösungen zu Test 144

1 (7 Punkte):

There is a large airport near London which/that is called Heathrow.
The London Eye is an attraction which/that many tourists like.
The Thames is the river which/that flows through the city.
Virginia Woolf was a writer who/that wrote her books in London.
London has always been the city which/that has been the capital of England.
There's a museum for figures which/that are made out of wax.
The Queen is the only one who/that may rule from Buckingham Palace.

Lösungen zu Test 145

1 (4 Punkte):

I watched the movie that you've told me about.
Have you seen the pencil that was in my bag?
What's the name of the teacher who/that we will get in English next year?
Basketball is a popular game that younger and older people like to play.

2 (3 Punkte):

Jenny didn't know the people who/that were visiting/visited her parents.
Will James and Ian watch the football game that is on TV today?
Do you know the writer who/that writes so much about London?

Lösungen zu Test 146

1 (4 Punkte):

Angekreuzt werden müssen:
A. Mit *who* wird das Subjekt bezeichnet. Es kann nicht weggelassen werden.
(Die Linie bleibt frei.)
B. Mit *who* wird das Objekt bezeichnet. Es kann weggelassen werden.
Isn't that the girl we met last week?

Regel:
Übrigens: Ein *who*, das als Objekt im Relativsatz steht, kann auch als whom eingesetzt werden: *That is the girl whom we met.* Diese Form ist heute aber unüblcher geworden.

2 (3 Punkte):

Where is that DVD ~~that~~ we wanted to watch?
I bought the book ~~which~~ you told me about.
Isn't that the pen ~~that~~ I bought for you?

Regel:
Wenn Relativpronomen in notwendigen Relativsätzen als Objekt stehen, dürfen sie weggelassen werden, z. B. „Sie ist die Lehrerin, *die* ich am liebsten mag." (also *wen*) – *She is the teacher I like best.*

Lösungen zu Test 147

1 (8 Punkte):

Anita comes from a country that/which is very far from England.
Have you seen the picture -- Anthony gave to me?
I think she is the most beautiful girl -- I have ever met.
Art was the subject -- Cedric was best at.
Nina did not like the comedy show that/which was on TV last night.
I've got the CD -- they were looking for.
Did you spend all the money -- grandma gave you yesterday?
Will they show the film that/which was already on TV?

2 (4 Punkte):

Have you seen/did you see the dog Al bought?
I don't like the shoes Nicky was wearing.
Give the book to the boy who/that stands there.
I've got/have got a friend whose sister isn't/is not very nice to me.

Lösungen zu Test 148

1 (5 Punkte):

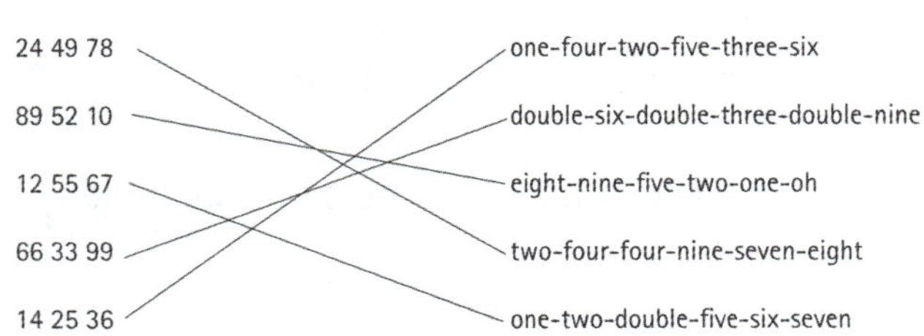

3 (4 Punkte):

twenty
nineteen
fifteen
thirty

2 (9 Punkte):

eight	seventeen	twenty-one
fifty-five	twelve	forty-eight
sixty-seven	thirteen	ninety-six

Regel:
Mit den Grundzahlen werden Dinge gezählt. Englische Zahlen, die aus Zehner- und Einerzahl zusammengesetzt sind, werden als Zahlwort mit Bindestrich geschrieben.

Lösungen zu Test 149

1 (8 Punkte):
one hundred/a hundred
three hundred and forty-five
seven hundred and seventy-seven
one thousand/a thousand
four thousand
thirty-three thousand
two hundred thousand
one million/a million

2 (4 Punkte):
twenty, twenty-five, thirty
thirty-two, forty-two, fifty-two
nine, twelve, fifteen, eighteen
fifty, one hundred/a hundred, one hundred and fifty/ a hundred and fifty, two hundred

Regel:
Die englischen Zahlwörter für 100, 1000 und 1 Million werden nur mit *a* oder *one* vorweg verwendet: *one hundred, one thousand, one million.*

3 (3 Punkte):
64 = sixty-four
31 = thirty-one
41 = forty-one

Lösungen zu Test 150

1 (14 Punkte):

first	fifth
forty-second	twelfth
eighty-third	ninth
twenty-fourth	thirtieth
fifteenth	eleventh
thirteenth	eighth
sixth	seventeenth

2 (3 Punkte):
sixteenth
forty-fourth
eightieth

Regel:
Ordnungszahlen geben eine Reihenfolge an: „Erste(r)", „Zweite(r)" usw. Die ersten drei lauten auf Englisch: *1st/first, 2nd/second, 3rd/third.* Die folgenden Ordnungszahlen bekommen die Endung *-th*. Besondere Schreibung gilt bei: *fifth, eighth, ninth, twelfth.*

Lösungen zu Test 151

1 (9 Punkte):
The first day of the week is Monday.
May is the fifth month of the year.
Christmas day is on the twenty-fifth of December.
The third day of the week is Wednesday.
Nine is the ninth number.
Thursday is the fourth day of the week.
Their parents are usually the first people that babies see in their lives.
This coat is really old. I bought it second-hand.
I liked this bike best of all. It was my first choice.

2 (4 Punkte):
Charlene is my 2nd girlfriend.
Will this band win the 1st prize?
Nick was 16th in the queue/in line.
This was your 3rd try!

Regel:
Endet die Grundzahl auf *-y*, dann wird daraus in der Ordnungszahl *-ieth*, z. B. *twentieth*.

Lösungen zu Test 152

1 (8 Punkte):

It's four o'clock.
It's eight o'clock.
It's half past one.
It's ten to three.
It's twenty past nine.
It's twelve o'clock./It's noon/It's midnight.
It's a quarter past ten.
It's three minutes past seven.

Regel:
Volle Stundenzeiten werden im Englischen mit *o'clock* bezeichnet. Minuten nach der vollen und bis zur halben Stunde werden mit *past* („nach") angegeben, solche von der halben bis zur nächsten vollen Stunde mit *to* („vor"). Bei Minutenangaben in 5er-Schritten wird das Wort *minutes* weggelassen.

2 (8 Punkte):

It's a quarter to eight.

It's five past nine.

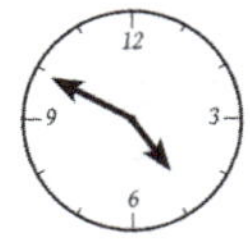
It's ten to five.

It's twelve minutes past eleven.

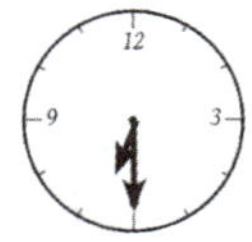
It's half past six.

It's twenty-five to one.

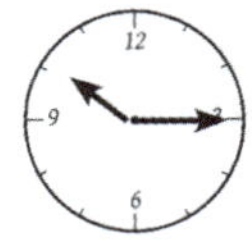
It's a quarter past ten.

It's two minutes to four.

Lösungen zu Test 153

1 (14 Punkte):

Lizzy has maths from ten to nine to twenty to ten. Lizzy has English from a quarter to ten to twenty-five to eleven. The first break is from twenty-five to eleven to ten to eleven. History is from five to eleven to a quarter to twelve. Lizzy has PE from ten to twelve to twenty to one. Lunch break is from twenty to one to twenty to two. Lizzy has music from a quarter to two to half past two.

Erläuterung:
Das englische Fach *PE* steht für *Physical Education* und bedeutet wörtlich „körperliche Erziehung" – also Sportunterricht!

2 (5 Punkte):

9.19 a.m.
9.30 p.m.
11.27 a.m.
7.10 p.m.
5.15 p.m.

Regel:
Im Englischen wird der Tag in zwei Einheiten zu je 12 Stunden aufgeteilt. Solche bis zum Mittag werden von der Abkürzung *a.m.* (steht für „vor Mittag") gefolgt, solche von Mittag bis Mitternacht mit *p.m.* („nach Mittag") gekennzeichnet.

Lösungen zu Test 154

1 (9 Punkte):

1600	sixteen hundred
1998	nineteen (hundred and) ninety-eight
2000	two thousand
2011	two thousand (and) eleven
1794	seventeen (hundred and) ninety-four
1566	fifteen (hundred and) sixty-six
1986	nineteen (hundred and) eighty-six
1882	eighteen (hundred and) eighty-two
2034	two thousand (and) thirty-four

2 (3 Punkte):

Seventeen (hundred and) ninety-four was an important year.
In nineteen (hundred and) forty-five the war ended./
The war ended in nineteen (hundred and) forty-five.
You will leave school in two thousand (and) eighteen.

Lösungen zu Test 154 (fortgesetzt)

3 (1 Punkt):

Angekreuzt werden muss:
in

Regel:
Jahreszahlen können in Zehnergruppen oder mit einem *and* verbunden ausgeschrieben/ausgesprochen werden: 1968 = *nineteen sixty-eight* oder *nineteen hundred and sixty-eight*. Im Gegensatz zum Deutschen verwendet man Jahresangaben, in denen ein Geschehen stattfindet, im Englischen immer mit der Präposition *in*, z. B. „Ich wurde 2001 geboren." = *I was born in 2001*.

Lösungen zu Test 155

1 (4 Punkte):

Maya's birthday is on the second of May.
Jonas' birthday is on the first of April.
Julian's birthday is on the twenty-third of September.
Connie's birthday is on the sixteenth of October.

Regel:
Das Datum kann im Englischen entweder mit Monat zuerst und Tag danach oder umgekehrt notiert werden: *June 1st*, gesprochen *June the first*, oder *1st May, 2012* gesprochen *the first of May*. Die Jahreszahl wird immer mit Komma abgetrennt. Sowohl Monate als auch Wochentage werden im Englischen immer groß geschrieben.

2 (4 Punkte):

May 20th, 1998 – May the twentieth, nineteen (hundred and) ninety-eight
March 1st, 2011 – March the first, two thousand (and) eleven
August, 10th, 2018 – August the tenth, two thousand (and) eighteen
June 12th, 2002 – June the twelfth, two thousand (and) two

Lösungen zu Test 156

1 (4 Punkte):

Easter Ostern	Christmas Weihnachten
New Year's Eve Silvester	New Year's Day Neujahr

3 (4 Punkte):

Christmas Day is on the twenty-fifth of December.
Boxing Day is on the twenty-sixth of December.
May Day is on the first of May.
New Year's Day is on the first of January.

2 (6 Punkte):

Halloween is in October.
Christmas is in December.
Easter is in March or in April.
New Year's Eve is in December.
New Year's Day is in January.

Regel:
Die englischen Monatsnamen der Reihenfolge nach:
January – February – March – April – May – June – July – August – September – October – November – December

Lösungen zu Test 157

1 (9 Punkte):

Folgende Verbindungen sind möglich:
a pound of carrots/sugar
a pair of socks
a spoonful of soup/sugar/apple juice
a piece of cake
a pot of tea/soup/sugar
a glass of apple juice
a bag of crisps/carrots
a bowl of soup/sugar
a group of children

2 (6 Punkte):

Folgende Verbindungen sind möglich:
a bottle/cup of water
a cup of coffee
a box/pack of cookies
a kilo of oranges
a box/pack of tissues
a slice of bread

Regel:
Anders als im Deutschen verlangen englische Mengenangaben das Wörtchen *of* vor ihrem zughörigen Substantiv – zählbare ebenso wie nicht zählbare.

Lösungen zu Test 158

1 (5 Punkte):

I have got ten toes.
There are twenty-four hours in a day.
Two shoes are a pair.
A pig has got four feet.
A spider has got eight legs.

2 (6 Punkte):

There are sixty minutes in an hour.
She ran the distance of fifty metres in eight seconds.
He was so cold that he wore two shirts and a pullover.
I can hold my breath for one/a minute.
Her older brother is twelve years old.

Lösungen zu Test 159

1 (18 Punkte):

much food	much sugar
many dogs	many women
much milk	many birthdays
many pictures	many pens
many cups	much rice
many numbers	many bananas
many peas	many fingers
much money	much hair
many coins	much noise

2 (8 Punkte):

How many windows are there in the classroom?
How much time have we got?
How much money have you got?
How many children are in that room?
How much does that game cost?
How much water will we need?
How many apples are there in the bag?
How many subjects do you have at school?

Regel:
Die Angaben *much* und *many* bedeuten beide „viel(e)". *Many* wird bei zählbaren Substantiven im Plural gebraucht, *much* hingegen bei unzählbaren Substantiven und solchen, die im Englischen keinen Plural haben, z. B. *much information.*

Lösungen zu Test 160

1 (2 Punkte):

They went to many parties.
They had much fun.

Lösungen zu Test 160 (fortgesetzt)

2 (13 Punkte):

How many eggs are there in the fridge?
Jane hasn't got much/a lot of time.
Do you know many/a lot of/lots of English words?
There was too much wood in the fireplace.
How many lessons do you have on Friday?
You cannot see many/a lot of/lots of stars tonight.
There is too much water in the bucket.
How many brothers has Timmy got?
There were many/a lot of/lots of ships at the harbour.
He put too much salt in the food.
Grandpa hasn't got much/a lot of hair.
I have never seen so many cats before.
There are too many poor people in the world.

Regel:
„Viel(e)" lässt sich auch durch die Ausdrücke *a lot of* oder *lots of* wiedergeben. Nach *how, so* und *too* aber dürfen nur *much* oder *many* folgen.

Lösungen zu Test 161

1 (11 Punkte):

There aren't any sweets left.
Why aren't there any flowers on the table?
Jamie went to the movies with some friends.
We will need water and some glasses.
She doesn't need any help.
Do you know any actors?
Cindy doesn't own any pets.
Do you need any nails with that hammer?
Here are some grapes for you.
Has Matthew got any sisters?
Linda doesn't want any presents for her birthday.

2 (10 Punkte):

Sue is a vegetarian. She does not eat any meat.
I've been working all week. Now I want to have some fun.
Here is your coffee. Only I haven't got any sugar.
Tomorrow is mum's birthday. Have you bought any presents yet?
Sorry, I can't stay. I haven't got any time.

Regel:
Die Mengenangabe *some* steht für „etwas" (vor einem Substantiv im Singular) bzw. „einige" (vor einem Substantiv im Plural). *Any* bedeutet dasselbe, wird aber in verneinten Aussagesätzen und Fragen verwendet, während *some* vor allem in bejahten Aussagen, Vorschlägen oder Antworten zum Einsatz kommt. Die Verneinung *not any* bedeutet immer „kein/e".

Lösungen zu Test 162

1 (8 Punkte):

einige/ein paar Teller
kein Essen
keine Milch
(irgendwelchen) Zucker
etwas Marmelade
keine Löffel
keine Messer
nicht viele Servietten

2 (6 Punkte):

A. richtig
B. falsch
C. richtig
D. falsch
E. richtig
F. falsch

Lösungen zu Test 163

1 (4 Punkte):

something somebody
someone
somewhere

Regel:
Dieselben Regeln wie für *some* und *any* gelten ebenso für all ihre zusammengesetzten Begriffe wie *somebody/someone, something* oder *somewhere.*

2 (12 Punkte):

We need to paint the kitchen. Can someone/somebody please help me? I really need some help.
Does she need any help?
Yes, we must do something to help her.

Are there any cookies left? I can't find them anywhere.
I cannot find any cookies either. Someone must have eaten them all.
Okay, let's bake some new ones then.

Dad, may I have some money for new shoes, please?
No, I won't give you any more money. Go and ask someone/somebody else.

Lösungen zu Test 164

1 (4 Punkte):

Our neighbour has gone. Did anyone/anybody know her?
Did anyone/anybody talk to her?
Did she do anything wrong?
Did she go anywhere?

2 (15 Punkte):

– I need some glue. Can you give me any glue?
– No, I haven't got any. Go and ask Emma. She may have some glue left from last week.
– I already asked her. She hasn't got any glue either.
– Oh, poor you! You're not having any/much luck today, are you?

– Is there any good party in town tonight?
– Yes, but I haven't got any/much money. Have you got any other ideas?
– Perhaps Sally can lend us some money. I think she has got some.

– Let me ask you some questions. You haven't read your newspaper for days now. Don't you need to know any news?
– I didn't want to read so much. I don't need any/much information.

Lösungen zu Test 165

1 (13 Punkte):

Ich habe eine Frage. / Darf ich eine Frage stellen?
Das verstehe ich nicht.
Können Sie das (bitte) an die Tafel schreiben?
Ist das (so) richtig?
Was haben wir auf?
Darf ich (bitte) auf Toilette gehen?
Ich bin Ihrer/deiner Meinung. / Ich bin nicht Ihrer/deiner Meinung.
Mir ist schlecht.
Wie schreibt man das?
Ich finde das interessant / langweilig.

Deine Lösungen müssen bei dieser Aufgabe nicht wörtlich, sondern sinngemäß übereinstimmen!

Lösungen zu Test 166

1 (30 Punkte):

STU	CDE	TUV	LMN	ABC
VWX	PQR	OPQ	HIJ	DEF
JKL	EFG	MNO	KLM	XYZ

2 (18 Punkte):

AC	UW	FH	WY	KM	HJ
VX	TV	JL	RT	MO	DF
CE	OQ	XZ	EG	SU	GI

Regel:
Zweisprachige Wörterbücher geben die Übersetzung von Wörtern aus dem Englischen ins Deutsche und aus dem Deutschen ins Englische an. Die Einträge sind alphabetisch geordnet. Das englische Alphabet ist das gleiche wie unseres, nur fehlen dort die Umlaute (und die Buchstaben werden anders ausgesprochen).

3 (11 Punkte):

her – ~~hectic~~ – herring – ~~honey~~ – hidden – ~~holy~~
hen – highlight – ~~hit~~ – ~~hay~~ – ~~human~~ – hippo

mistake – mixer – ~~mind~~ – modern – ~~menu~~ – ~~must~~
money – moan – ~~my~~ – mission – ~~mouth~~

Regel:
In Wörterbüchern steht auf der linken Seite ganz oben links fett gedruckt immer das erste Wort der Seite, auf der rechten Seite ganz oben rechts immer das letzte Wort der Seite. Man nennt diese beiden Wörter **Leitwörter**. So kannst du mit einem Blick nach oben gleich erkennen, welche Wörter zwischen den beiden auf der Doppelseite zu finden sind.

4 (6 Punkte):

paperback	paperclip
background	backpain
come back	come up

Lösungen zu Abschlusstest 1

1 (14 Punkte):

boys
geese
<u>bridges</u>
wives
feet
<u>churches</u>
ladies
mice
<u>noses</u>
<u>foxes</u>

2 (10 Punkte):

zählbar (countable)	**nicht zählbar (uncountable)**
mouse	information
phone	milk
egg	food
foot	honey
	wood
	bread

3 (5 Punkte):

Nina's bicycle
my brother's shirt
my parents' house
the children's pencils
the baby's hair

Lösungen zu Abschlusstest 2

1 (3 Punkte):

Rock concerts are louder than flute players./
Flute players are not as loud as rock concerts.
The Alps are higher than the hills of Shropshire./
The hills of Shropshire are not as high as the Alps.
Cambridge is more beautiful than Manchester./
Manchester is not as beautiful as Cambridge.

2 (7 Punkte):

Does Jen feel better today than yesterday?
Watch out, children! Don't run on the street so carelessly!
Oh no, this must be the worst movie that I ever watched!
John smiled at me happily. He had nice eyes.
Aunt Dora is a careful driver. She never goes faster than she is allowed.

3 (7 Punkte):

Where is Victoria? I can't see her. Is she not here?
I still have her keys. She will need them.
What about the others? Can you find them ?
Their train will leave soon. I must go too,
and I haven't got my bags yet.

Lösungen zu Abschlusstest 3

1 (9 Punkte):

Do you watch television all the time?
May I leave the classroom now?
The sun didn't/did not shine a lot last year.
You two cannot/are not allowed to have sweets every day!
Sebastian has just finished cleaning his room.
People must not/are not allowed to touch the paintings in museums!
Julia wasn't able to/was not able to/couldn't/could not find her umbrella yesterday.
Will our car have to get some new tires next year?
Milly and Pete haven't/have not been able to do their homework yet.

Lösungen zu Abschlusstest 4

1 (3 Punkte):
Look here! The bus is coming.
Anne usually goes for a walk on weekends.
I'm/am doing my homework right now.

2 (8 Punkte):
When I was sitting on the sofa last night, the cat jumped on my lap.
Evie has learnt three new dances since last week.
Josh was riding his bike, when it suddenly started to rain.
Our class has already read two stories by Roald Dahl.
Last summer I and two friends went on holiday to a cottage in Denmark. Our parents drove us there.

3 (2 Punkte):
Kylie's birthday will be on a Saturday this October.
Are Nathan and Wyatt going to meet Tina this weekend?

Lösungen zu Abschlusstest 5

1 (2 Punkte):
Did Kayla go shopping? Did she spend a lot of money?
Sam can come home early tonight.

2 (6 Punkte):
I will not buy these boots, although they are cheap.
I often went skiing, but I never went ice-skating.
I don't like horror movies, because they scare me.

3 (2 Punkte):
Marlon is a good friend (who/that) you can trust.
That's my aunt whose name is Susie.

4 (2 Punkte):
When school is out, I will go home at once.
If it snows, we will build a snowman.

Lösungen zu Abschlusstest 6

1 (3 Punkte):
Mira's birthday is on the third of September, two thousand.
Noah's birthday is on the first of February, two thousand (and) one
Sophie's birthday is on the ninth of October, nineteen (hundred and) ninety-eight

2 (8 Punkte):
How many teeth are there in your mouth?
Dylan cannot buy this CD, he hasn't got so much money.
Does he know any/many famous people?
Although it was noon, they couldn't see any/many people in the streets.
My soup doesn't taste good, I need some salt.
Have you got any cats or dogs at home?
Ms Jordan would like some cream in her coffee.
Is there any cake left?

3 (4 Punkte):
a cup of hot chocolate
a bottle of orange juice
a pound of meat
a minute of silence

Punktetabelle: Notiere deinen Fortschritt

Notiere hier Datum und Punktzahl deiner bearbeiteten Tests.

	Datum	Punktzahl		Datum	Punktzahl
Test 1:			Test 23:		
Test 2:			Test 24:		
Test 3:			Test 25:		
Test 4:			Test 26:		
Test 5:			Test 27:		
Test 6:			Test 28:		
Test 7:			Test 29:		
Test 8:			Test 30:		
Test 9:			Test 31:		
Test 10:			Test 32:		
Test 11:			Test 33:		
Test 12:			Test 34:		
Test 13:			Test 35:		
Test 14:			Test 36:		
Test 15:			Test 37:		
Test 16:			Test 38:		
Test 17:			Test 39:		
Test 18:			Test 40:		
Test 19:			Test 41:		
Test 20:			Test 42:		
Test 21:			Test 43:		
Test 22:			Test 44:		

Punktetabelle: Notiere deinen Fortschritt

	Datum	Punktzahl		Datum	Punktzahl
Test 45:			Test 68:		
Test 46:			Test 69:		
Test 47:			Test 70:		
Test 48:			Test 71:		
Test 49:			Test 72:		
Test 50:			Test 73:		
Test 51:			Test 74:		
Test 52:			Test 75:		
Test 53:			Test 76:		
Test 54:			Test 77:		
Test 55:			Test 78:		
Test 56:			Test 79:		
Test 57:			Test 80:		
Test 58:			Test 81:		
Test 59:			Test 82:		
Test 60:			Test 83:		
Test 61:			Test 84:		
Test 62:			Test 85:		
Test 63:			Test 86:		
Test 64:			Test 87:		
Test 65:			Test 88:		
Test 66:			Test 89:		
Test 67:			Test 90:		

Punktetabelle: Notiere deinen Fortschritt

	Datum	Punktzahl
Test 91:		
Test 92:		
Test 93:		
Test 94		
Test 95:		
Test 96:		
Test 97:		
Test 98:		
Test 99:		
Test 100:		
Test 101:		
Test 102:		
Test 103:		
Test 104:		
Test 105:		
Test 106:		
Test 107:		
Test 108		
Test 109:		
Test 110:		
Test 111:		
Test 112		
Test 113:		

	Datum	Punktzahl
Test 114:		
Test 115:		
Test 116:		
Test 117:		
Test 118:		
Test 119:		
Test 120:		
Test 121:		
Test 122:		
Test 123:		
Test 124:		
Test 125:		
Test 126:		
Test 127:		
Test 128:		
Test 129:		
Test 130:		
Test 131:		
Test 132:		
Test 133:		
Test 134:		
Test 135:		
Test 136:		

Punktetabelle: Notiere deinen Fortschritt

	Datum	Punktzahl
Test 137:		
Test 138:		
Test 139:		
Test 140:		
Test 141:		
Test 142:		
Test 143:		
Test 144:		
Test 145:		
Test 146:		
Test 147:		
Test 148:		
Test 149:		
Test 150:		
Test 151:		
Test 152:		
Test 153:		
Test 154:		
Test 155:		
Test 156:		
Test 157:		
Test 158:		
Test 159:		

	Datum	Punktzahl
Test 160:		
Test 162:		
Test 163:		
Test 164:		
Test 165:		
Test 166:		
Abschlusstest 1		
Abschlusstest 2		
Abschlusstest 3		
Abschlusstest 4		
Abschlusstest 5		
Abschlusstest 6		

Platz für deine Notizen

Klassenarbeiten

Hinweise

- Nimm diese Klassenarbeit ohne die dazugehörigen Lösungen aus dem Testblock heraus.
- Suche dir einen ruhigen Ort, an dem du ungestört bist.
- Nimm einen Stift und etwas Schmierpapier zur Hand. Gern kannst du auch die Notizseiten am Ende des Heftes benutzen.
- Die Bearbeitungszeit, die du pro Klassenarbeit hast, ist immer ganz am Anfang der Arbeit angegeben.
- Stelle dir am besten einen Wecker, der klingelt, wenn die Zeit um ist.
- Dann beginne mit den Aufgaben.
- Wenn du alle Aufgaben gelöst hast, überprüfe deine Antworten noch einmal.
- Wenn die Zeit um ist, überprüfe deine Antworten mithilfe der Lösungen und schau im Notenspiegel nach, welcher Zensur deine Gesamtpunktzahl entspricht.
- Bitte beachte: Die Punktetabellen für die Noten der Klassenarbeiten in diesem Buch sind Richtwerte, mit denen du deine Leistung ungefähr einschätzen kannst. Deine Lehrerin oder dein Lehrer bewertet möglicherweise auf einer anderen Grundlage.

Und nun viel Erfolg!

Name:	Klasse:	Datum:

Klassenarbeit 1

Du hast 45 Minuten Zeit, die Aufgaben zu lösen.

1

Bilde den Plural der Substantive.

egg	______	foot	______	city	______
wish	______	penny	______	wife	______
sheep	______	river	______	bus	______
woman	______	potato	______	tooth	______
box	______	sock	______		

14 Punkte

2

Welche Substantive sind zählbar? Kennzeichne alle, die man nicht zählen kann, mit einem *u* für *uncountable* und alle, die man zählen kann, mit einem c für *countable*.

tea ☐ cup ☐ money ☐ air ☐ apple ☐ juice ☐ plane ☐

purse ☐ love ☐ pot ☐ rice ☐ kiss ☐

12 Punkte

3

***A* oder *an*? Trage die Begriffe aus der Reihe oben in die richtige Tabellenspalte ein.**

letter	young child	bag	unit	illness	orange	ball	strong arm	exercise book	old dog

a	*an*

10 Punkte

4

***My, your, his, her, our, their*? Trage die passenden Possessivbegleiter ein.**

Tara: So this is ____________ room, Bella? Bella: Yes, it is. And this is ____________ new desk. My old desk is for my little sister . It's in __________ room now.

Tara: And there is a comic book on the floor. Is that ____________ book?

Bella: No, it belongs to my brother Jacob. It's ____________ favourite comic book.

Tara: Are ____________ parents at work? Bella: Yes, they work in the same office.

Tara: Where is ____________ office?

Bella: In the city. Shall we do ________ homework now?

8 Punkte

5 Ergänze die Sätze mit dem korrekten *s*-Genitiv der Wörter in Klammern.

________________________ (Oliver) shorts are green.

The ________________________ (Jacksons) dog is named Blackjack.

The ________________________ (firemen) new uniform is black.

3 Punkte

6 Antworte auf die Fragen in Kurzform. Dabei steht ☺ für ja als Antwort, ☹ bedeutet nein.

Have you got a new smartphone? ☺ Yes, I ________________________.

Has your sister got her own TV set? ☹ ________________________.

Can you make breakfast today? ☺ ________________________.

Is your room very tidy? ☹ ________________________.

4 Punkte

7 Stelle zu den Antworten passende Fragen mit Fragewörtern.

This is our new maths teacher. Who ________________________?

Amelia is in the classroom. ________________________?

My favourite pets are cats. ________________________?

We are her friends. ________________________?

8 Punkte

8 Übersetze die Sätze.

Ethans Freund hat viele weiße Mäuse und einen Hamster.

____

________________________.

Eine Tante fragt: „Wer füttert sie jeden Tag?"

____

____

4 Punkte

Punkte: ____ |63 Note: ____

Klassenarbeit 1

Lösungen

Achtung: Bei Punktebewertungen mit mehreren Punkten pro Antwort kannst du dir einen Teil der Punkte auch dann geben, wenn nicht alles an deiner Antwort richtig ist. Beispielsweise könnten deine Zeitformen in dem Antwortsatz stimmen, aber eine Schreibweise nicht. Dann kannst du dir die korrekte Zeitform zum Beispiel mit 1 Punkt von 2 möglichen Punkten anrechnen.

1

egg	eggs	foot	feet	city	cities
wish	wishes	penny	pennies	wife	wives
sheep	sheep	river	rivers	bus	buses
woman	women	potato	potatoes	tooth	teeth
box	boxes	sock	socks		

14 Punkte

2

tea u	cup c	money u	air u	apple c	juice u	plane c
purse c	love u	pot c	rice u	kiss c		

12 Punkte

3

a	*an*
letter	illness
young child	orange
bag	exercise book
unit	old dog
ball	
strong arm	

10 Punkte

4

Tara: So this is your room, Bella? Bella: Yes, it is. And this is my new desk. My old desk is for my little sister . It's in her room now.
Tara: And there is a comic book on the floor. Is that your book?
Bella: No, it belongs to my brother Jacob. It's his favourite comic book.
Tara: Are your parents at work? Bella: Yes, they work in the same office.
Tara: Where is their office?
Bella : In the city. Shall we do our homework now?

8 Punkte

5

Oliver's shorts are green.

The Jacksons' dog is named Blackjack.

The firemen's new uniform is black.

3 Punkte

6

Have you got a new smartphone?	Yes, I have.
Has your sister got her own TV set?	No, she hasn't.
Can you make breakfast today?	Yes, I can.
Is your room very tidy?	No, it isn't .

4 Punkte

7

Jede korrekte Frage zählt 2 Punkte.

Who is this?

Where is Amelia? / Who is in the classroom?

What are your favourite pets?

Who are you?

8 Punkte

8

Jede korrekte Zeile zählt 2 Punkte.

Ethan's friend has (got) many white mice and a hamster.

An aunt asks: "Who feeds them every day?"

4 Punkte

Punkte	58–63	51–57	42–50	31–41	18–30	0–17
Note	1	2	3	4	5	6

Name:	Klasse:	Datum:

Klassenarbeit 2

Du hast 45 Minuten Zeit, die Aufgaben zu lösen.

1

Ergänze die Sätze mit dem korrekten *s*-Genitiv der Wörter in Klammern.

Ms. Appleton is ______________________________ (Kayla) art teacher.

The ______________________________ (pupils) uniform is white and grey.

Harry is asleep in his ______________________ (parents) bedroom.

3 Punkte

2

Much oder *many*? Sortiere die Wörter in die passende Tabellenspalte.

time	smartphones	water	ideas	words	traffic	money	friends

much	*many*

8 Punkte

3

Trage die passenden Pronomen oder Possessivbegleiter ein.

Mum, I cannot find ___________ left shoe. Can ___________ help me find it?

The cats are hungry, Annie. Can you feed ___________ ? ___________ food is in the fridge.

Is that ___________ new bike, Kyle? ___________ looks fantastic!

Hey, we cannot keep up. Please wait for ___________ !

7 Punkte

4

Ergänze die Aussagen in der korrekten Form des *simple present*. ☺ steht für eine bejahende Aussage, ☹ bedeutet eine Verneinung.

☺ : Stella ___________ (feed) the dog every morning.

☹ : Paul ___________ (drink) lemonade every day.

☺ : After school I ___________ (be) so tired, I always ___________ (sleep) first.

☹ : Our teachers ___________ (give) us homework to ___________ (do) on weekends.

☹ : Mum ___________ (make) dessert for us every day, but that ___________ (be) so bad.

8 Punkte

5

Stelle zu den Antworten passende Fragen. Benutze für die mit F gekennzeichneten Fragen Fragewörter.

Yes, my arm really hurts. ______________________________ ?

No, they don't play the flute. ______________________________ ?

I eat lunch at 12 o'clock. F: ______________________________ ?

Paige buys her sneakers at the sports shop. F: ______________________________ ?

Tom buys twelve balloons. F: ______________________________ ?

10 Punkte

6

Füge die Satzteile zu vollständigen Sätzen im *present progressive* zusammen. Bilde Fragesätze, wo Fragezeichen stehen.

David and Joseph / play / tennis / at the moment

______________________________ .

Phoebe / not help / parents / right now

______________________________ .

Phil / watch / TV / in his room

______________________________ ?

Sam / do / the dishes / downstairs

______________________________ ?

8 Punkte

7

Simple present oder *present progressive*? Übersetze die Sätze in der richtigen Zeitform.

Robbie ist im Krankenhaus.

______________________________ .

Seine Mutter spricht gerade mit ihm.

______________________________ .

Er muss jeden Tag Pillen nehmen.

______________________________ .

6 Punkte

Punkte: ____ |50 Note: ____

Klassenarbeit 2

Lösungen

Achtung: Bei Punktebewertungen mit mehreren Punkten pro Antwort kannst du dir einen Teil der Punkte auch dann geben, wenn nicht alles an deiner Antwort richtig ist. Beispielsweise könnten deine Zeitformen in dem Antwortsatz stimmen, aber eine Schreibweise nicht. Dann kannst du dir die korrekte Zeitform zum Beispiel mit 1 Punkt von 2 möglichen Punkten anrechnen.

1

Ms. Appleton is Kayla's art teacher.

The pupils' uniform is white and grey.

Harry is asleep in his parents' bedroom.

3 Punkte

2

much	*many*
time	smartphones
water	ideas
traffic	words
money	friends

8 Punkte

3

Mum, I cannot find my left shoe. Can you help me find it?

The cats are hungry, Annie. Can you feed them? Their food is in the fridge.

Is that your new bike, Kyle? It looks fantastic!

Hey, we cannot keep up. Please wait for us!

7 Punkte

4

Stella feeds the dog every morning.

Paul does not drink lemonade every day.

After school I am so tired, I always sleep first.

Our teachers don't/do not give us homework to do on weekends.

Mum doesn't/does not make dessert for us every day, but that isn't / is not so bad.

8 Punkte

5

Jede korrekte Frage zählt 2 Punkte.

Does your arm (really) hurt?

Do they play the flute?

When do you eat lunch? / What do you do at 12 o'clock?

Where does Paige buy her sneakers? / What does Paige buy at the sports shop?

How many balloons does Tom buy? / What does Tom buy?

10 Punkte

6

Jeder korrekte Satz zählt 2 Punkte.

David and Joseph are playing tennis at the moment.

Phoebe is not helping her parents right now.

Is Phil watching TV in his room?

Is Sam doing the dishes downstairs?

8 Punkte

7

Robbie is in the hospital.

His mother is (just) talking to/with him.

He must/has to take pills every day.

6 Punkte

Punkte	46–50	40–45	33–39	25–32	15–24	0–14
Note	1	2	3	4	5	6

Name:	Klasse:	Datum:

Klassenarbeit 3

Du hast 45 Minuten Zeit, die Aufgaben zu lösen.

1 *Some* oder *any*? Ergänze die Sätze.

– Let's go to that store. I think they have ____________ nice clothes.

– I don't know. I can't see ____________ great tops in the window. Just ____________ boring T-shirts. Haven't they got ____________ pretty blouses?

4 Punkte

2 *Can* oder *must*? *Can't*, *needn't* oder *mustn't*? Trage die passenden Hilfsverben ein.

Come on now, Shannon, we ____________ hurry. I don't want to be late!

Grace is so cool! She ____________ play football very well.

Josh ____________ walk his dog every day. He ____________ forget it, so the dog ____________ get out every day.

Nick ____________ meet his friends, because he is ill. He ____________ help his mother today, because he feels sick.

7 Punkte

3 Ergänze die Tabelle mit den Stammformen der unregelmäßigen Verben und einer deutschen Übersetzung.

infinitive	*simple past*	*past participle*	Deutsch
swim			schwimmen
		lost	
come			
			sich treffen
throw			
	sent		
			sein
		hurt	

23 Punkte

4 *Simple past* oder *past progressive*? Setze die Verben in der passenden Zeitform ein.

Last summer we ______________________ (take) a trip to London.

Nathan ______________________ (walk) on the street, when his phone ______________________ (go) off.

While I ______________________ (read) John's text message last night, our cat ______________________ (jump) at my phone.

10 Punkte

5 Stelle genau zu den Antworten passende Fragen.

Yes, she went to a friend's house. ______________________________________ ?

Yes, I was waiting for her. ______________________________________ ?

No, she didn't call me. ______________________________________ ?

No, I wasn't angry. ______________________________________ ?

Yes, I was watching TV all afternoon. ______________________________________ ?

10 Punkte

6 Setze die passende Präposition ein.

____________ the right

____________ exactly five o' clock

____________ summer

____________ Sundays

4 Punkte

7 Übersetze die Sätze in der passenden Zeitform. Achte dabei auf Signalwörter.

Hast du gestern Rebecca getroffen?

____ ?

Ja, während ihr den Film gesehen habt.

____ .

4 Punkte

Punkte: ______ |62 Note: ______

Klassenarbeit 3

Lösungen

Achtung: Bei Punktebewertungen mit mehreren Punkten pro Antwort kannst du dir einen Teil der Punkte auch dann geben, wenn nicht alles an deiner Antwort richtig ist. Beispielsweise könnten deine Zeitformen in dem Antwortsatz stimmen, aber eine Schreibweise nicht. Dann kannst du dir die korrekte Zeitform zum Beispiel mit 1 Punkt von 2 möglichen Punkten anrechnen.

1

– Let's go to that store. I think they have some nice clothes.

– I don't know. I can't see any great tops in the window. Just some boring T-shirts. Haven't they got any pretty blouses?

4 Punkte

2

Come on now, Shannon, we must hurry. I don't want to be late!

Grace is so cool! She can play football very well.

Josh must walk his dog every day. He mustn't forget it, so the dog can get out every day.

Nick can't/mustn't meet his friends, because he is ill. He needn't help his mother today, because he feels sick.

7 Punkte

3

swim	swam	swum	schwimmen
lose	lost	lost	verlieren
come	came	come	kommen
meet	met	met	sich treffen
throw	threw	thrown	werfen
send	sent	sent	schicken
be	was	been	sein
hurt	hurt	hurt	wehtun

23 Punkte

4

Jede richtige Zeitform zählt 2 Punkte.

Last summer we took a trip to London.

Nathan was walking on the street, when his phone went off.

While I was reading John's text message last night, our cat jumped at my phone.

10 Punkte

5

Jede korrekte Frage zählt 2 Punkte.

Yes, she went to a friend's house.	Did she go to a friend's house?
Yes, I was waiting for her.	Were you waiting for her?
No, she didn't call me.	Did she call you?
No, I wasn't angry.	Were you angry?
Yes, I was watching TV all afternoon.	Were you watching TV (all afternoon)?

10 Punkte

6

on the right

in/before/after/during summer

at exactly five o' clock

on Sundays

4 Punkte

7

Jeder korrekte Satz zählt 2 Punkte.

Did you meet/see Rebecca yesterday?

Yes, while you were watching the film.

4 Punkte

Punkte	57–62	50–56	41–49	31–40	18–30	0–17
Note	1	2	3	4	5	6

Name:	Klasse:	Datum:

Klassenarbeit 4

Du hast **45 Minuten Zeit,** die Aufgaben zu lösen.

1 Trage *since* oder *for* in die Lücken ein.

Megan has been watching TV ____________ hours.

I haven't gone swimming ____________ two years.

Ms Bright has been answering e-mails ____________ 9 a.m.

The Smiths have never stopped for petrol __________ they left London.

4 Punkte

2 Ergänze die Verbformen im *present perfect.*

I ______________________ never ______________________ (see) Edinburgh castle.

______________________ you ever ______________________ (be) to Scotland?

______________________ your parents ______________________ (listen) to Adele's new album yet?

That album ______________________ already ______________________ (sell) four million copies.

Lucy ______________________ ______________________ (learn) five new dance moves since last week.

She _______________ just ________________ (finish) exercising.

12 Punkte

3 Ergänze die Tabelle mit den Stammformen der unregelmäßigen Verben und einer Übersetzung.

infinitive	*simple past*	*past participle*	Deutsch
		seen	
			weggehen, verlassen
	gave		
buy			
			essen
fly			
		taken	
			haben

24 Punkte

4

Simple past oder *present perfect?* Setze die richtige Verbform ein.

I ____________________ (be) a member of the riding club for three years and I am still a member.

Last week Liv ____________________ (cannot find) her sunglasses. Her dad ____________________ (find) them on Friday.

The company ____________________ (just / open) a new café in Luton.

Grandma ____________________ (not have) such a nice holiday since 2005.

10 Punkte

5

Fülle die Lücken mit den passenden Steigerungsformen der Adjektive.

Timothy has a ____________________ (nice) smile than Julian.

Wow, this is the ____________________ (good) pasta that I've ever tried!

Poor Jasmine! She feels ____________________ (bad) than yesterday.

Mr Gaynor is the ____________________ (boring) teacher of the whole school.

4 Punkte

6

Übersetze die Sätze.

Ich bin größer als mein kleiner Bruder.

____.

Lewis hat seit drei Tagen nicht genug geschlafen.

____.

Jess ist um 7 Uhr aufgewacht.

____.

6 Punkte

Punkte: |60 Note:

Klassenarbeit 4

Lösungen

Achtung: Bei Punktebewertungen mit mehreren Punkten pro Antwort kannst du dir einen Teil der Punkte auch dann geben, wenn nicht alles an deiner Antwort richtig ist. Beispielsweise könnten deine Zeitformen in dem Antwortsatz stimmen, aber eine Schreibweise nicht. Dann kannst du dir die korrekte Zeitform zum Beispiel mit 1 Punkt von 2 möglichen Punkten anrechnen.

1

Megan has been watching TV for hours.

I haven't gone swimming for two years.

Ms Bright has been answering e-mails since 9 a.m.

The Smiths have never stopped for petrol since they left London.

4 Punkte

2

I've / I have never seen Edinburgh castle. Have you ever been to Scotland?

Have your parents listened to Adele's new album yet?

That album has already sold four million copies.

Lucy has learned five new dance moves since last week.

She has just finished exercising.

12 Punkte

3

see	saw	seen	sehen
leave	left	left	weggehen, verlassen
give	gave	given	geben
buy	bought	bought	kaufen
eat	ate	eaten	essen
fly	flew	flown	fliegen
take	took	taken	nehmen
have	had	had	haben

24 Punkte

4

Jeder komplett richtige Satz zählt 2 Punkte.

I have been a member of the riding club for three years and I am still a member.

Last week Liv couldn't/could not find her sunglasses. Her dad found them on Friday.

The company has just opened a new café in Luton.

Grandma hasn't/has not had such a nice holiday since 2005.

10 Punkte

5

Timothy has a nicer smile than Julian.

Wow, this is the best pasta that I've ever tried!

Poor Jasmine! She feels worse than yesterday.

Mr Gaynor is the most boring teacher of the whole school.

4 Punkte

6

Jeder richtige Satz zählt 2 Punkte.

I am taller/bigger than my little brother.

Lewis hasn't/has not slept enough for three days.

Jess woke up at 7 o'clock.

6 Punkte

Punkte	55–60	48–54	40–47	30–39	18–29	0–17
Note	1	2	3	4	5	6

Name:	Klasse:	Datum:

Klassenarbeit 5

Du hast **60 Minuten Zeit,** die Aufgaben zu lösen.

1 Setze die richtigen Präpositionen ein.

James was born __________ 2005.

The kitten is hiding __________ the couch.

Ella's dad goes __________ work __________ the morning.

4 Punkte

2 Trage die fehlenden Possessivpronomen aus der Reihe oben in die Lücken ein. Achtung: Nicht alle kommen in den Sätzen vor.

mine	yours	hers	his	ours	theirs

Caitlin is looking at the pens. She doesn't know which one is ____________ .

Is this your suitcase? Sorry, I didn't know it was ____________ . I took it because I thought it was ____________ .

The book Tyler read isn't ____________ . It's from the school library.

Sorry, but these seats are __________ . We've got the tickets for them.

5 Punkte

3 *It's* oder *its*? Ergänze die Sätze.

This egg fell out of __________ box. __________ broken.

Look, __________ that bike over there! __________ price seems okay.

4 Punkte

4 Fülle die Lücken mit den Verben im *will future*.

______________________________ (you / come) to my birthday party on Saturday?

No, I ___________________________ (be) there, sorry. I ___________________________ (help) my older brother with his car.

3 Punkte

5 *If* oder *when*? Ergänze die Sätze.

____________ we don't hurry now, we'll miss our bus. ____________ the bus stops next, we'll have to get off.

My parents will worry, ____________ I stay out too long.

3 Punkte

6 Bilde Sätze mit *will* oder *won't*.

Luke's family – move – Wales – next year

____ .

He – play – in a football club – there

____ .

that – be – fine

He thinks ____ .

his old friends – not forget – him

He hopes ______________________________ .

8 Punkte

7 Fülle die Lücken mit den passenden Verben aus der Reihe oben in der richtigen Zeitform.

invite	sweep	tell	buy	help

If you ask Emily, she ____________________ you with your maths homework.

Will you be sad if Lily doesn't ____________________ you to her party?

You won't believe me if I ____________________ you the truth.

Their dad ____________________ Declan and Mel ice cream if they ____________________ the front yard.

10 Punkte

8 Übersetze ins Englische mit *if* oder *when*. Beachte die richtige Zeitform für Bedingungssätze.

Wenn (sobald) ich das Geld habe, kaufe ich ein neues Waveboard.

____ .

____ .

Wenn (falls) alles okay ist, gebe ich es nicht zurück.

____ .

____ .

Wenn du willst, lass ich es dich benutzen.

____ .

______________________________ .

6 Punkte

Punkte: |43 Note:

Klassenarbeit 5

Lösungen

Achtung: Bei Punktebewertungen mit mehreren Punkten pro Antwort kannst du dir einen Teil der Punkte auch dann geben, wenn nicht alles an deiner Antwort richtig ist. Beispielsweise könnten deine Zeitformen in dem Antwortsatz stimmen, aber eine Schreibweise nicht. Dann kannst du dir die korrekte Zeitform zum Beispiel mit 1 Punkt von 2 möglichen Punkten anrechnen.

1

James was born in 2005.

The kitten is hiding under/behind/next to/on the couch.

Ella's dad goes to work in the morning.

4 Punkte

2

Caitlin is looking at the pens. She doesn't know which one is hers.

Is this your suitcase? Sorry, I didn't know it was yours . I took it because I thought it was mine.

The book Tyler read isn't his . It's from the school library.

Sorry, but these seats are ours. We've got the tickets for them.

5 Punkte

3

This egg fell out of its box. It's broken.

Look, it's that bike over there. Its price seems okay.

4 Punkte

4

Will you come to my birthday party on Saturday?

No, I won't/will not be there, sorry. I'll/I will help my older brother with his car.

3 Punkte

5

If we don't hurry now, we'll miss our bus.

When the bus stops next, we'll have to get off.

My parents will worry, if I stay out too long.

3 Punkte

6

Jeder korrekte Satz zählt 2 Punkte.

Luke's family will move to Wales next year.

He will play in a football club there.

He thinks that will be fine.

He hopes his old friends won't/will not forget him.

8 Punkte

7

Jede richtige Zeitform zählt 2 Punkte.

If you ask Emily, she will help you with your maths homework.

Will you be sad if Lily doesn't invite you to her party?

You won't believe me if I tell you the truth.

Their dad will buy Declan and Mel ice cream if they sweep the front yard.

10 Punkte

8

Jeder korrekte Satz zählt 2 Punkte.

When I have the money, I'll/I will buy a new waveboard.

If everything is okay, I won't/will not give it back.

If you want, I'll/I will let you use it.

6 Punkte

Punkte	40–43	35–39	29–34	21–28	13–20	0–12
Note	1	2	3	4	5	6

Notizen

Notizen

Notizen